OVERSIZED                146550

959.704q
Vie        The Vietnam experience:
             South Vietnam on
v.10         trial

# South Vietnam on Trial

# The Vietnam Experience

# South Vietnam on Trial

## Mid-1970 to 1972

by David Fulghum, Terrence Maitland,
and the editors of Boston Publishing Company

Boston Publishing Company/Boston, MA

959.704 g
Vie
[v. 10]

## Boston Publishing Company

President and Publisher: Robert J. George
Vice President: Richard S. Perkins, Jr.
Editor-in-Chief: Robert Manning
Managing Editor: Paul Dreyfus

Senior Writers:
Clark Dougan, Edward Doyle, David Fulghum, Samuel Lipsman, Terrence Maitland, Stephen Weiss
Senior Picture Editor: Julene Fischer

Researchers: Kerstin Gorham (Chief), Sandra M. Jacobs, Christy Virginia Keeny, Denis Kennedy, Carole Rulnick, Ted Steinberg, Nicole van Ackere

Picture Editors: Wendy Johnson, Lanng Tamura
Assistant Picture Editor: Kathleen A. Reidy
Picture Researchers: Nancy Katz Colman, Robert Ebbs, Tracey Rogers, Nana Elisabeth Stern, Shirley L. Green (Washington, D.C.), Kate Lewin (Paris)
Picture Department Assistants: Suzanne M. Spencer, Kathryn J. Steeves

Historical Consultants: Vincent H. Demma, Lee Ewing
Picture Consultant: Ngo Vinh Long

Production Editor: Patricia Leal Welch
Assistant Editor: Karen E. English
Editorial Production: Sarah E. Burns, Pamela George, Elizabeth C. Peters, Theresa M. Slomkowski, Amy P. Wilson

Design: Designworks, Sally Bindari

Marketing Director: Jeanne C. Gibson
Business Staff: Amy Pelletier

## About the editors and authors

Editor-in-Chief *Robert Manning*, a long-time journalist, has previously been editor-in-chief of the *Atlantic Monthly* magazine and its press. He served as assistant secretary of state for public affairs under Presidents John F. Kennedy and Lyndon B. Johnson. He has also been a fellow at the Institute of Politics at the John F. Kennedy School of Government at Harvard University.

Authors: *David Fulghum* has been a senior writer with the U.S. News & World Report Book Division. A veteran of the U.S. Navy, he received his B.A. from Angelo State University in Texas and has done graduate studies in military and diplomatic history at Texas A&M and Georgetown Universities. *Terrence Maitland* has written for several publications, including *Newsweek* magazine and the *Boston Globe*, and has coauthored other volumes in *The Vietnam Experience*. He is a graduate of Holy Cross College and has a M.S. from Boston University.

Historical Consultants: *Vincent H. Demma*, an historian with the U.S. Army Center of Military History, is director of the center's history of the Vietnam conflict. *Lee Ewing*, editor of *Army Times*, served two years in Vietnam as a combat intelligence officer with the U.S. Military Assistance Command, Vietnam (MACV) and the 101st Airborne Division.

Picture Consultant: *Ngo Vinh Long* is a social historian specializing in China and Vietnam. Born in Vietnam, he returned there most recently in 1980. His books include *Before the Revolution: The Vietnamese Peasants Under the French* and *Report From a Vietnamese Village*.

**Cover photo:**
First ARVN Division troops search for a machine gun harassing Firebase O'Reilly north of the A Shau Valley in September 1970.

Library of Congress Catalog Card Number: 84-71522

ISBN: 0-939526-10-7

10 9 8 7 6
5 4 3 2 1

# Contents

# Soldiering On

In late March 1971, Fire Support Base Mary Ann, the westernmost outpost of the U.S. 23d Infantry (Americal) Division in Quang Tin Province, was about to become the property of the Army of the Republic of Vietnam (ARVN). Under the two-year-old program of Vietnamization, the United States, as it gradually withdrew, was turning over its bases to the Vietnamese armed forces— expanded, better equipped, and better trained than ever before. As the U.S. combat participation receded in the longest war in American history, these improved Vietnamese forces had to play the primary role in defending their country.

Based at Mary Ann, the Americal's 1st Battalion, 46th Infantry, part of the 196th Brigade, had been patrolling the western highlands fifty kilometers west of Chu Lai, seeking out North Vietnamese Main Force units as part of Operation Middlesex Peak. Apart from discovering two weapons caches along supply trails leading from

Laos, the 1st Battalion had encountered no evidence of NVA regulars. Throughout Vietnam the war had ebbed in late 1970 and early 1971, and it seemed to have by-passed the 1st Battalion's area altogether. Firebase Mary Ann had taken a few mortar rounds during the year of its existence, but it had not even been probed by the enemy. The 1st Battalion had already shipped some of its men, artillery, and mortars to a new base farther east and therefore had not built up its ammunition stocks. "When the war is starting to wind down, keeping the troops alert, keeping them on their toes is a very difficult problem . . . ," 196th Brigade commander Colonel William S. Hathaway cautioned. "This is the time when it's easy to get complacent."

Mary Ann's defenders had grown careless and their defenses inadequate. Surrounded by three rings of concertina barbed wire, the firebase, like every other base, had a defense plan, but few people in the understrength rifle companies (Charlie Company had only seventy-five men) knew exactly what it was. The base defenses had failed two inspections, and on March 27 Col. Hathaway conducted another inspection. He walked the perimeter and, apart from remarking on some loose ammo, announced that Mary Ann was "greatly improved . . . a hundred percent improved." Since no enemy units were operating in the vicinity, however, the organization of defenses seemed unimportant. As battalion commander Lieutenant Colonel William P. Doyle asked, "Who in his right mind would attack it?"

## Night raid

The answer: the 2d Company of the 409th NVA Main Force Sapper Battalion, "a bunch of real pros," as Hathaway later conceded. During the night of March 28, the sappers (estimates range widely from 40 to more than 100), dressed only in black shorts and their bodies smeared with black grease, crept up to the perimeter of Firebase Mary Ann, which they had been observing for weeks. They carried satchel charges, hand grenades and grenade launchers, rifles, tear gas canisters, and gas masks. They stepped carefully over the flare and claymore trip wires. None of the guards in the twenty-two perimeter bunkers saw the sappers as they approached.

At 2:30 A.M. the sappers cut through the last ring of perimeter wire in four locations, and, under cover of a barrage of 82MM mortar rounds, they swarmed over Firebase Mary Ann. The night erupted. Explosions seemed to occur simultaneously all over the base, and a cloud of tear gas soon blanketed the hill. One group of sappers rushed for

the artillery emplacements, damaging the 155MM howitzers with satchel charges. Another group threw tear gas, hand grenades, and satchel charges into the tactical operations center. A lone sapper raced toward Col. Doyle's bunker near the TOC and threw a forty-pound satchel charge just as Doyle spotted him and fired his .45 automatic. He hit the sapper, but the charge exploded, temporarily deafening Doyle and wounding him in the legs. Captain Paul Spilberg had rushed to the TOC; now he was driven out by the tear gas and explosions. Armed only with a .45 pistol, he fell into a trench outside. He heard explosions going off all over the perimeter. A grenade landed near him and shrapnel tore into his back.

With their bodies blackened, the sappers moved like wraiths through the darkness. A nearby firebase fired an illumination round over Mary Ann seventeen minutes after the attack began; still, some men saw only shadows. Others came face to face with the NVA. Soldiers scrambling to get out of their bunkers and into the trenches ran into sappers already in fighting positions, firing and throwing charges. Lieutenant Carl McGee took on several NVA soldiers by himself. His body was found surrounded by dead sappers, his hands locked around one of them.

Moving south to north, the sappers swept across Mary Ann in half an hour. More enemy mortar shells began to fall, covering the sappers' exit on the north side of the base. A gunship arriving overhead fired through the smoke and flames and killed several North Vietnamese trying to escape through the wire.

In the morning the haze and smoke cleared over the greatest American combat loss from a single attack in four years. Of the 231 Americans at the base, the sappers had killed 30 and wounded 82. Most of the officers had been killed or wounded. Only one of the twenty ARVN soldiers at Mary Ann was wounded. One medevac pilot described the destruction as "the worst carnage I have ever seen at an American installation. . . . Some [bodies were] burned to charcoal. . . . There were nine body bags full of bits and pieces of flesh." Fifteen sappers had also been killed, and several of their bodies were hauled to the trash dump where they were burned at the order of acting battalion commander Major Donald C. Potter.

The massacre at Firebase Mary Ann provoked a succession of investigations—by Hathaway's 196th Brigade, by Major General James L. Baldwin's 23d Division, and by U.S. Commander General Creighton Abrams's own inspector general. In assessing the "effectiveness of the functioning of command" within the 1st Battalion, the 196th Brigade, and the 23d Infantry Division, the MACV investigators interviewed most Mary Ann survivors and pursued matters up the chain of command to the level of division commander.

With the June 1971 submission of the panel's report—large portions of which remained classified more than a dozen years later—several military careers were blighted.

The most senior officer affected was General Baldwin, who in July was relieved of command of the 23d Division. The MACV report seemed to hold Baldwin partly responsible for the burned enemy bodies, a war crime in clear violation of the Geneva Convention, which prohibits maltreatment of the enemy dead. When he learned of the burning four days after the event, Baldwin testified, he ordered the charred bodies buried, but he neither reported the crime to his superiors nor meted out punishment to those responsible. Four other officers, including brigade commander Hathaway and battalion commander Doyle, were demoted or reprimanded in administrative actions. Doyle, who had compiled a nearly flawless record during eighteen years in the army, requested a court-martial to rebut charges of his "substandard performance." The request was never granted. "They were looking to hang anybody they could," Captain Spilberg later said, "and that's what they did."

In addition to its harsh assessment of culpability for the events at Firebase Mary Ann, the MACV report, signed by Colonel Arthur E. Sikes, sounded an alarm about the false sense of security that prevailed among combat units in Vietnam. The fate of Mary Ann, the report suggested, could easily afflict other units. It continued:

The reduced level of combat activity and the increasing publicity by the news media focused upon ending of the war tend to create great complacency among both the troops and their commanders. Coupled with this is the effect of anti-Vietnam and anti-military attitudes [in the United States] and the growth of permissiveness within the military establishment. All of these factors confront a commander in Vietnam today with a formidable task (challenge) of maintaining a high state of discipline and alertness among his troops.

The accuracy of this criticism was borne out by comments made by survivors immediately after the event. "Man, we thought the war was over for us," muttered one soldier. The attack at Mary Ann had dramatically proven the contrary. In spite of the fact that the war was winding down, said Specialist 4 Dennis Schulte, "We sleep in the rain, we eat out of cans, we stay wet ten or twelve days, until our bodies look like wrinkled prunes. The people back in the States think this war is over. It isn't."

## Seeking peace with honor

President Richard Nixon and his national security adviser, Henry Kissinger, did not count themselves among those in the United States who thought the Vietnam War was over. For them the war was a frustration they could neither end nor bring under control. From the beginning of his administration, Nixon had been seeking ways to quit Vietnam without seeming to capitulate, to achieve the illusive "peace with honor," and yet he had accomplished little more than to perpetuate the endless stalemate he had in-

herited, albeit with fewer and fewer U.S. troops. "If winding down the war is my greatest satisfaction in foreign policy," Nixon said in early 1971, "the failure to end it is my deepest disappointment." As the United States continued to withdraw unilaterally from the battlefield, the problem facing the administration, said Kissinger, was to make the withdrawal "an expression of policy and not ... a collapse."

That policy, developed in 1969 and 1970, was predicated on the pursuit of two goals—Vietnamization and successful negotiations with the North: Prepare the South Vietnamese to fight the war on their own while working out with Hanoi a political settlement that took the U.S. out of Vietnam. There was a serious tension within the administration between these dual approaches. From Kissinger's point of view, the continuing withdrawal of U.S. troops reduced the bargaining power he brought to the negotiating table. Kissinger observed, "There was simply no negotiating scheme that would possibly work with the cold-eyed planners in Hanoi unless it was related to some calculus of the balance of forces." Yet the Department of Defense, principally Secretary Melvin Laird, believed that the negotiations might stretch on endlessly without result and that bringing home the U.S. troops was Nixon's domestic political mandate. As Kissinger sought to slow the rate of U.S. troop withdrawals, Laird, an astute politician and bureaucratic infighter, worked to hasten them regardless of the diplomatic and battlefield ramifications. Laird's pressure in the summer of 1970 was dictated by the turbulent events of the spring that had dramatized the growing American impatience with the war.

The combined U.S.-South Vietnamese invasion of Cambodia had touched off a frenzy of protest that sent shivers through the administration. Antiwar protesters marched, universities closed down after four students died at Kent State, and government employees, including some cabinet officers, voiced their disapproval of the widening of the war. The Senate was also active, in June repealing the six-year-old Gulf of Tonkin resolution and passing, after nearly 300 floor speeches, the Cooper-Church amendment. Had it been approved by the House of Representatives, the amendment would have prohibited the president from spending money for American troops, advisers, or air support in Cambodia. The more conservative House killed it, but a watered-down version did pass both houses of Congress and became law in December, long after U.S. troops had departed Cambodia. The new law permitted continued American aid to Cambodia and its Lon Nol government but barred U.S. ground combat troops from Laos and Cambodia.

On June 30, 1970, the last U.S. troops left Cambodia after a two-month foray, exactly on the schedule announced by the administration. With the Cambodia issue thus defused, public outcry subsided; after two months of rage, antiwar protesters seemed to have expended their

*President Nixon greets members of the 1st Infantry Division during a visit to Vietnam in July 1969, a month after announcing the start of troop withdrawals. The 1st rotated home the next April.*

energies, and the movement slipped into the summer doldrums. As the country regained its equanimity throughout the summer and fall of 1970, the Nixon administration undertook a reexamination of its strategy. After the capable South Vietnamese performance in Cambodia, Nixon was convinced that ARVN was improving and Vietnamization was working. Ultimately the ARVN might be able to stand on its own. Peace negotiations, on the other hand, had come to a halt. The North Vietnamese and Vietcong delegates had boycotted the Paris peace talks at the start of the Cambodian incursion, promising not to return until U.S. troops had left Cambodia. On July 1, 1970, in an effort to get the talks going again, Nixon named the highly respected diplomat David Bruce as head of the U.S. delegation to Paris, a post that had been vacant for six months.

Next, the Vietnam Special Studies Group, comprising representatives from the State and Defense Departments, the CIA, and Joint Chiefs, and chaired by Henry Kissinger, developed the idea of a "cease-fire in place." Nixon had initially opposed this because it would undermine the Thieu regime, but the success of the Cambodian incursion changed his mind. In a television address on October 7, which he described in advance as "the most comprehensive statement ever made on this subject since the beginning of this difficult war," Nixon proposed the cease-fire in place. Although well received by the public (the *New York Times* called it a "major new peace initiative"), the proposal was immediately rejected by the North Vietnamese because it called for an eventual mutual withdrawal of forces. Based on the premise that North and South Vietnam were one country, Hanoi insisted on keeping its presence in the South after the cessation of hostilities. A National Security Council study concluded late in 1970 that the United States could neither persuade nor force North Vietnam to withdraw its troops from the South.

Faced with this reality, Nixon and Laird leaned toward a faster withdrawal of U.S. troops, linked, however, with a naval quarantine of North Vietnam and the resumption of the kind of large-scale bombing of the North that had ceased in November 1968 when President Johnson ended Rolling Thunder. Kissinger counseled patience, reasoning that a more rapid withdrawal of U.S. troops could destabilize the South Vietnamese government in advance of the presidential elections that Saigon had scheduled for October 1971. Kissinger preferred continuing negotiations toward a cease-fire while maintaining phased American troop withdrawals at their current rate, which would take the last U.S. combat forces out of Vietnam just before the 1972 U.S. presidential elections. Kissinger envisaged the events of the next two years in this way: If the North Vietnamese refused to accept a cease-fire sometime in 1971, it would mean they were planning a spring dry season offensive in 1972 when U.S. troops would have been for the most part gone. Then the outcome of the war would depend on the ability of the South Vietnamese, aided by U.S.

In May 1970 "hardhat" construction workers in New York protest the Cooper-Church amendment, curbing American aid to Cambodia, which the Senate passed the next month.

11

air power, to repel the offensive. Kissinger clearly doubted that by then ARVN would be able to do that. In sum, Kissinger said, peace would come "at the end of 1971 or at the end of 1972, either by negotiation or by a South Vietnamese collapse." In order to see a cease-fire as a welcome alternative, he reasoned, the North Vietnamese had to be weakened militarily.

## Hanoi's Cambodian front

North Vietnam had other reasons for rejecting Nixon's cease-fire in place proposal. In fact, the North Vietnamese feared that a cease-fire would leave them in a strategic imbalance because they did not have enough troops in place in the South. Hanoi had yet to make up all its losses from the 1968 Tet offensive (an estimated 45,000 killed, mostly VC Main Forces), losses so substantial that the Communists had been forced onto the defensive. Their tactics were spelled out in the 1969 COSVN Resolution 14,

"On Guerilla Warfare," which called for breaking down Main and Local Force units into companies of sappers wherever possible. The new Communist approach was to continue guerrilla activities and periodic attacks, thereby maintaining pressure on the South Vietnamese and the departing Americans, but to curtail conventional actions, which always risked large losses. The strategy was one of "economy of force" punctuated by two- or three-day periods of intense enemy activity the Americans called "high points." As Politburo member Truong Chinh said in a radio address after the Tet offensive, "We must shift to the defensive to gain time, dishearten the enemy, and build our forces to prepare for a new offensive."

Events in Cambodia in 1970 had further complicated Hanoi's plans for rebuilding its forces. The overthrow of Prince Norodom Sihanouk in March 1970 by pro-American General Lon Nol threatened Hanoi with the loss of its sanctuaries and closed the port of Sihanoukville to the Communists, thus disrupting the supply lines to the sanc-

### The War in Cambodia

The March 1970 fall of Cambodia's Prince Norodom Sihanouk—and the subsequent incursion by U.S. and ARVN forces—provoked a flurry of organizing activity among Communists. At Hanoi's order, four NVA divisions left South Vietnam's battlefields and plunged deep into Cambodia, joining forces with the Khmers Rouges (the "Red Cambodians"). Together they raised and trained an army to oppose the U.S.-backed government of Lon Nol, who had deposed Sihanouk. With the Khmers Rouges doing much of the recruiting, and the North Vietnamese providing training, the Communists fielded a native Cambodian army of some 15,000 men within a year. These photographs, obtained from the Khmers Rouges, show the new army in action.

Right. *Soldiers armed with an assortment of U.S.-made carbines and Soviet-style AK47 assault rifles, do battle in 1970.*

Far right. *In a village setting, Communist trainers instruct a group of recruits in hand grenade throwing.*

tuaries. The ability to move supplies through Sihanoukville to NVA troops along Vietnam's border was essential to carrying on guerrilla warfare in the South.

Reacting to its Cambodia crisis, Hanoi, in March 1970, had hastily planned and begun to execute what it termed "Campaign X." It redeployed four divisions from Vietnam and the border sanctuaries to perform a three-part "emergency mission" deep in Cambodia: protection of the vital LOCs, expansion of Communist liberated zones, and expansion of the insurgent Cambodia Liberation Army. The *Front Unifie Nationale de Kampuchea* (FUNK) was to carry on the fight against the Lon Nol government, as the Vietcong had carried on Hanoi's fight in South Vietnam in the early years of the war. Campaign X amounted in effect to an invasion of Cambodia by some 60,000 soldiers and cadres—the 5th and 9th VC Divisions and the 1st and 7th NVA Divisions—and the creation of an organization similar to the one it had put together in South Vietnam years before.

In short, while the United States was "Vietnamizing" the war in South Vietnam to permit its own withdrawal, Hanoi was attempting to "North Vietnamize" the widening war in Cambodia to insure its own continued use of the eastern half of that country. As it had in South Vietnam, Hanoi sent agit-prop teams consisting of an armed squad, a medic, political cadres, and Khmer interpreters through the hamlets and villages to persuade the people of the Communist cause and to seek military recruits. These recruits received basic military instruction at camps established by the North Vietnamese in provinces under partial or complete Communist control. After basic training the Cambodian soldiers joined NVA units for combat training. All did not pass smoothly; enmity between the Khmers and the Vietnamese was long-standing, so there was much suspicion and, in several instances, fighting. The North Vietnamese took pains to equip their distrustful Cambodian allies with obsolete weapons and carefully rationed ammunition lest one day the guns be turned on them.

Nevertheless, the North Vietnamese managed to build an army and eventually formed autonomous FUNK battalions with NVA/VC cadres as advisers. By the end of 1970, total FUNK strength had grown to 12,000 to 15,000 trained and equipped Cambodians, backed up by several NVA divisions. The regular Cambodian army had more men on paper, but its recruits, with little training or experience, were no match for the Communists, as was soon to become evident.

By invading Cambodia in April 1970, the United States and South Vietnam had hoped to drive the North Vietnamese out of their sanctuaries and to bring some measure of peace to the Vietnamese battlefields. They had accomplished that goal, but instead of eliminating the North Vietnamese they had only driven them deeper into Cambodia, destabilizing an already weak country. As a staff member of the Senate Foreign Relations Committee had warned in a report at the height of the incursion in May 1970, "Saigon's dreams [of security] may prove to be Phnom Penh's nightmares." He proved to be prescient.

Hanoi's Campaign X dealt not only with Cambodia, it also called for continued pressures against South Vietnam. But the withdrawal of four NVA divisions from South Vietnam's battlefields meant that Vietnamization and pacification programs could proceed virtually unimpeded in the southern part of Vietnam. By late 1970 the Communist Lao Dong party conceded in internal documents that Saigon had made great strides and gained wide control of the land and people. Still Hanoi knew that it could take this risk because time was its ally, inasmuch as antiwar sentiment in the United States necessitated the continued withdrawal of U.S. troops no matter how prepared South Vietnam was to assume the burden of its own defense.

## The "one war" concept

When he took command of U.S. forces in Vietnam in June 1968, General Creighton Abrams had first to devise, then to apply, strategy and tactics in a war different from what he had experienced as an aggressive World War II tank commander. Defense Secretary Laird, who gave marching orders to Abrams early in the Nixon administration, admitted:

Militarily, we both realized, Abrams faced an impossible task. He had been engaged in a limited war, using limited means, with a limited objective, against an enemy whose objectives were not limited. Now he would have to continue fighting this war and, at the same time, guide the withdrawal of our men and train the South Vietnamese army.

During the first four years of American involvement in the Vietnam War, the major task of U.S. troops had been to search out and destroy enemy Main Force units while leaving pacification and civil duties to the South Vietnamese. But Abrams combined the various facets—destroying enemy forces, providing security, and nation-building—into a "one war" concept whose principal goal was to protect the civilian population so that the government could reestablish its authority. Quick-hitting, multi-battalion search and destroy operations of the Westmoreland era, such as Masher/White Wing, Hastings, and Junction City, gave way to longer-range, more diffuse operations in which U.S. and ARVN worked together to provide population security. In I Corps, for example, the 101st Airborne Division coordinated with the 1st ARVN Division in three consecutive operations from 1969 through 1971. In Operations Randolph Glen, Texas Star, and Jefferson Glen, the Americans and ARVN provided a shield of security in the populated lowlands of Thua Thien Province, while other U.S. troops conducted offensive actions against the Main Forces in the western highlands of Thua Thien and Quang Tri provinces. These operations produced far fewer enemy casualties than the large operations of early years, but success was now measured not in body counts but in pacification gains and in the de-

struction of enemy supplies. General Abrams recognized that enemy forays from the sanctuaries into Vietnam were always preceded by a logistical build-up of enough supplies to support the attack. The North Vietnamese carried these supplies forward, caching them along the trails and near the scene of intended battle. Abrams characterized this enemy practice as sticking out a "logistics nose" and defined the countertactic of cutting it off. With his supply system disrupted, the enemy was less able to attack.

## Tactics of the withdrawal army

The Vietnam War had been largely a war of ambushes. Ninety percent of U.S. combat casualties occurred in company-sized engagements—usually in the first few minutes of battle. Now with the shift away from major search and destroy actions, the war shrank to even smaller clashes. General Abrams encouraged adoption of enemy tactics, relying on U.S. mobility to maneuver faster than the enemy and on firepower to eliminate him. "We work in small patrols because that's how the enemy moves—in groups of four and five," said Abrams. "When he fights in squad size, we now fight in squad size. When he cuts to half a squad, so do we."

This change transferred an enormous responsibility to the platoon leaders, usually first lieutenants, and the non-commissioned officers who served as squad leaders. They now conducted the "shooting war," and success often hinged on the speed and instincts of their reactions. "In many cases a platoon action is a major [battle]," said 196th Brigade commander Col. Hathaway.

They are of very short duration, very violent. There's very little anybody can do except maybe the squad leader or maybe the platoon leader to influence the outcome of this. . . . The only thing that the battalion commander, the brigade commander, or anybody else for that matter, can do is make sure that the people are well prepared, that they have artillery cover, that they have the necessary supplies, that you have medical evacuation available.

The one thing most units lacked, which commanders were incapable of supplying, was an adequate number of soldiers. Steady U.S. withdrawals and stringent controls on the number of soldiers who could be sent to Vietnam produced a serious manpower shortage. Units in the field had difficulty getting replacements for all their wounded or killed soldiers or for those who rotated home at the conclusion of their tours. As a result, companies and platoons went into the field at half or even less than half strength. First Lieutenant William Joy, a platoon leader with the 101st Airborne Division in 1971, had an average of 21 men in his platoon (authorized strength was 41) and never had more than 33. Captain Steve Adolph, a Special Forces veteran of the Tet offensive, commanded a company (ideally six officers and 158 enlisted men) in the 25th Division during his third tour in late 1970. "I was going into the field with fifty or sixty men and two officers," he said.

Beyond the manpower problem, the disengagement years of 1970 and 1971 saw the army itself deteriorate. It sometimes seemed to be little more than a ragtag band of men wearing bandannas, peace symbols, and floppy bush hats with little or no fight left in it; many officers and NCOs on whom so much depended had done little or no fighting. Most small-unit leaders—lieutenants not long past Officer Candidate Schools or "shake 'n bake" sergeants who had been rushed through school and given high enlisted ranks to fill vacancies—had no experience in combat and neither had their soldiers. "Things had died down enough that they had not seen much combat," said Captain Adolph. "When I took over the company they were going into the field with three M-16 magazines each." In earlier years, soldiers on patrol packed a dozen or more. "You are supposed to put the most experienced person on point, so when we patrolled I walked the point," Adolph said. The shortage of experienced noncommissioned officers resulted from the long war and the one-year tour, so that the seasoned veterans had done their one or two or three tours and had rotated out, leaving younger men to carry the burden.

Major David L. Ogilvy, a New Zealand army veteran of jungle warfare and an expert in counterinsurgency tactics who rose from the enlisted ranks to a commission, went on patrol with units of the Americal Division in 1971. With an outsider's perspective he observed some of the problems with American army small-unit leadership. "Because the platoon commander and the sergeant are essentially the same age, they have the same experience in this army," he said. "Neither can rely on the other for help. . . . A sergeant is paid for his responsibility. It seems to me that some of the sergeants I've seen here don't warrant their pay." According to Ogilvy, the squad leaders failed to enforce discipline or proper tactics. He gave this example:

A weapon should be carried without a sling, with both hands on the weapon. One hand around the forward part of the woodwork, the command hand around the small of the butt, one finger on the trigger and the thumb against the safety catch so there's only a split second of time before you can use your weapon. I never saw one fellow with both hands on his weapon at any time.

In the seconds it took to unsling and position the weapon, Ogilvy said, "a fleeting target in the jungle, the opposition, can go." Ogilvy also noticed troops were noisy, tended to use incorrect gear and camouflage, and relied on loose patrolling techniques, bunching up instead of maintaining proper spacing between men to reduce potential booby trap casualties.

For many American units in this seeming "wind down" period of the war, the absence of opposition was welcome. They practiced what was called "search and evade" tactics, consciously staying out of harm's way. "We passed by the NVA or VC," said army medic Scott Gauthier. "They'd be going one way and we'd be going the other so we'd just pass them. We didn't want to open fire. Nobody wanted to die. Nobody wanted anything to happen." The men in army Captain William Paris's unit accepted the pronouncement of Commander in Chief Richard Nixon, who had said the U.S. Army was in Vietnam to support the ARVN. "Any fighting [was] incidental to helping them . . . ," said Paris. "Anyone who was in the infantry after November or December of 1970 really didn't have much to do. Any fighting they got into was totally by mistake."

Many officers and NCOs came to consider their primary responsibility to be to return their men safely home rather than to hunt the enemy or to carry out a tactical mission. On patrol that meant keeping on the move, since to remain in one place often invited attack. Lt. William Joy knew of some three-man scout teams in his battalion who "would sit there for three or four days, right where they were let off the helicopter. They would almost always get hit." Joy's platoon patrolled endlessly in the hills above the huge U.S. base at Cam Ranh Bay to prevent infiltration of enemy units. To avoid booby traps, Joy, a Special Forces-trained officer, sometimes took point, leading his platoon through the jungle rather than along trails. Joy violated his own rules of constant movement when on some afternoons it became too hot to continue through the jungle. Then he occasionally took the platoon into a bamboo thicket and put claymore mines and trip wires all around. The men rested or slept during the stifling afternoon. "After a while we picked up and moved on," Joy said.

As the number of American units in Vietnam decreased, the tactic of splitting companies into platoons and platoons into squads permitted wider and quicker coverage of territory. But if it was to be effective the patrolling had to be aggressive. A firebase located on high ground brought an area within range of U.S. guns, but without active patrolling enemy units might simply by-pass the firebase, setting booby traps as they passed through the area. The best means of discouraging the enemy, according to New Zealand's Major Ogilvy, was to do precisely what more and more Americans were refusing to do:

[set up] dozens of ambushes. Go out by night, by foot. Move by night, set up the ambush, stay out there for six, seven, nine, ten days, be within artillery range and have available air support. Instead of the enemy dominating the ground by booby traps and our fear of going out there, let us dominate it by ambushes. I realize that we're now in a defense posture here and probably the idea is to restrict casualties. I think we could probably restrict casualties and do this defensive withdrawal by carrying out this large number of ambushes.

On the contrary, more units, when sent to patrol areas outside the firebases and to set ambushes, often moved so noisily as to scare away the enemy or did not move at all. "We basically went out there and hid," said James E. Willard, a draftee in the 25th Division in 1970. "If you got shot at, you'd shoot back. That was about it. I wasn't looking to kill anyone if I could help it."

As the U.S. combat presence declined, large search and destroy operations gave way to small-unit patrols in an effort to keep the enemy off balance and to find and destroy his supply caches. General Abrams called it cutting off the enemy's logistics nose. Although enemy activity, and the likelihood of ambush, had lessened, the tension for soldiers on patrol did

## On Patrol

not slacken. Mines and booby traps laced the overgrown trails and roads into villages. Also, sniper fire could erupt at any moment. Below, packing gear and rations to last several days, men of the 3d Brigade, 101st Airborne Division, patrol near Camp Evans in northern Thua Thien Province, late 1969.

Right. *Near Xuan Loc, Long Khanh Province, in December 1971, troops of the 3d Brigade, 1st Cavalry Division (Airmobile), pause to listen for any unusual noises. Wide spacing between the men reduced the risk of more than one soldier being harmed by a booby trap or mine.*

Below. *After four days on patrol without meeting the enemy—though they did find one supply cache—the 1st Cav troopers check map coordinates so they can call in helicopters to return them to base.*

Above. *Their Americal Division unit under sniper attack southeast of Chu Lai in January 1971, PFC Rickey McClean (right) returns fire with his M16 rifle while PFC David Wright (left) follows suit with an M60 machine gun.*

Left. *A soldier from the 101st Airborne Division emerges from a camouflaged enemy bunker, one of ninety-three the Americans discovered while on patrol near the A Shau Valley in late spring 1971.*

## Firebases under attack

The North Vietnamese did not lose their compulsion to kill Americans and South Vietnamese, especially those who chose to sit in static positions. Throughout the country, the North Vietnamese and Vietcong kept up a steady level of harassment and attack by "indirect" fire, that is, by mortars or artillery whose shells travel to an unseen target on a preplotted trajectory. To disrupt pacification and Vietnamization programs, the enemy increasingly attacked civilians and Territorial Forces. South Vietnamese Regional and Popular Forces suffered 30 percent of all "friendly" deaths by indirect fire in 1970, compared to 23 percent in 1968 and 17 percent in 1969. Together civilians and the RF/PF Forces who defended them suffered 66 percent of their casualties by indirect fire from 1968 through 1970. The intensity of these attacks—the number of rounds fired—rose in 1970, especially in I Corps Tactical Zone.

Enemy ground attacks also increased. In one combined attack on June 11, Communists shelled the friendly hamlet of Thanh My, thirty kilometers southeast of Da Nang, with 60MM and 82MM mortars. Then 200 soldiers dashed through the hamlet tossing grenades and satchel charges and pinning down the defenders with rifle fire. When the terror ended, most of Thanh My had been destroyed, and seventy-four civilians lay dead. The attackers lost only seven men killed.

U.S. firebases made inviting targets, both for indirect fire and ground attacks, such as the combined assault mounted against the 101st Airborne Division's FSB Ripcord in July 1970. The 2d Battalion, 506th Infantry, of the division's 3d Brigade, had constructed Ripcord in April, just northeast of the NVA bastion in the rugged A Shau Valley. It was to be a forward base for a U.S. summer offensive, in concert with the 3d Regiment of the 1st ARVN Division, against the supply caches and base areas of the 29th and 803d Regiments of the 324th NVA Division. For two months the 2d Battalion patrolled around the base and set up ambushes but found few enemy soldiers.

That changed dramatically in July after the 6th NVA Regiment had deployed to the area around Ripcord, supporting the 29th and 803d Regiments. With the equivalent of a division loosely surrounding Ripcord, the NVA stepped up attacks by fire using mortars, including the fearsome 120MM, and recoilless rifles. Patrolling U.S. units engaged in twenty-three firefights with NVA forces around Ripcord in the first week of July alone. They also brought up more antiaircraft weapons, especially 12.7MM machine guns, to attack helicopters carrying reinforcements and supplies. On the afternoon of July 18, NVA gunners shot down a twin-rotor CH-47 Chinook, which crashed into a 105MM howitzer battery setting off the stored ammunition, causing a major fire within the base and destroying six howitzers in the bargain. Mortar attacks continued for the next several days, and twice com-

panies on patrol were pinned down for several hours outside the base, suffering numerous killed and wounded.

By July 22, 3d Brigade commander Colonel Benjamin L. Harrison concluded that it was costing him too much to defend and supply Ripcord and he ordered its evacuation. On the following day, beginning at 5:45 A.M., artillerymen from nearby bases fired more than 2,200 rounds to cover the extraction by helicopter. The NVA nevertheless managed to lob several hundred mortar rounds into the base, and the evacuation took place under continuous fire. Another CH-47 Chinook fell to 12.7MM ground fire, and eight others (of a total of fourteen involved in the evacuation) were hit. The Americans retreated from Ripcord after having lost sixty-one men killed and 345 wounded in a little over three weeks.

After forcing the Americans out of Ripcord, the 1,500-man 6th NVA Regiment trekked eight kilometers north to attack Firebase O'Reilly, manned by the 1st ARVN Regi-

ment of the 1st ARVN Division. Predicting an "all-out effort to get O'Reilly," division commander Major General Ngo Quang Truong reinforced with another regiment. The South Vietnamese defended the base for two months against fierce enemy attacks, but in September they decided to abandon O'Reilly and another embattled firebase, Barnett, farther north and close to the Laos border.

Despite these many instances of attack by fire and by sappers, many U.S. commanders and men in the American firebases were lax in their security precautions. Lieutenant Colonel Richard J. Kattar, who served as a 1st Cavalry Division brigade inspector general before taking over a battalion, made repeated tours of firebases and observed "downright incompetent" tendencies. He found troops using bangalore torpedoes (charges shaped to explode upward in order to blow through barbed wire) to clear brush for a firebase, walking about without steel helmets, and failing to shift crew-served weapons, such as

howitzers, around the perimeter to confuse the enemy's efforts to pinpoint locations for eventual attack.

The men of Company D, 2d Battalion, 327th Infantry, 101st Airborne, provided a praiseworthy illustration of good security when they repulsed a sapper attack against FSB Tomahawk on June 10, 1970. After reconnoitering the lowlands firebase in Thua Thien Province for a week, an estimated seventy sappers from the 31st Sapper Company, 4th NVA Regiment, launched a three-pronged assault against Tomahawk. Their main objectives were three 155MM howitzers. To assure surprise, the enemy chose not to precede their attack with the usual preparatory fires and simply crept up to the wire, by-passing trip flares, and began to cut their way through.

---

*Under attack at Firebase O'Reilly. Ducking machine-gun fire, ARVN 1st Division troops move against an NVA mortar harassing the base west of Hue in September 1970.*

According to proper procedure, the company commander always had one officer or NCO walking the perimeter at night to keep the men on guard duty awake and alert. The company had also recently rehearsed the defensive plan three times. The patrolling platoon sergeant spotted one sapper in the wire and killed him. At the sound of gunfire, the men leaped to their positions, hurriedly bringing up artillery fire and mortars and firing their rifles. During the thirty-five-minute fight, none of the sappers penetrated the base and twenty-eight were killed. One U.S. soldier died when a dud illumination canister fell on him. In the division report the company was lauded for its performance, but it was criticized for not having patrolled for nine days, thus allowing the enemy to get a fix on the base.

U.S. Commander General Abrams was especially impatient with lapses in firebase security, believing that his officers should eliminate complacency and keep soldiers in a state of alertness and preparedness. When visiting a firebase, Abrams often conducted his own inspection, usually bending over to test the tautness of tangle-foot wire, which was stretched outside the concertina in a crisscross pattern. The highly publicized attack on FSB Mary Ann in March 1971 persuaded Abrams to pursue the investigation until several officers had been punished. But less than two months after Mary Ann, a dinner-time rocket attack on Firebase Charlie 2, near the demilitarized zone, killed twenty-nine soldiers and wounded fifty more. One rocket scored a direct hit on a bunker adjacent to the mess hall where the men had scurried for shelter. The rocket, with a time-delay fuse, drove through six feet of overhead cover before detonating.

When informed of the Charlie 2 attack, Abrams delivered a "broadside" tirade at his staff, hitting them, according to an aide, "with all eight stars"—the two groups of four general's stars on each side of his collar. The men of the 1st Brigade, 5th Mechanized Division, at Charlie 2 had ignored a fundamental rule by taking shelter in one bunker, by "bunching up" when they should have scattered. "An atmosphere and climate begin to prevail, and with it comes a certain amount of laxity," Abrams later said to newsmen. "It just requires a lot of attention, a herculean effort to keep alertness up."

Abrams's message filtered down through the ranks. When Colonel Thomas Ware took over the 101st Airborne Division's 2d Brigade a few weeks later and reported for his briefing, division commander Major General Thomas M. Tarpley told him that officers in every layer would be relieved if any firebase suffered heavy casualties through carelessness. Tarpley also said, "The day is past when U.S. units will engage in bloody combat for reasons not clear to the United States public and president." The division commander warned Ware not to get into a situation in which faulty tactics and planning resulted in heavy casualties.

Beginning his third tour in Vietnam, Colonel Ware faced the formidable task of keeping under control the men on the brigade's large base of Phu Bai, which had a fourteen-kilometer circumference. Tarpley reminded him that things had changed since his previous tour in 1967, when just two men in his battalion had been found with marijuana. Now the attack on drugs had become a priority of the division. Tarpley advised him to break up gaggles of men, split up replacements and transfers, and forbid men from congregating because idle men in groups seemed trouble-prone. "Everybody belongs to somebody," said Tarpley. "Find his unit." Within the first few days on the job, Ware understood Tarpley's message. He saw that the training and motivation of the soldiers had declined, that the NCOs had been in the army only slightly longer than the soldiers they were supposedly leading. Ware formed quick impressions of his officers. "The good leaders had effective units," he said. "Average leaders had poor units. A poor leader had a mob on his hands."

## 1st of the 5th Cav

During the years of Vietnamization, while the United States was winding down the war and the military had difficulties maintaining discipline, leadership ranged from good to poor, and units varied of necessity between effective and undistinguished. The 1st Battalion, 5th Cavalry, 1st Cavalry Division (Airmobile), and its commander in early 1971, Lt. Col. Richard Kattar, was one example of a unit that remained effective and disciplined.

When Kattar took command of the 1st Battalion, 5th Cavalry, in III Corps Tactical Zone, his men received a jolt. "He energized the battalion," said Captain Eugene J. White, Jr., Company A commander. "He pulled me out of the field and brought me back to the base and said, 'My name's Kattar. Here's what you can expect from me, and here's what I expect from you.' That's the first time a battalion commander had talked to me like that." Already close to the end of his one-year tour, White extended the tour in order to remain with the battalion. Company B commander Captain Hugh Foster at first was skeptical. Kattar came on too strong for Foster. "But he was supportive and he gave his people credit for common sense," said Foster. Many of the troops at the time grumbled about going into the field. But Kattar told operations officer Lieutenant John D. Stube, "We cannot have that attitude. People will be sloppy, make mistakes and get killed."

Kattar immediately improved firebase security. He ordered more patrolling and required his men to change the positions of the 105MM howitzers after dark. He had them loaded with fléchette rounds (an antipersonnel round containing short, nail-like projectiles) for direct fire against any attackers. Units returning from patrol were given additional tasks to keep them busy on the base; the prior habit of "flopping out" had raised the level of boredom.

In his second tour after serving as an adviser in 1963–64, Kattar believed that the soldiers "deserved to be inspired, to believe in a cause," and their own survival was an excellent cause. Kattar visited each company separately and gave the men a version of the following speech:

No one in his right mind wants to be shot at, indeed killed. Unless you're a crackpot, and I'm certainly not a crackpot. But I am a professional soldier. I've been here before, I've been shot at before, and I have lived as you live, on the trail with my whole life on my back. I am not here to demonstrate courage under fire. Because I'm scared to death every time somebody shoots at me. The only thing I'm delighted with is that the army took the time to train me well enough so I react properly under fire. Because that's all it is—a reaction. No one really thinks about what the hell they're doing.

Now I have a beautiful wife, three lovely children and a great life ahead of me. I want to get this done and get back to that. The things I can guarantee you are that I will die for you, if it's necessary, and that I will never experiment with you, and that if you listen to what I tell you and do as I say and am prepared to do with you, then your opportunity to fight and win will be the greatest, will be maximized. Because it makes no sense to me at all for someone to draw the conclusion that they're giving themselves an opportunity to get back home by walking around the jungle in a stupor, either because of dope or preoccupation of mind. The best way to get home is to be a superb infantryman. When you walk through that jungle, you'll walk through there sharp and intent upon insuring that if that sonofabitch raises his goddam ugly head to blow you away, you're going to blow him away first.

And then we're going home.

Kattar forbade the wearing of bandannas and required his men to wear steel helmets. He also put a stop to one of the characteristic "grunt" symbols of the war—the wearing of "Pancho Villa" bandoliers of M60 ammunition crossed over the shoulders. The steel links in the belt tended to rust, and when a soldier flattened on the ground, dirt got into the ammo links. Also, under fire a soldier had difficulty getting the belt off to pass it to the machine gunner. Henceforth only the gunner carried ammunition that way; the remainder was carried in an M60 ammunition box. Kattar required company commanders to attach "secure" scrambler devices to the standard PRC–77 radio for communications security; for a long time the practice had been to dispense with them because they were heavy.

Under the prevailing circumstances of 1971, Kattar's insistence on tight discipline and "by-the-book" procedures might have made him a candidate for "fragging" by disgruntled troops. But most of the men responded to his leadership. "He took care of the soldiers," said Captain Foster. Operating from Firebases Apache and Mace, the 1st Battalion's mission was to pursue the 33d NVA Regiment. "Kattar always came out into the field," Foster said. "He talked with the soldiers. He went out on sweeps with the company. He showed that he shared the risks."

# U.S. Army Troop Withdrawals
## 1969-1972

| | Major Combat Unit | Withdrawal | Total U.S. forces remaining in Vietnam (estimated) |
|---|---|---|---|
| | 9th Infantry Division, 1st Brigade, 2d Brigade (3d Brigade) | August 1969 (September 1970) | 519,000 |
| | 1st Infantry Division | April 1970 | 434,000 |
| | 199th Infantry Brigade (Light) | October 1970 | 384,000 |
| | 25th Infantry Division 1st Brigade, 3d Brigade (2d Brigade) | December 1970 (April 1971) | |
| | 4th Infantry Division 1st Brigade, 2d Brigade (3d Brigade) | December 1970 (April 1970) | 344,000 |
| | 1st Cavalry Division (Airmobile)* 1st Brigade, 2d Brigade | April 1971 | |
| | 11th Armored Cavalry Regiment | April 1971 | 284,000 |
| | 1st Brigade 5th Infantry Division (Mechanized) | August 1971 | 226,000 |
| | 173d Airborne Brigade | September 1971 | 198,000 |
| | 23d Infantry Division (American)* 11th Brigade (Light) 198th Brigade (Light) | November 1971 | 184,000 |
| | 101st Airborne Division | January 1972 | 139,000 |
| | 3d Brigade *1st Cavalry Division 196th Brigade (Light) 23d Infantry Division | June 1972 | 49,000 |

Note: U.S. Marine Corps divisions withdrew as follows:

| 3d Marine Division | November 1969 |
|---|---|
| 1st Marine Division | April 1971 |

The 1st Battalion also had its share of the problems of the times—combat refusals, drug problems, racial strife—which the weakened "system" proved incapable of resolving. Punishments for offenses that once were considered to be serious had become lenient. A squad leader who had refused Foster's order to stake out an ambush was court-martialed and found guilty, fined only $100, and was not demoted. Another soldier, a machine gunner, threatened to kill a squad leader if he forced his men to advance down a certain trail. Sent to the rear for prosecution, the man returned shortly without having been court-martialed. The legal authorities said that since he had not fired his weapon, he had committed no offense. Captain Foster attempted to isolate his problems in Company B. "I took all the slugs I had and put them together in one platoon," he said. "I kept them away from the rest of the men. I said if you guys want to smoke dope and get yourselves killed and the system won't help me, then just go off by yourselves and do it."

## Valedictory to Vietnam

In February of 1971, officers of the 1st of the 5th Cavalry got word that the war would end for them in late March, and they informed their troops that they were going to "stand down" in a month. Normally units with such information worked very cautiously indeed, but Kattar permitted no slack. A few days before the battalion left the field, intelligence suggested the presence of a small contingent of the 33d NVA Regiment, and Kattar planned to attack it. Wringing permission from a somewhat reluctant division commander, Major General George W. Putnam, Jr., Kattar mounted a full battalion assault as the 1/5's valedictory action in Vietnam. "I don't recall a single soldier saying, 'I'm not going,'" said Captain White of Company A.

Kattar sent White's company on a difficult night march to link up with F Troop of the 11th Armored Cavalry Regiment, which was attached to the battalion. By daylight they swung off Highway 1 and moved west into the jungle. Artillery fire drowned the sound of the armored vehicles. Kattar's plan was to send the armored column toward the suspected enemy camp, which ought to cause them to move. To catch them in a pincer, at last light Companies C and D assaulted by helicopter several kilometers to the west of White and the armored column. Foster's Company B acted as battalion reserve.

During the night the North Vietnamese started to scatter. At midday Captain William Brownell's Company D got into some small firefights, and Kattar committed Foster's company to reinforce. Shooting was desultory as the enemy scurried out of the trap in groups of twos and threes. At nightfall the men set up "automatic" ambushes using claymore mines. At 3:00 A.M. enemy soldiers tripped one of White's ambushes, and he called in additional artillery on the area. In the morning the men found four enemy bodies. Other units discovered numerous blood trails and perhaps twenty enemy weapons but no more bodies. The body count held little significance for Kattar, he said later. What mattered was the pride his men felt after accomplishing a difficult operation. "They weren't backing out of Vietnam, licking their wounds," he said. "They were doing their jobs." One man of the battalion was killed (by a dud mortar round that exploded during disposal) and several were wounded.

As the battalion came off the helicopter pad at Bien Hoa to stand down prior to leaving Vietnam, the troops were enthusiastic, shouting "All the way!" and "Airborne!" as they left the war behind them. General Putnam, who had come out to the airfield, was clearly moved by the sight, remarking that it was the picture he wished people would remember of the U.S. soldier in Vietnam. "They were aggressive right up to the day they stood down," said Putnam. A writer from the division historical office, also out to watch the 1st of the 5th come in from the field, asked operations officer Lt. Stube how the battalion commander had managed to get these troops to act as they did. "He is the finest leader I have ever known," Stube answered. "He motivated soldiers and officers to do the right thing."

## Standing down

In the kind of formal ceremony marked by speeches and flag-lowering rituals that became familiar throughout Vietnam, the 1st Battalion, 5th Cavalry, stood down at Bien Hoa the day after returning from the field. Other battalions of the 1st Cavalry Division soon did likewise. "Standing down is disintegrating," said General Putnam. "The 1st Cav was a magnificent organization, and I was watching it disintegrate." At the end of April, General Putnam carried the division's colors to Fort Hood, Texas, the Cav's permanent home, and delivered them to the division's next commander. The "First Team," which had brought airmobility to Vietnam in the late summer of 1965, was gone, leaving only a separate brigade.

The marines who had first come over Red Beach in Da Nang in March 1965 left at the same time. The marine headquarters, called III Marine Amphibious Force (or III MAF), had served as a corps-level headquarters in I Corps Tactical Zone for most of the war—controlling marines, army, and navy units that totaled 150,000 men at peak strength in 1968. In a ceremony on April 14 that featured a parade, with marine aircraft flying overhead, III MAF commander Lieutenant General Donn J. Robertson lauded the marines for what they had done in Vietnam. "Results of our combined efforts surround us in the security in the hillsides, construction of buildings and prosperity of the people," he said. "I am proud to have been a partner in that effort." Two other units that had come early to the Vietnam War joined the 1971 exodus. The 5th Special

Forces Group turned over the last of its camps to the Vietnamese and departed on March 1, 1971. The 173d Airborne Brigade, the first army combat unit to arrive in Vietnam, left in August.

In October, the conclusion of the 101st Division's Operation Jefferson Glen brought to an end the participation of U.S. ground combat units in major operations. On Veterans Day, November 11, 1971, the 23d Infantry (American) Division—less the 196th Brigade, which remained until the next June—closed out its role in Vietnam, and the following day President Nixon affirmed the defensive posture of U.S. forces. "American troops are now in a defensive position . . . in a defensive role," he said. "The offensive activities of search and destroy are now being undertaken by the South Vietnamese." As they watched their comrades stand down, the men of the 196th Brigade, left behind to provide security in the Da Nang region, seemed to accept their fate resolutely. "It's just a job we have to do," said Sp4 Steve Dondero. "It doesn't make my day any shorter to know that all the other grunts are going home." But a senior brigade officer spoke more to the point when he said, behind the cloak of anonymity, "Nobody in the brigade gives a damn about this war anymore, including me. We will be happy to get home and when we do the enemy will march down out of the hills and take over."

That senior officer's bitter statement was widely shared among the departing American soldiers. The Vietnam experience had carried U.S. armed forces to the point of disintegration. Said army Captain Steve Adolph, a veteran of three tours, "When I came home, I didn't think the U.S. Army could whip the North Vietnamese Boy Scouts, and I wasn't sure about the Girl Scouts either." Brigadier General Theodore C. Mataxis, who had served as a corps adviser, brigade commander, and acting division commander, summed up the army's tortuous journey this way: "It's been the opposite of Korea. There we went in with a bad army and came out with a good one. In Vietnam we went in with a good army and came out with a bad one."

*Snapshots of the 1/5 Cavalry, at Firebase Apache. Left. Company B commander Capt. Hugh Foster and First Sgt. Ben Reynolds hoist the company guidon.*

Above. *Foster in the company B command post.*

Below left. *An overview of Firebase Apache.*

# An Army Departs

Withdrawal took many GIs from jungle post to home base in the States in a matter of days. "Out-processing" for a unit started with stand-down ceremonies during which the colors were lowered and the unit formally redeployed. Departing troops then cleaned and turned in their field gear, had haircuts if they needed them, and claimed their "souvenirs"; war trophies, excluding live ordnance, could be taken home. After June 1971, soldiers also submitted to urinalyses, which detected drug addiction. A major stop on the trail home was the huge U.S. complex at Long Binh. The base outside of Saigon, which had once received thousands of in-

Men of the 101st Airborne Division go home in January 1972. Left. The men arrive at Phu Bai, division HQ. Above. They pass through the "Freedom Arch" at Long Binh.

coming troops a week, now served as the processing center for the departure of an army. From Long Binh troops traveled to Bien Hoa, Tan Son Nhut, or some other airfield, where "Freedom Birds" waited to transport them back to "the World," as many troops called home.

At the end of World War II, U.S. forces had abandoned huge amounts of equipment and weapons on the ground or dumped them over the sides of ships. The military had no intention of doing the same in Vietnam. Virtually everything, from helicopters to crates of C-rations, had to be accounted for. Equipment was repaired, if possible, and transported to bases in the States or in Asia or given to U.S. allies, primarily South Vietnam. By mid-July 1971, the U.S. had turned over to South Vietnam nearly 240 bases and other installations, most of them small camps and outposts in border regions.

*Packing up and moving out. At Da Nang, the "comforts of home" go into storage.*

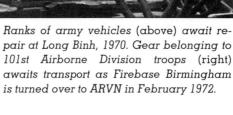

*Ranks of army vehicles (above) await repair at Long Binh, 1970. Gear belonging to 101st Airborne Division troops (right) awaits transport as Firebase Birmingham is turned over to ARVN in February 1972.*

Final moments in 'Nam. Top. Two Americans receive tearful good-byes from their Vietnamese girlfriends at Bien Hoa.

Above. Soldiers polish their boots before departing Long Binh.

Right. In fresh uniforms, GIs aboard a "Freedom Bird" at Bien Hoa air base take off for home, 1971.

Left. *Sixteen hours after taking off from Vietnam, returning GIs of the 101st Airborne and American Divisions disembark at McChord Air Force Base, near Tacoma, Washington, in November 1971. Above. Men of 101st await a flight home from Seattle-Tacoma Airport.*

GIs returned from Vietnam more quickly than soldiers had from any other war. There was little time in which they could prepare for what lay ahead. Upon landing at an air base in the U.S., GIs were usually greeted by a huge sign reading, "Welcome Home Soldier—U.S.A. is Proud of You," a steak dinner, and much paperwork. Many soldiers faced months of what they called "Mickey Mouse" duty to fill the unexpired time of their tours. But most drew their final pay, separated from the service, and headed for home. Their welcome was often less than hospitable. Unemployment was high, GI benefits were paltry, and the American people seemed unwilling to listen to their experiences or recognize their sacrifices.

# Crisis in Command

The army the United States sent to Vietnam contained, in the opinion of General William Westmoreland, "the toughest, best trained, most dedicated American servicemen in history." Even given a commander's tendency to overpraise his men, Westmoreland may not have exaggerated; certainly he was not alone in his view. Retired Brigadier General S.L.A. Marshall, combat veteran of World War I and front-line chronicler of the Second World War and Korea, paid a lengthy visit to Vietnam in 1966, during which he operated with men in the field. He said, "My overall estimate was that the morale of the troops and the level of discipline of the Army were higher than I had ever known them in any of our wars. There was no lack of will to fight and the average soldier withstood the stress of engagement better than ever before."

Marshall also ticked off several items that nagged at him from that early trip. He wrote:

Our marksmanship and musketry were deplorably bad, and furthermore it was my reckoning that about one-third of our losses were our own fault, owing to carelessness about security. We were paying an excessive price for rotation; the average captain on the line was given too little time with his company. Hardly was he broken in when he was sent elsewhere.

Several of Marshall's critical comments—on security, rotation policies, even, to a certain extent, on marksmanship that might have improved through better training or stricter fire control—fell within the purview of the officers corps, the body of men (and women) from second lieutenants to four-star generals commissioned to lead the army. A strong supporter of the army, but also an astute critic, Marshall had identified problems in 1966 that later took on great import for the army and the American effort in Vietnam. Marshall had praised the will of the U.S. soldier and reproached his leaders for their handling of the war.

The faulty strategy of a limited war of attrition had produced a stalemate in Vietnam by the end of 1968, and infantry tactics had generally deteriorated through an overreliance on artillery and air power. In a practice that stemmed from the political consideration to hold down casualties, ground commanders from the start were encouraged to use firepower lavishly in order to conserve lives. Rather than using traditional infantry tactics to attack the enemy, U.S. units in contact increasingly resorted to rolling up into a defensive perimeter and calling for supporting artillery fire and air support. As one military critic wrote, "By 1967 only a foolhardy or desperate commander would ever engage hostile elements by any means other than with firepower." That defensive orientation, and the political need to limit casualties, led during the withdrawal years to an increased dependence on firebases. U.S. units holed up in their hilltop "castles," in effect ceding territory and movement to the mobile enemy. General Westmoreland came to criticize this "firebase psychosis" and predicted that for future wars such a narrow tactical doctrine would have to be bred out of young officers whose experience of warfare was restricted to Vietnam.

While these changes were taking place, the character of the army was also changing. Beginning in late 1969 and early 1970, the army was increasingly beset with problems that grew more severe over the next three years. In the field, soldiers refused orders to patrol a certain trail, climb a certain hill, to attack the enemy. Some unpopular officers were "fragged," or killed, by their own disgruntled men. In rear areas drug problems were rife, and blacks and whites battled. As the climate in the United States grew increasingly polarized, new soldiers, many of them

draftees coming from the society, brought their heightened political consciousnesses—and their drug problems and disrespect for authority—with them. They argued against the legality and brutality of the war, and many participated in political workshops, lectures, and discussion groups. Each service—army, marines, navy, air force—experienced varying measures of deterioration in Vietnam. But the problems of the army, as the preponderant force, gained the most exposure and generated the most scrutiny and commentary, both inside and outside the army.

The army's senior generals were among the last to recognize these changes. General Bruce Palmer, vice chief of staff during the army's most turbulent years, 1968–72, believed that it took approximately two years for knowledge of change in the field to filter up to leaders in Washington. It took roughly a year, according to Palmer, for events at the grassroots level, in small units, to come to the attention of the senior officers in a theater. This was probably because small-unit leaders (up to battalion commander) did not know how to react to the restlessness of the troops and hence did not report it. Then another year might elapse, Palmer felt, before the news of change in the theater reached Washington. The state of the army did not really come to the attention of the army's top leadership until the time of the Cambodian incursion in May 1970. "All of a sudden, you're blindsided," Palmer said. "But it wasn't sudden at all. It had probably been going on for a year, a year and a half. We were slow catching on."

Evidence for Palmer's frank admission existed in the statements of top officers in Vietnam who often seemed oblivious to problems, heedless to change. A common refrain of commanders in Vietnam was that "it" may be happening but not in my outfit. After the war many commanders persisted in the fantasy. As one 1971 division commander wrongly asserted, "I didn't have the troubles they were having at that time." Such officers were wearing blinders. And for every high-ranking officer who denied having "trouble," numerous captains, lieutenants, and NCOs either had to deal with it, go along with it, or let it slide, leaving the accumulation of problems for the next officer rotating through.

One opinion with which everyone seemed to agree, however, was that the 23d Infantry Division (American) had "troubles." Hastily constituted in September 1967 from three separate outfits—the 11th, 196th, and 198th Infantry Brigades—the American encountered problems almost from its start. Brigadier General Andy A. Lipscomb later said that the 11th Infantry Brigade was not ready for combat when he took it to Vietnam. Inquiries revealed that the soldiers of the 11th were relatively unschooled in the Geneva Convention and negligent in reporting civilian casualties. To create a division staff, the American sought officers from other units; those units viewed the "draft" of staff officers as an opportunity to dispose of deadwood. In the American planning and operations staff, for example, there was only one major among field grade officers (major, lieutenant colonel, colonel) who had graduated from the Army Command and General Staff College. Of the majors, all but two had been passed over for promotion to lieutenant colonel.

The 23d's first commander, Samuel W. Koster, was a newly promoted and untried major general who, after commanding a battalion in World War II, had performed mainly staff work. To whip such a mongrel group of independent brigades and new staff officers into a coherent division with an *esprit de corps* was to prove beyond the abilities of those who led the Americal Division. Nowhere was the failure of leadership in Vietnam more apparent than during the killings of civilians in the hamlet of My Lai-4 on March 16, 1968, and in the Americal Division after the event. In the later years of the war the division reverted to calling itself the 23d Infantry Division, in an effort to divorce itself from the shame of the Americal.

The My Lai incident left an indelible stain on the performance of the U.S. Army in Vietnam, leading to criticism of strategy, tactics, and leadership, and, by extension, raising questions about the entire U.S. effort in Vietnam. My Lai became perhaps the most deeply probed and widely publicized event of the war. Throughout late 1970 and 1971 the trials of some participants took place in the harsh glare of national publicity. In mid-1970, about the same time that General Palmer suggested that the top army leadership was first becoming aware of deep-seated problems within the army, the public was also learning about the grisly events that occurred at My Lai.

# The Peers Commission

The atrocities at My Lai first came to the army's attention in March 1969, when ex-GI Ron Ridenhour wrote a letter to the army, to Defense Secretary Laird, and to some congressmen. He alleged that one year earlier Charlie Company, 1st Battalion, 20th Infantry, of the Americal, had committed "dark and bloody" deeds in a village nicknamed "Pinkville" in Quang Ngai Province. Although not a member of the unit, Ridenhour reconstructed events based on conversations he had had with participants. The men, he said, had orders "to destroy the trouble spot and all its inhabitants," and as a consequence perhaps 400 civilians had been massacred. Company commander Captain Ernest Medina had been "hesitant" in issuing the orders, "as if it were something he didn't want to do but had to."

According to the battalion after action report, the sweep through My Lai that day had resulted in 128 Vietcong dead and three weapons captured. That only three rifles were recovered from such a large number of enemy dead apparently aroused few suspicions as the report traveled up through the chain of command, although a follow-up report completed a month later by brigade commander Colonel Oran Henderson concluded that twenty civilians may have been killed by artillery "preparatory fires and by the cross fires of the US and VC forces." Based on the favorable after action report, the staff of General Westmoreland, commander of U.S. forces in Vietnam in March 1968, sent congratulations to "officers and men of C-1-20 for outstanding action" that had "dealt [the] enemy [a] heavy blow."

General Westmoreland was the army's chief of staff when, a year later, Ridenhour's letter arrived on his desk. Both he and Vice Chief of Staff General Palmer, who was the U.S. Army commander in Vietnam at the time of My Lai, were shocked by the allegations. They assigned the army's Criminal Investigation Division to look into the case, and by September enough evidence had been uncovered to charge Lieutenant William L. Calley, Jr., with murdering 109 civilians at My Lai. As the officer in command of the 2d Platoon, Calley was alleged to have taken over a machine gun and fired when a soldier balked at his order to cut down a group of villagers he had herded together. While the criminal investigation continued, Westmoreland ordered Lieutenant General William R. Peers in November 1969 to conduct a formal inquiry into the reporting systems that had failed to divulge the affair at My Lai—in short, an investigation of the cover-up.

Westmoreland chose Gen. Peers, a former division and corps commander, not only for his Vietnam experience and his probity, but also because he had not attended West Point and thus was not a "ring knocker," as academy grads were called for wearing their heavy, and highly visible, class rings. "Because he had entered the Army through ROTC at the University of California at Los Angeles," Westmoreland wrote, "there could be no presumption that ties among brother officers from West Point would be involved." With the army investigating itself, Westmoreland was sensitive to potential criticism involving the imaginary "West Point Protective Association." Critics, some of them disgruntled officers passed over in their careers, claim that graduates of the military academy tend to look out for one another, receive choice assignments and inflated officer efficiency reports, and in general advance higher and more rapidly than officers who enter the army through Officer Candidate School or Reserve Officers Training Corps. Others, often those with a West Point pedigree, argue that the military academy commission bestows no advantage. As Brigadier General Peter M. Dawkins, a West Point graduate, wrote in a doctoral dissertation critical of the army bureaucracy, "[Some] claim that every senior officer who displays a modicum of favoritism toward fellow graduates is more than compensated for by others who impose more demanding standards, on the belief that West Point graduates should be expected to perform better." Whatever the merits of the perennial argument, Westmoreland chose to sidestep the issue and strive for maximum objectivity by appointing a non-West Pointer.

*The Peers Commission in Vietnam. A security officer leads Lt. Gen. William Peers* (center) *and civilian counsel Robert Mac-Crate* (right) *through the hamlet of My Lai-4 on a site inspection trip in January 1970.*

The Peers Commission, with a staff that grew to ninety-two people, labored for nearly four months, interviewing 398 witnesses and making a field trip to the scene in Vietnam. Lt. Calley appeared before the panel just once and kept his silence, except to deny that his battalion or brigade commander had ever asked him about the events at My Lai. On March 15, 1970, two years less a day after the incident itself, and hours before a two-year statute of limitations on the military offenses would have expired, General Peers submitted a damning report to General Westmoreland. It had ramifications extending far beyond the issue of My Lai itself. General Peers summarized the panel's findings, writing:

The My Lai incident was a black mark in the annals of American military history. In analyzing the entire episode we found that the principal breakdown was in leadership. Failures occurred at every level within the chain of command, from individual non-commissioned-officer squad leaders to the command group of the division. It was an illegal operation in violation of military regulations and of human rights, starting with the planning, continuing through the brutal, destructive acts of many of the men who were involved, and culminating in aborted efforts to investigate and, finally, the suppression of the truth.

## An army in deep trouble

The breakdown in leadership cited by Peers found its most infamous personification in Lt. William Calley, a poorly trained officer of marginal intelligence. Calley's own lawyer argued that the army must share culpability for the My Lai affair since a man like Calley, whom one rifleman characterized as "just one of those guys they take off the street," would never have earned a commission under normal circumstances. Many of the army's thoughtful officers agreed.

The circumstances when Calley graduated from Officer

Candidate School in 1967 were anything but usual. In the manpower build-up between the 1965 arrival of U.S. forces in Vietnam and the 1968 Tet offensive, the number of army officers worldwide increased from 111,541 to 165,595, or 48 percent, while enlisted strength ballooned from 1,079,700 to 1,357,000, an increase of 26 percent. College students who would normally have filled the officer rolls remained on college campuses with draft deferments, and graduates sought other means to avoid the draft. Calling up the reserves or National Guard would have made trained officers and enlisted men available to the services in Vietnam, but President Johnson chose for domestic political reasons not to do so. "The failure to mobilize was one of President Johnson's major blunders," said General Palmer, who watched the army deplete itself and weaken its posture worldwide by using all army units, especially the 7th Army stationed in Germany, as replacement depots to fill its needs in Vietnam. At the war's height the army had some 365,000 men in Vietnam, each serving a one-year tour. Thus the army had to replace that number each year out of a pool of fewer than 1 million soldiers available for transfer. The army was so hungry for officers and enlisted men that it necessarily relaxed its standards to take men who would formerly have been screened out. After the disclosures of My Lai, one colonel at Fort Benning, home of the Officer Candidate School, remarked, "We have at least two or three thousand more Calleys in the army just waiting for the next calamity."

Calley was the first person tried for crimes at My Lai. His court-martial took place from November 1970 to March 1971. Convicted of killing "at least twenty-two" civilians, he received a sentence of life imprisonment. Calley was also the first—and the only—U.S. serviceman convicted of murder in Vietnam to benefit from presidential intervention when President Nixon decided to review his case. (Throughout the war 137 servicemen were convicted of murder or manslaughter of civilians.) Although Nixon took no action himself, Calley's sentence was later reduced by the secretary of the army and he gained parole in 1974.

Twenty-five men in all were charged with war crimes and related acts, such as perjury and contributing to the My Lai cover-up. Most had charges against them dismissed. Three officers other than Calley stood trial in courts-martial and were acquitted. The most senior officer tried, brigade commander Col. Oran Henderson, was charged with dereliction of duty in failing to conduct a proper investigation, failing to report a war crime, and lying before the Peers panel. Henderson epitomized the problems facing the army as it tried to unravel the truth about My Lai and assign blame. After appearing before the Peers panel, Henderson, in a magnanimous but foolish effort to protect the tarnished image of the army, wrote to Gen. Westmoreland offering to accept complete responsibility for events at My Lai. He added, "I continue to main-

tain the highest admiration, confidence, and faith in the integrity, fighting qualities and courage of the officers and men . . . present during the alleged incident." Gens. Westmoreland and Peers of course rejected Henderson's suggestion, and his acquittal after a trial two years later came as a great surprise to Gen. Peers. "From what I know of his performance and on the basis of what I would have expected of an officer of his grade and experience, I cannot agree with the verdict," Peers wrote. "If his actions are to be judged as acceptable standards for an officer in his position, the Army is indeed in deep trouble."

## From duty, honor to CYA

That trouble extended directly to the army's ivory tower, where the Americal Division commander at the time of My Lai, Samuel W. Koster, now occupied the army's most honored major general billet—superintendent of West Point, an office formerly held by such examples of rectitude as Robert E. Lee, Douglas MacArthur, and William C. Westmoreland. Charged by the Peers panel with dereliction of duty in failing to investigate civilian casualties, Koster resigned his post. Although some superintendents had taken leave in ceremonies that included full dress parades, in Koster's case the cadets simply filed past his house in quiet respect. The leveling of charges against Koster and other officers might have been expected to spark debate on duty and responsibility at the academy, which is considered to be the conscience of the army and is ruled by a personal honor code. Said Lieutenant Colonel John H. Johns, associate professor of military psychology and leadership at West Point, "I wanted an uproar around here. But there wasn't any. I even tried to provoke one, and got nowhere." The absence of criticism was due in part to the fact that many cadets and faculty seemed to feel that Koster had been made a scapegoat.

After a further investigation into General Koster's actions, the army dismissed all charges but issued a letter of censure and took back one star, leaving Koster a brigadier general. The army's internal report, according to a chagrined General Peers, "acknowledged that he may have been remiss in not reporting the twenty known civilian casualties and in not ordering a proper investigation, [but] it stressed General Koster's fine character and his long career of outstanding service, which somehow excused these derelictions." Officers at all levels questioned why the senior officers should have gotten off while junior officers had had to stand trial, and Jerome Walsh, civilian counsel to the Peers panel, went so far as to call the dismissal of charges against Koster "a whitewash of the top man." Walsh added, "General officers are given great power and responsibility. They should be held strictly to account when they fail."

One theme to emerge from testimony before the Peers panel was that the army's lofty ideal of "Duty, honor,

# The Long Gray Line

At the U.S. Military Academy at West Point, cadets bartered four years of free education for five years of active duty, though many graduates went on to careers in the army. Upon graduation, the cadets joined the "Long Gray Line" of those educated at West Point. The West Point years steeped the future officers in military discipline and ideals, and, increasingly, in the science and technology needed to operate the sophisticated machines of war. The army's tumultuous passage through the war in Vietnam, however, shook the traditions celebrated by General Douglas MacArthur when he told the student body in 1962, "In war there is no substitute for victory ... if you lose, the nation will be destroyed ... the very obsession of your public service must be duty, honor, country."

*Above. The seal of the academy, featuring the West Point motto and the helmet of Pallas Athena, patron of Athens and goddess of wisdom. Right. Cadets in gray full dress uniforms march in a Saturday morning drill in October 1967.*

Three plebes, or first-year students, pull each other's shirts tight for inspection.

Upperclassman Charles Williams barks at newly arrived plebe Gregory Moeller, ordering him to get his hair cut.

*Americal Division officers Major General Samuel W. Koster (above) and Colonel Oran Henderson, both charged with dereliction of duty, in the wake of My Lai.*

country," the West Point motto, seemed to have metamorphosed into the bureaucratic practice of "CYA—Cover Your Ass." To persistent questioning about why they had done nothing to expose the My Lai incident, several witnesses answered that the prevailing attitude was "Don't do anything to rock the boat—CYA." The acronym CYA was widely used around army installations in the late 1960s and early 1970s (though it did not appear as graffiti as frequently as the more negative and profane FTA, which stood for F--- the Army). People had become conditioned to doing the minimum, to meeting their narrowly defined responsibilities, to passing problems along.

Since World War II the U.S. military had been gradually adopting the practices of the modern business corporation, and an increasing number of officers pursued graduate work in business administration and management. The appointment in 1961 of Ford Motor Company President Robert S. McNamara as secretary of defense brought to the Pentagon a businesslike cast. Systems analysis, cost benefit analysis, and career management became the department's buzz words. As one study critical of the transformation in the army noted, "The traditional aspects of the 'military way' collapsed under the impact of new administrative skills, staff reorganizations and computer models of decision making." In the process, many officers caught up in trying to exist and advance in the huge army bureaucracy came to confuse leadership and management.

## Study on military professionalism

General Peers took special note of the problems of operating in Vietnam when he sent an additional memorandum to General Westmoreland outlining what he perceived of as "Leadership Requirements in a Counterinsurgency Environment." Among the many aspects of command responsibilities that he enumerated for the field and rear, Peers included this pet peeve: "Leadership is most effective when it is conducted on a person–to–person, face–to–face basis; it cannot effectively be practiced over a telephone [or] radio." At My Lai, no commander above company level had landed his helicopter that day to communicate with ground forces even though a major battle was said to be taking place. In fact Peers's philosophy of command and leadership was so distinctly at odds with what had occurred at My Lai that Westmoreland ordered the Army War College at Carlisle, Pennsylvania, to conduct a study on the state of military professionalism.

When the study was completed in June 1970, after lengthy questionnaires had been filled out and tabulated and interviews and group discussions held, its universally depressing results shocked many of the army's senior leaders. Military professionalism in the U.S. Army, it seemed, had reached its nadir. Officers at all grades recognized a "significant difference" between the ideal values and the actual values of the officer corps and felt that the army did nothing to insure that ideal values were practiced as well as hypocritically preached. As one internal army memorandum summed up the findings:

Officers [interviewed] saw a system that rewarded selfishness, incompetence and dishonesty. Commanders sought transitory, ephemeral gains at the expense of enduring benefits and replaced substance with statistics. Furthermore, senior commanders, as a result of their isolation (sometimes self-imposed) and absence of communication with subordinates, lacked any solid foundation from which to initiate necessary corrective action.

The study found that "careerism" was running rampant in the army, that officers concerned themselves more with career advancement than with the performance of their duties. According to the report, many shared the feeling that "If you are going to be a good officer, you must compete to be chief of staff." To attain even to the rank of colonel or brigadier general, an officer was under the impression he had to have a variety of experiences, like a manager in a high-powered business who climbs the corporate ladder by moving from department to division to subsidiary, turning in an impressive performance while on each rung. For an army officer, this meant that he needed to command men, work in a staff position, obtain a "civilian" master's degree in some subject, and attend the military war college and Command and General Staff College. Said one colonel quoted in the report (speakers are identified by rank only): "The Army has made it clear that an individual has to have 'certain tickets.' Without these he is in trouble as far as promotions and assignments are concerned." Added a major: "The tendency in the Officer Corps today is to get the 'ticket punched' regardless of the cost." A lieutenant colonel put careerism in further perspective: "Command of a battalion is sought not to make a contribution to the Army, not to lead troops and improve their performance," he said, "but to fulfill a requirement for the advancement of one's career."

In accumulating the "tickets" needed to become a well-rounded "general" officer, a man had to perform flawlessly at each step, and this expectation led to inflated officer efficiency reports (OER). Unless an officer from the time of his initial lieutenant's job were rated by his superior as virtually "the best officer I have ever seen," he risked falling behind in his career to those who obtained such ratings. A malicious boss, or one seeking to shunt responsibility, could damage a subordinate's career with something less than a stellar report. "The military requires success in everything, so success is reported," said one colonel. Making a mistake at any time in one's career,

On trial for killing 109 civilians at My Lai, First Lieutenant William "Rusty" Calley leaves a courtroom in Fort Benning, Georgia.

even one that could ultimately result in increased proficiency and learning, represented a career risk because "the officer [is] zapped by the OER," as one captain put it. If a "screw-up" occurred, no one owned up to it since an unsatisfactory OER became a permanent part of an officer's personal file and haunted the rest of his career. One colonel expressed the opinion that "buck passing" from higher levels down to the lower had lately become increasingly evident. "Endless CYA exercises create suspicion and distrust on the part of junior [officers]," he said. Another colonel agreed. "The present day commander looks upon his command tour as a mechanism to help him get ahead provided he does not rock the boat or make waves," he said. "As a result, subordinates are not being properly developed and there is a general feeling among junior officers that seniors are untouchable, unapproachable, unreasonable and constantly looking for mistakes."

These myriad problems afflicting military professionalism cried out for reform, and in fact the army soon began to address the problems and adopt some of the recommendations, such as revising the Officer Evaluation Report System, as proposed in the study. But those in the best position to enact reform, the army's senior generals, were the very men who had advanced and prospered under the current army system. Change came slowly to them; old habits died hard. The system had indeed grown more businesslike and efficient, but at the same time it had become corrupt, and many of its flaws had been manifested not harmlessly in some stateside garrison but on the battlefields of Vietnam. The damage had already been done; the army leadership had "managed" the war poorly. As Edward Luttwak, a prominent critic of the army, later wrote: "American forces in the Vietnam War were marvels of efficiency. Their communications were efficient, their logistics, their transportation, even their administration of firepower. Yes, our managers in uniform were very efficient—the only trouble is that they were not very combat effective."

## The one-year tour

As the U.S. role gradually increased in 1965 and American soldiers began pouring into Vietnam by the tens of thousands, MACV commander General Westmoreland

*A poster from an army officer recruitment campaign in 1968 plays on the army's corporate image. From 1965 to 1968 army officer ranks grew 48 percent.*

recommended that the new troops serve the same one-year tour of duty that had been set for the Americans who served as advisers. He did so because he foresaw a protracted war of attrition in which the will of America would be sorely tried and in which a tour of any longer than one year would, he wrote, "likely bring about a hue and cry to 'bring the boys home.'" Politically Westmoreland's judgment was astute (although he failed to anticipate that the inequitable draft law would result in manpower shortages). Militarily, however, his decision was open to question, for it resulted in the DEROS system (Date Eligible for Return from Overseas), which caused most soldiers to think more about crossing off 365 consecutive days on their calendars than about accomplishing a common military mission. After six months in action a soldier began to come down with "short-timer's fever" and to think about surviving to the end of his year. "We had a saying in Vietnam," recalled medic Scott Gauthier. "As soon as you set foot on Vietnamese soil, you're dead. Mark yourself as dead. And from that point on, all you are doing is fighting for the right to go home again, to live again. That was the incentive we had." As another soldier put it, "I'm fighting for number one, me."

In the early years of the war the one-year rotation policy may have bolstered the morale of the combat soldier, but the start of the U.S. withdrawal brought with it the common knowledge that the war was to end inconclusively and from that moment on the rotation system very likely worked against combat effectiveness. As one military expert wrote, "The low morale of the American ground forces after 1969 can be regarded as a kind of short-timer's fever writ large."

In one sense, the U.S. Army in Vietnam was an army of strangers. The steady rotation of troops inhibited the formation of personal bonds and unit cohesion that result from extended combat together. Statistically, in the average infantry company of perhaps 175 men, a man left almost every two days—and a new man arrived. Statistically, in any average week, another three or four men were taking their seven-day rest and recuperation (R&R) leaves. Other men might have been on sick call or back in a base area for any variety of personal or administrative reasons. When soldiers were killed or wounded and had to be replaced, of course, the sense of impermanence grew greater. The men barely got to know one another, let alone trust each other. Unlike other wars, the veterans failed to remain in touch afterward despite the intense closeness forged during combat. In most cases nothing more was heard in the field from the soldier who had "survived" and rotated home.

Some of these problems might have been alleviated, in the opinion of General Palmer, by the institution of a dual system of rotation—one for draftees, another for regular army. Palmer came to believe that it was a mistake to put regular army soldiers on the same rotation system as the draftees. "Career people should have served two or three years in Vietnam," Palmer said. "It would have created a more stable, more professional environment. We wouldn't have been learning the same lessons over and over, fighting the same battles over and over."

Some career officers and noncommissioned officers, including many combat veterans of Korea, accepted or even volunteered for second tours, but many served out their tours in the early years of the war and then tried to avoid further tours. Some resigned rather than return, and many of those ordered back to Vietnam sought out staff positions that kept them out of combat. So the army in the field was for the most part young and inexperienced, said New Zealand Major David Ogilvy, who worked with two brigades of the 23d Division in 1971. "Several of the soldiers that I spoke to made this comment: 'Why are we young ones here? . . . Where are the older soldiers, where are the experienced soldiers?' And they answered the questions themselves. 'They're all back in base.'"

## The Vietnam command ticket

For officers the one-year tour customarily meant six months in a combat command and six months in a staff position. While this presented more officers with opportunities to put their training into practice by commanding men in combat (and not incidentally punching their command "tickets"), it virtually guaranteed inexperience in the leadership of the small units that fought so many of the battles of the Vietnam War. As Westmoreland's operations chief in 1965, Major General William DePuy had had a hand in introducing search and destroy tactics to the U.S. Army effort in Vietnam. Only a year later, as commander of the 1st Infantry Division, DePuy had difficulty finding proficient lieutenants to act as platoon leaders. For the operations MACV had envisioned, excellent small-unit training, speed, and firepower were required, but DePuy found that it took too long to teach officers to use the firepower available to them. Colonel Donn A. Starry, 11th Armored Cavalry Regiment commander in 1969-70, summed up the situation this way: "We had a bunch of young, inexperienced NCOs leading a bunch of young, inexperienced soldiers, overwatched by a bunch of older, but equally inexperienced, lieutenant colonels, colonels

and generals. The result on the ground in the jungle just wasn't good at all."

The peculiar nature of the Vietnam War, particularly in the jungle terrain, produced a rationale for the six-month tour. When he commanded the 4th Infantry Division in 1967 in the rugged central highlands of II Corps Tactical Zone, William Peers, then a major general, found that officers quickly "burned out." Said Peers: "An individual battalion commander physically and mentally could not take over six months because he was on the move all day long and at night he had to get his people bedded down, and he would be up practically all hours of the night. He may get three or four hours sleep if he was lucky." Some officers disagreed with Peers's assessment. Lieutenant Colonel Richard Kattar, who had trekked through the jungles for a year as an adviser in 1964 before commanding a battalion in 1971, felt that a battalion commander had ample time to prepare himself mentally and physically for command. "I had spent the previous seventeen years getting ready to do this," he said. "I ought to have been prepared to do it. . . . Of course, I was under stress but I am trained. That's what an officer is supposed to do, operate best under stress, under adversity. What do you do, train for something that's tranquil and well-organized? No, you're supposed to be a manager of chaos."

Another damaging aspect of the six-month command tour was that it prevented development of an institutional memory, a body of experience passed from man to man by close association. No amount of after action reports and other documents filed at headquarters or buried in the bowels of the Pentagon could equal the true value of experiences that men could pass on if they had not been rotated back to the States. For example, when plans were formulated for a major incursion into Laos in 1971, an operation labeled Lam Son 719, the abandoned installation at Khe Sanh was designated the forward base for the invasion. This was the base where American marines had fought under siege for seventy-seven days in 1968, yet, according to Major William Dabney, who had served there in 1968, no marine veterans of that battle were consulted in the preparations for Lam Son 719. When an army officer reported to Major Dabney that road mines around Khe Sanh were taking a toll on his unit, Dabney informed him that the mines had not been emplaced by the enemy but were American mines that had been planted during the 1968 siege. Maps pinpointing the mines' locations could be found in III MAF files—if someone had chosen to look for them.

Brigadier General S.L.A. Marshall discovered a similar lapse in mid-1968 when he visited the Iron Triangle northwest of Saigon with 1st Division commander Major General Keith Ware. During the gigantic Operation Cedar Falls in January 1967, U.S. troops had killed over 700 Vietcong, leveled the stronghold village of Ben Suc, and mapped or destroyed several kilometers of tunnels and

*Captain Brian Utermahlen, commander of Company A, 1/8 Cavalry, 1st Cavalry Division, maneuvers his men in late 1970. A 1968 graduate of West Point, Utermahlen developed a special rapport with his troops. "They want intelligent leadership," he said. "It's not a democracy, but they want to have a say."*

fortifications. Now the houses were gone and the trees were flattened and leafless and looked from the air like burned match sticks. As the two left the helicopter and picked their way through the devastation, General Ware, who had only recently taken command of the division, said, "That story about a vast tunnel system underlying this place is all bunk. We have probed and found only a couple of small holes."

Marshall thought Ware was joking, for the engineer "tunnel rats" who had explored and mapped the four-kilometer-long complex had given him copies of the maps, which sat in his desk in his Detroit home. Marshall was incredulous that the commander whose division had responsibility for the Iron Triangle, indeed whose division under a former commander had spearheaded Operation Cedar Falls, was not aware that the tunnels had been explored. "This is the sort of lapse that occurs under rotations with too frequent changes of command," Marshall wrote. "On return home I sent him the [map]." Gen. Ware then sent his own units back into the Iron Triangle and not only found the tunnels but also learned that the Vietcong were still using them.

John Paul Vann, a retired army officer who remained in Vietnam as a civilian and rose to the position of II Corps senior adviser in 1971, condensed this problem into a simple and often-quoted epigram: "The United States has not been in Vietnam for ten years," he said, "but for one year ten times."

## Pressure to perform

With only six months, a career-minded officer had to produce results. This pressure to display aggressiveness and to perform for the satisfaction of the chain of command frequently led to unwise tactical decisions and sometimes to successes. According to the Peers Commission Report on My Lai, Task Force Barker had become frustrated in its attempts to bring the local VC force to battle. The report stated: "It appears that Lt. Col. Barker and his subordinate commanders probably viewed the Son My operation as a real opportunity to overcome their past failures (or lack of opportunity) to close effectively with and defeat a major identifiable enemy force."

Enlisted men, who spent a year in the field and often had more experience than their officers, tended to treat opportunists harshly. In the disengagement years, some enlisted men felt that the war was serving little more purpose than advancement of officers' careers, so they understandably preferred to be led by officers who cared more for the welfare of the men than for impressive battle results. "We had a good battalion commander," said Marty Cacioppo, a sergeant in the 25th Division in 1970. "He never really pushed a big body count. He knew maybe he would make colonel. But I don't think he really cared that much. He wasn't in there to get a bunch of medals."

Battlefield and service decorations constituted an integral part of a career-minded officer's performance. A hunger for medals led to medal inflation. Almost half the generals who served in Vietnam, few of whom consistently faced the perils of battle, nonetheless received one or more medals for bravery. In 1969, for example, twenty-six of the fifty-seven generals who returned from Vietnam had received either the Silver Star, the Distinguished Flying Cross, or the Bronze Star for valor. About one in ten average servicemen received similar awards. (After the Medal of Honor and Distinguished Service Cross, these awards are the highest army decorations for bravery in combat.) Fifty of the fifty-seven general officers received the Distinguished Service Medal, given for meritorious service in a position of great responsibility, not necessarily in a combat situation.

The devaluation of medals and the imaginative citations accompanying them turned scandalous in October 1970, when Brigadier General Eugene P. Forrester, assistant commander of the 1st Cavalry Division, was awarded a Silver Star for his actions during the Cambodian incursion. The citation described how on June 9, 1970, while flying in his command helicopter, he directed ground troops in a firefight. Although his helicopter was under enemy fire, he continued to observe and adjust artillery fire. He then flew to the nearby firebase to collect more ammunition and returned to the scene where he kicked out the supplies and evacuated the wounded. "Brigadier General Forrester's gallantry and leadership were deciding factors in turning a desperate situation into a defeat of a determined enemy force," the citation read.

The problem with General Forrester's Silver Star was that the actions cited never took place. As angry enlisted men in the awards and decorations office complained in letters to the House Armed Services Committee and the *New York Times*, they had fabricated the tale on orders from their superiors who wanted to present the general with a medal before he left the division. The men had borrowed some items from a genuine Silver Star citation on file in their office and had added some stock phrases, and they chose June 9 because it was one of the men's birthday. After an investigation provoked by publicity, Gen. Forrester's Silver Star was rescinded, and 1st Cavalry Division Chief of Staff Colonel George Newman, who instigated the award, received a reprimand.

In 1966 the so-called "Impact" award system was instituted, authorizing division and separate brigade commanders to award decorations, up to the coveted Silver Star, in the immediate aftermath of a battle. Naturally they relied on the testimony of subordinate commanders and staff officers. The rationale for this system was that courageous soldiers were honored promptly, while the event was fresh in the minds of those who had been there. Soon, however, this innovation was corrupted; many a Silver Star was pinned to the shirt of a commander who gave or-

The conviction of Lt. Calley in March 1971 convinced many in the army he had been made a scapegoat. Here, soldiers pause for religious services at Firebase Gladiator under an artillery piece that reflects their feelings. Gladiator is north of the NVA–held A Shau Valley.

ders from the relative safety of a helicopter during battle, landing only after the shooting had stopped.

As medals began to festoon officers' chests, respect for the awards degenerated. Said one disgusted major in 1970, "The only current decorations I admire are the Distinguished Service Cross and the Medal of Honor. All others are tainted by too often being awarded to people who do not deserve them." A captain who had been a helicopter pilot in Vietnam agreed. "It's the biggest farce going," he said. "Commanders give themselves the medals. They need the medals to advance their careers." Despite the widespread knowledge of medal inflation, however, an officer who did not receive such awards risked slipping a rung on the career ladder. As Brigadier General Peter Dawkins observed, "A general attitude develops that any officer who has served in the combat theater and has not received certain medals is presumed to have somehow performed inadequately."

## A call for renewal

With the phased withdrawal of U.S. troops in 1970–72, the Vietnam "career machine" began to wind down. Although many experienced and motivated officers served in Vietnam during this period, in general the army had used up many of its best officers. High-caliber officers once attracted to Vietnam had already done one or two tours, and they had little inclination to put in for more service. Earlier in the war officers had sought combat commands as much to do the job they were trained for as to punch their tickets. But in the later period many career-minded officers shied away from combat battalion and brigade commands because an undistinguished performance by his troops, a majority of whom were draftees and marginally disciplined, could result in a blemished record and a hindrance to promotion.

The Vietnam War had glaringly exposed severe failings in the leadership of the army. Businesslike attitudes had not resulted in combat effectiveness, and the corruption in the officer corps had been shockingly revealed in the Study on Military Professionalism. Such deep-seated problems had to be addressed, but few reforms could proceed in the milieu—Vietnam—that had brought them into bold relief and in many cases had brought them into being. As McGeorge Bundy, national security adviser to Presidents Kennedy and Johnson, declared in a private talk in May 1971, "Extrication from Vietnam is now the necessary precondition of the renewal of the U.S. Army as an institution."

In May 1971, however, 284,000 U.S. servicemen—of whom 213,000 were army—remained in Vietnam, manning the bases, patrolling and dying, training and advising. Most of them hoped that the program called Vietnamization—training the Vietnamese to fight their own war—would soon take hold.

# Vietnamization

For the name of an ambitious program that combined many of the Nixon administration's plans
to wind down the war, "Vietnamization" had a
rather casual origin. In March 1969, early in the
Nixon administration, General Abrams's deputy,
General Andrew Goodpaster, informed a full-
dress meeting of the National Security Council
that the Republic of Vietnam Armed Forces
(RVNAF) had improved to the point where the
United States might soon begin "de-Americanizing" the war. Secretary of State Melvin Laird, a
skillful politician, reflected on the public relations
impact of that cumbersome word. "I [don't agree]
with your term 'de-Americanizing,'" he said.
"What we need is a term like 'Vietnamizing' to
put the emphasis on the right issues." President
Nixon immediately concurred. "That's a good
point, Mel," he said, and thus the ungainly word
"Vietnamization" was coined.

The ground war was in fact going to be "de-
Americanized," but such a word carried the con-

notation that America was simply abandoning its ally. The Nixon administration wanted to avoid that charge and instead shift the focus to the growing ability of the RVNAF to accept military responsibility. But the RVNAF's increasing self-sufficiency, of course, would permit the United States to withdraw gradually. The two courses of action—RVNAF improvement and U.S. withdrawal—were inextricably linked. Hence the Nixon policy of Vietnamization, which commenced July 1, 1969, combined both RVNAF improvement and U.S. withdrawal in its three-stage plan. In Phase I ground combat responsibility would be turned over to the improved RVNAF. During Phase II the RVNAF would develop its combat support capability, with specialists completing the complex training required to maintain the sophisticated machines of war. In the third phase the American presence would be reduced to a military advisory mission.

Despite the rightness of the word "Vietnamization" for Laird and President Nixon, the Vietnamese took exception to the term, for they had borne the brunt of fighting the Communists since long before the Americans had taken any meaningful interest in the war. Even though American combat troops had taken on the Communist main forces, South Vietnamese casualties had always greatly exceeded those of U.S. troops. The Vietnamese, said ARVN Major General Nguyen Van Hinh, had always "suffered and sacrificed the most." President Nguyen Van Thieu, himself a crafty politician, thought the term Vietnamization appropriate only for American domestic consumption; it certainly should not be used in Vietnam where it was likely to fit into the propaganda schemes of Hanoi, which always demeaned Saigon's soldiers by referring to them as the "puppet troops" of the American imperialists. The government and press ceased referring to the program openly. But many Vietnamese called it "Ba Tu," which literally translates as "the three selves"—self-recovering, self-powering, and self-sustaining. Because it frowned on the implications of Vietnamization, Saigon designed no additional programs of its own. "Old plans and programs [of RVNAF improvement] were kept unchanged," wrote General Hinh, "except for a new sense of urgency and emphasis instilled by the U.S. decision to phase down and eventually withdraw its forces."

The U.S. withdrawal was irreversible and proceeded in more or less regular installments. This irked National Security Adviser Henry Kissinger, who believed that bringing troops home from Vietnam was like offering "salted peanuts" to the American public, which would keep demanding more until they were all home. That would leave Kissinger with little leverage at the bargaining table in his search for a negotiated settlement. But peace talks were bogged down in Paris, and Vietnamization rapidly became the key to an honorable American extrication from the longest war in its history. As one Nixon aide later recalled, "We started out saying that Vietnamization was not a substitute but a spur to negotiations. When nothing happened in the talks, Vietnamization and not negotiations constituted our plan to end the war."

Defense Secretary Laird persuaded the Joint Chiefs of Staff of the necessity of withdrawal and Vietnamization by pointing out that the continuing war was eroding the military's capability to defend vital interests elsewhere in the world. The more resources the services employed in Vietnam, the less they would have available for their worldwide commitments. Laird also developed a close working relationship with General Abrams, to whom he gave, as Kissinger wrote, "one of the most thankless tasks ever assigned an American general"—to dismantle a force more than half a million men strong, while maintaining security and training another army to take over. Abrams stolidly accepted his task. "Contrary to mythology, the military rarely oppose their Commander-in-Chief, even privately," Kissinger observed. "If they can conjure up a halfway plausible justification, they will overcome their misgivings and support a presidential decision. It was painful to see General Abrams, epitome of the combat commander, obviously unhappy, yet nevertheless agreeing to a withdrawal."

Military men in the field were divided over the potential of Vietnamization. Assuming the simultaneous withdrawal of U.S. and NVA forces, the program was originally designed to prepare the RVNAF to face Vietcong units that remained after the departure of NVA troops. But as the possibility of an NVA withdrawal grew increasingly remote, the emphasis on Vietnamization changed, and some military men doubted that a conventional army, which only a few years earlier had been on the verge of falling to a guerrilla force, could be improved to a level where it might withstand highly professional North Vietnamese main forces. Privately they called the program "alleged" or "pretended" Vietnamization, simply a cover for the U.S. withdrawal. The South Vietnamese, they said, could never hack it alone.

But for every soldier who doubted the ability or fortitude of the RVNAF, there were others who, accepting the political reality of withdrawal, believed that Vietnamization was a responsible means of giving the South Vietnamese a chance at survival. To Lieutenant Colonel Frank Benedict, a MACV plans officer who worked on the RVNAF Improvement and Modernization Program, Vietnamization meant that "instead of just saying we're going to bug out, we will take the hard road and we will train, we'll equip, and we'll leave the South Vietnamese in a good position to defend themselves." Because of the phased withdrawal, time constraints imposed an urgency, and while many military men believed that Vietnamization would succeed,

---

Preceding page. *ARVN Rangers prepare to land in a combat area in IV Corps in 1969.*

*The victim of a Vietcong ambush fifty kilometers north of Saigon in August 1969, an ARVN Ranger is helped by a U.S. adviser to a waiting medevac helicopter.*

that belief rested more on hope than on reason. "I think the idea was that we would do what we could in the time allotted to us," said Vice Admiral Robert S. Salzer, commander of U.S. naval forces in Vietnam in 1971, "and that somehow things would work out."

For all the aplomb they displayed in public, the South Vietnamese had little experience at running the war themselves, and many found the prospect daunting. Although the Vietnamese Joint General Staff (JGS) was entirely independent, the RVNAF had grown accustomed to relying on U.S. combat troops, logistical support, and on the leadership of MACV itself. For all intents and purposes, the Vietnamese "were integrated in the whole U.S. armed forces," observed a pragmatic Vietnamese colonel on the Joint General Staff. "When . . . part of that integrated force leaves, the remaining Vietnamese forces have lack of support, lack of leadership, lack of coordination." Some younger Vietnamese were far less analytical in examining the meaning and impact of Vietnamization. They saw a dark future. Said a captain in the Vietnam Armored Cavalry after the war, "We officers felt Vietnamization was just a way for the U.S. to get out . . . and [leave] the South Vietnamese armed forces to take the responsibility of defeat."

## Vietnamization in action

To arm and train an expanded RVNAF, the U.S. brought to bear enormous resources. Enacted in several phases—the third and final phase was called Consolidated RVNAF Improvement and Modernization Program, or CRIMP—Vietnamization resulted in the transfer to Vietnamese control of 855,000 individual and crew-served weapons, 1,880 tanks and artillery pieces, 44,000 radio sets, and over 1,000 helicopters and fixed-wing aircraft. By late 1971 the RVNAF had grown to over 1 million men from a 1968 level of 717,000. ARVN consisted of 450,000 men in thirteen divisions that contained 171 maneuver battalions supported by fifty-eight artillery battalions and nineteen battalion-sized armored units. The number of Ranger battalions more than doubled, increasing from 20 to 45. But whereas ARVN had always been sizable (it grew by 92,000 men between 1968 and 1972), most expansion took place in the air force, navy, and territorial forces. The air force (VNAF) grew from 19,000 airmen in 1968 to 64,000 in 1972, while the navy (VNN) rose from a strength of 19,000 to 43,000 sailors operating 1,680 coastal craft in that same year.

Territorial militias, the Regional and Popular Forces that operated in the provinces and districts respectively, made up about half of RVNAF strength, and they formed the first line of defense against enemy attack. These totaled over 550,000 men by 1971, an increase of some 200,000 since 1968. More important, RF/PF equipment was upgraded, with M16 rifles replacing obsolescent M1 rifles and carbines and Thompson submachine guns. Browning Automatic Rifles and World War I model .30-caliber machine guns gave way to modern M60s. Their old weapons went to the People's Self-Defense Forces in local villages. The new armaments enhanced the morale of the RF/PF Forces, for now they had the firepower to match that of local Vietcong who had long possessed AK47 rifles.

Under CRIMP the lot of soldiers and their dependents improved slightly, a necessity to counteract the astronomical rates of desertion. In 1969, 125,000 soldiers had walked away from their units, and the following year 150,000 men—over 15 percent of the RVNAF rolls—went over the hill. Such attrition destroyed the cohesion of the military units. Military service was a hardship for many soldiers since it took them out of their fields and left their tightly knit families with little source of income. Most of the deserters returned to their homes, and many of them ultimately joined local militias. There was no evidence that many had joined the Communists. Some deserters—one-sixth of the 1970 total of 150,000—reported back to their units after visiting home.

To address some of these familial problems, the U.S. and GVN in 1970 jointly inaugurated a program to con-

struct 200,000 homes for military dependents. The U.S. provided material support for half of the homes slated to be built between 1970 and 1974. In addition, President Nixon agreed to send $42 million of free canned food between 1971 and 1973 to supplement servicemen's pay. At U.S. urging, salaries were raised 19 percent across the board in 1970, bringing military pay scales closer to those of the civil service. But the pay was still paltry and scarcely kept pace with an inflation fueled by the infusion of American GIs' dollars into South Vietnam's marketplace. In early 1971 an ARVN private with a dependent child received forty dollars a month.

## New emphasis on training

Training the South Vietnamese had in theory received high priority under Vietnamization, but in practice too little attention was paid to the programs during 1969. MACV had made numerous proposals to the Vietnamese Joint General Staff and Central Training Command (CTC) for improving the personnel capacity and effectiveness of the training facilities, but such recommendations got little support from the Vietnamese high command. As the MACV Command Overview stated, "Despite CTC and MACV efforts, very little progress was made in 1969 in these areas due to the complex personnel changes required, JGS reluctance to give the program a high priority, and refusal by RVN field commanders to release experienced officers and NCOs from operational responsibilities."

Early in 1970 a U.S. Army fact-finding team led by Brigadier General Donnelly Bolton toured Vietnam's training facilities and found the efforts of both the Vietnamese and United States to be inadequate. The MACV Training Directorate was operating at only 70 percent of assigned strength, and all the U.S. training advisory detachments in the field were likewise understrength. The quality of advice was also found wanting, since training had often been left in the hands of soldiers thought unfit to serve in more prestigious operational and staff positions. "It was clear that top professionals were not being assigned to training advisory duties," wrote then Colonel Stan L. McClellan, a member of the Bolton team adding:

*Not knowing when— or if—he will see them again, a South Vietnamese conscript bids a painful farewell to members of his family at a training camp near Saigon.*

As a consequence of selecting the wrong people to handle the job, training centers and schools throughout the country had operated on a poorly programmed, mostly unfunded basis. Corruption, inefficiency, overcrowded living conditions, outmoded instructional standards—all of these were predictable results of such a system.

General Abrams agreed with the Bolton team's findings and urged the members on their return home to lobby the Joint Chiefs of Staff to send highly professional training advisers to Vietnam. According to McClellan, Abrams told the team, "It's time that they [the Joint Chiefs] recognize in Washington that the day of the U.S. fighting force involvement in South Vietnam is at an end. All we have time for now is to complete the preparation of South Vietnam to carry on the task."

At the same time that General Abrams tried to coax more support from the Joint Chiefs of Staff, he also attempted to wheedle more cooperation from Vietnamese leaders. In a letter to General Cao Van Vien, chairman of the Joint General Staff, in March 1970, Abrams urged that an adequate number of officers and noncommissioned officers be assigned to training centers and that senior Vietnamese commanders get behind the training programs. "Arrangements for support of CTC activities must be widened and accelerated," Abrams wrote. "As a first order of effort it is essential to enlist the personal interest and assistance of corps, division tactical area, and sector commanders each of whom . . . is a user of the product of the training system and should contribute to improving the quality of the product."

During 1970, training programs finally gained the needed momentum, in large part because of the influence of General Abrams. The United States began to send, in Colonel McClellan's words, "an infusion of top-flight military professionals into South Vietnam's training advisory effort." To consolidate and standardize the training, the number of national centers was reduced from the twenty-three that existed in 1968 to ten by 1971. The United States contributed $28 million to expanding and improving these centers. And the South Vietnamese took a significant step forward when they began to transfer experienced officers and noncommissioned officers into training slots. Although field commanders only reluctantly gave up their veteran small-unit leaders, by the end of 1971 nearly half of the South Vietnamese training instructors were men with combat experience.

## A foot soldier's war

The departure of U.S. forces, and the anticipated dwindling of U.S. military aid, forced the South Vietnamese to review their military doctrine and tactics and hence redesign their training. In a war in which the Americans had been lavish in their expenditure of firepower—B-52 bombers used in tactical support, landing zones prepped with

1,000 rounds of artillery, gunships available in a matter of minutes, riflemen firing their M16s on full automatic—the South Vietnamese had acquired bad habits by example, if not actually from training or the lack of it. As Major General Hinh wrote, "It had become common practice for infantry units to hold back, wait for the target to be torn apart by fire and then just move in to count enemy bodies." But such practices had to change, principally because the firepower was one day no longer going to be available to them. "Dammit, they've got to learn they can't do it all with air [power]," General Abrams said. "They've got to do it on the ground with infantry. If they don't, it's all been in vain."

Although they were in essence learning the American way of war, the Vietnamese had to grow accustomed to fighting without the benefits of airmobility or lavish firepower. They had to make do with 400 or 500 helicopters, for example, whereas U.S. forces at their peak had employed about eight times that number. The opposing North Vietnamese had no helicopters, of course, but the NVA, as the offensive army, had the option of massing its men for attack. As the defensive force, the South Vietnamese needed mobility to react and move troops rapidly to the point of attack. That mobility had formerly been provided primarily by American-operated helicopters. ARVN now had to prepare to fight a foot soldier's war, at which its enemies were extremely proficient.

In their combat arms training, the South Vietnamese began to emphasize three traditional infantry skills: marching, marksmanship with the M16 rifle, and close combat. Marching hardened the troops for walking long distances, when trucks and helicopters were unavailable, and also improved a unit's ability to maneuver quickly on the battlefield. Marksmanship conserved ammunition, while close combat training, according to General Hinh, "was a much needed shot in the arm to enhance combat prowess among troops." To counter the enemy when he was most active, the South Vietnamese placed more emphasis on night training, and by 1971 one-third of the training at combat arms schools took place at night.

As the training of South Vietnamese improved, MACV grew more and more confident of the RVNAF's ability to perform in combat. "Accomplishments within the RVNAF training establishment . . . were so many, and so positive, as to be astonishing," wrote Stan McClellan, who as a brigadier general returned to Vietnam in 1971 as MACV director of training. One American observer who toured Vietnam and evaluated the stepped-up RVNAF training wrote, "Our allies are fighting much better; the foremost reason for this may be better training. There are improvements in facilities, professionalism at all levels, and military security." It seemed certain that sometime in 1971 Phase I of the Vietnamization program would be declared achieved, and all ground combat responsibility would be handed over to the RVNAF.

In spite of the battle readiness of RVNAF troops, however, an imponderable of South Vietnamese self-sufficiency remained that of leadership. As a U.S. Army postwar study concluded:

Unit for unit and man for man, the combat forces of South Vietnam repeatedly proved themselves superior to their adversaries. Missing, however, were inspired civil and military leadership at the highest levels. ... The required leadership was certainly available in the South Vietnamese armed forces, but it was not allowed to surface and take charge in enough situations.

## Questions of leadership

In an understatement that applied to armies through the ages, a Defense Department study declared early in 1970, "There is a high correlation between combat effectiveness and the leadership in ARVN infantry." Indeed, one of the most pressing requirements of Vietnamization and of the U.S. advisory effort was to improve the quality of leadership among RVNAF officers from corps commanders down to noncommissioned officers. More to the point, the MACV Command Overview stated, "The deficiency in leadership manifested itself in many ways, the most serious of which was lack of aggressiveness when units were in contact with the enemy."

The officer corps fell short not only in quality but also in quantity. The rapid pace of RVNAF expansion thinned out the ranks of experienced officers and NCOs who transferred to command positions in new units. Reserve officers might once have helped fill that gap, but during the national mobilization of 1968 all reserve officers had been called to active duty. To alleviate this shortage at every level, the RVNAF attempted to step up promotions and to move more officer candidates through its training schools. This latter program met with success, as the ranks of lieutenants grew by 13,627 to 44,194 in 1969, bringing the number of junior officers above the desired quota.

The RVNAF plan to promote qualified officers in senior ranks (captain, major, lieutenant colonel, colonel) was, however, far less successful. At these levels promotion was determined more by politics and connections to senior generals than by military ability. Although recommendations for annual and special promotions were made by promotion boards and unit commanders, respectively, the actual promotions were decided only by high-ranking authorities. President Nguyen Van Thieu appointed all generals. The prime minister named permanent colonels, and the minister of defense had authority for functional (or temporary) colonels and permanent majors. General Tran Thien Khiem held both these portfolios in 1970. General Staff Chairman Cao Van Vien promoted temporary majors and captains. Only General Vien delegated a portion of his promotion authority to subordinate commanders. Such a subjective system invariably moved slowly, since politicians in a country that had seen so many coups were

leery of promoting political opponents into positions where they commanded thousands of troops. Inaction left thousands of senior officer slots vacant. As a U.S. Defense Department study noted, "The steady expansion in the size of the RVNAF has overtaken army politics in the sense that the need for more officers, and hence promotions, has outstripped the capacity of the RVNAF political system to sanction such promotions." In 1969 alone the senior officer rolls were only 62 percent of assigned strength; RVNAF had 6,857 fewer senior officers than required and the vast majority of vacancies existed, naturally, in captain and major positions at the bottom of the senior officer pyramid.

The shortage of qualified senior officers resulted in the assignment of men to duties for which their rank and experience would normally have disqualified them. In mid-1970, for example, 60 percent of the ARVN battalions were commanded by captains rather than lieutenant colonels. Several South Vietnamese brigadier generals and colonels commanded divisions, a job normally held by a major general. In fact only three ARVN divisions had major general commanders in early 1970.

The inequities of the political system created resentment between the "combat officers" who had slowly earned their rank by leadership in battle and the "political officers" who advanced quickly because they had sponsors in high places. The political officers invariably outranked contemporaries who held combat commands; indeed the political appointees occupied many field grade positions and filled out planning staffs that dictated operational orders to the combat units. As appointees of the president, many general officers failed to earn the respect of subordinates because of their lack of tactical and combat experience. The resulting effect on leadership, morale, military discipline, and the chain of command was bound to be harmful. "Only a handful of generals had the confidence of lower-ranking officers, who in turn felt that the generals were more concerned about their own personal welfare than that of the country," wrote Brigadier General Douglas Kinnard, U.S. II Field Force chief of staff in 1970.

The problem of leadership was intertwined with that of class. There had been social progress since the days of the French when a respectful private could not have looked his battalion commander in the eye, but the army still was hindered by class distinctions. Officers, usually urban, often Catholic, and possessing at least a high school education, looked down on their enlisted men, who were normally rural Buddhists. Any effort to close the gap required breaking down class barriers that had been erected over centuries. In one program designed to promote veteran NCOs to commissioned officers, trainers spent time on social conventions as well as military topics. "These former noncoms don't need much training in tactics," said Colonel Emanuel Burack, American senior adviser to the school. "What we try to give them is the social graces. Many of them come from poor peasant homes and don't have much education, so we try to teach them how to get along with other officers. Some of the courses included the proper form of writing letters and orders, how to address a senior officer and how to act with confidence while talking to troops."

Such class distinctions between officers and enlisted men impeded unit cohesion and the possibility of developing an *esprit de corps*, a necessity for an effective fighting force. Haughtiness on the part of officers, who benefited so much more from the privileged society, made enlisted men understandably reluctant to risk their lives.

As products of a relatively classless society, American advisers often failed to come to grips with class consciousness in the Vietnamese military. One of the primary themes of leadership for the effective U.S. officer is that the well-being of his men must come first. U.S. advisers threw up their hands at failures in leadership on the part of Vietnamese officers when they displayed callousness toward

*Colonel Le Chi Cuong, chief of An Xuyen Province, and a veteran paratrooper, proudly displays his medals.*

their men. During a bombardment one American lieutenant colonel, an adviser to a Vietnamese regiment, witnessed a captain "chewing out" a seriously wounded enlisted man for bleeding on the floor of the command bunker. In a letter to his wife, the adviser blasted the "incompetence, corruption, timidity, and the Mandarin attitude of the officers who have absolutely no concern for the welfare of their men." Under such leadership the men often responded with lackluster performance.

Admiral Robert Salzer found little to complain about with South Vietnamese servicemen. The problem was with leadership. "If you found mediocre leadership you were rather happy with it; poor leadership or no leadership was the rule," he said after the war. "The South Vietnamese sailor or soldier . . . responded to leadership or the lack thereof; the leadership just wasn't there."

The critical absence of leadership, according to Salzer, was in large part the fault of the United States, which instituted Vietnamization only after the U.S. decided to phase out of Vietnam. "To train the officers, to imbue them with the elements of leadership is a job that takes time . . ." Salzer said. "To do that kind of a job in a three-year time frame is very risky. The bread just cannot be baked all the way through. We should have started this process . . . much earlier, and continued it much longer."

## Superhuman task

Problems of time and cultural differences also hindered the training and qualification of pilots, technicians, and specialists to operate and maintain a modern American-style war machine. "It is quite a challenge for the Vietnamese to learn how to maintain an airplane," said U.S. Air Force Lieutenant Colonel Jimmie R. Osborne, a maintenance adviser. "They did not develop their mechanical aptitude as most Americans do in childhood fixing a bicycle or a pair of skates." Yet their pride made the Vietnamese loath to admit to their technical backwardness. "Take two basic mechanics—a VNAF 'wrench turner' and a USAF 'wrench turner'—and the Vietnamese will match most any American," said Colonel Roy D. Broadway, chief of an air force advisory team in 1971. "But bring in technical equipment and the VNAF are forced to display ignorance—and even the smallest show of ignorance is a loss of face."

The language barrier oftentimes appeared insurmountable. Instruction by U.S. trainers took place in English; thus the initial chore was for the Vietnamese to learn the language. For many who had a working knowledge of French, English was their third language. Some technicians and most pilots went to the United States for training in English and then in their specialties. But the process proved time-consuming, since a language course lasted six to nine months before the Vietnamese grasped basic grammar and a technical vocabulary. Then technical

*Officer-trainee Bui Huu Chanh inspects his men's gear. Chanh, twenty-five years old, has been drafted from college to become a platoon leader in the officer-poor ARVN.*

training required another eight to nine months, so it took up to two years to produce a trained pilot. The rapid pace of Vietnamization scarcely accommodated such a luxury of time.

An alternative means was to translate maintenance and repair manuals into Vietnamese so that instruction might proceed with the help of interpreters. But the Vietnamese language, reflecting its society, had not developed words for sophisticated technology. The language could come no closer to the M48 tank's "ballistic computer," for example, than to render it as an "adding machine." As late as May 1971, almost 6,000 pages of helicopter maintenance and repair manuals had yet to be translated. These manuals, according to Lieutenant Colonel Donald Marshall, a member of Secretary Laird's Vietnam Task Force, were "difficult enough for an English speaker with a reasonable education to read in the first place." For a Vietnamese who might not even be highly literate, the prospect was "fantastically difficult."

Even after their training was completed, the language barrier continued to plague Vietnamese maintenance men and pilots as they worked with U.S. equipment and advisers. At Bien Hoa airfield, for example, helicopter log books contained what was called a "discrepancy list" that technicians filled out on the condition of the machine. But, said U.S. adviser Sergeant First Class John Keith, "when we write in English what is wrong, the Vietnamese don't understand, and when they write in Vietnamese what they have done about it, it's Greek to us. Sometimes they just make out a fresh discrepancy list, with nothing on it, so

# Two Fighting Generals

Great generals lead great armies, or so it has seemed throughout history. In Vietnam neither the fledgling ARVN nor its often corrupt and highly politicized leadership appeared destined for greatness. Yet to succeed in building an army capable of withstanding the North Vietnamese, ARVN needed generals able to inspire war-weary troops, leaders who could somehow stretch their own personalities to help fill the gaps left by the withdrawal of U.S. forces.

When MACV issued a "report card" on Vietnamese division commanders in early 1970, many of the ARVN generals received failing grades. Quoting anonymous U.S. senior advisers, the report minced no words in its descriptions. A few of the evaluations read, "coward," "super defensive," "weak," "the Vietnamese generals ... hate his guts," and "domineering—scares his commanders." Paradoxically, an effective and popular general with loyal troops often came to be considered a political threat in a country that had experienced more than its share of military coups. "This is a country that won't allow anyone to remain a hero very long," an American observer in Saigon explained. "But they sure could use one."

For a time, ARVN got its hero; in fact two outstanding fighting (as opposed to political) generals emerged from the pack of mediocre officers to take command of III and IV Corps shortly after the 1968 Tet offensive. Both young, confident, and aggressive, Lieutenant General Do Cao Tri and Major General Nguyen Viet Thanh proved themselves capable military strategists and inspiring leaders.

*Lieutenant General Do Cao Tri on the battlefield in 1970.*

In the post-Tet shakedown of the ARVN officer corps—part anticorruption campaign, part political maneuver by President Thieu to remove officers loyal to Vice President Nguyen Cao Ky—Generals Tri and Thanh received command of the two densely populated and politically sensitive southern corps tactical zones. They faced daunting problems. Though rated best of the three divisions in IV Corps, the 7th Division, from which Gen. Thanh was promoted, was unable to shake the reputation it had picked up as the "Search and Avoid Division." The other IV Corps divisions, the 9th and the 21st, performed no better.

Despite the 7th's lackluster record, Thanh had earned high praise from General William C. Westmoreland as the best ARVN division commander. Westmoreland and senior U.S. advisers had high hopes for him, but they feared that obvious American "sponsorship" might taint Thanh in the eyes of political and military leaders in Saigon. Fortunately, President Thieu not only recognized Thanh's dynamic leadership, but he also appreciated his lack of political ambition and so backed the general wholeheartedly.

Thanh commanded the loyalty of his troops, and during the Tet offensive Thanh's popularity nearly cost him his life. In an attempt to exploit the 7th Division's devotion to its commanding general, Vietcong troops took Thanh and his family prisoner, hoping to induce the demoralized troops to defect. But their ploy failed, and, curiously, Thanh was released unharmed.

Gen. Thanh's senior IV Corps adviser in 1968 and 1969, Major General George S. Eckhardt, recounted another tale of Thanh's popularity. On one occasion the two generals flew to My Tho, Thanh's for-that our remarks don't appear." Pilots often had difficulty understanding English as it crackled over the radio from U.S. air controllers. At one air base, Vietnamese-piloted helicopters collided twice in one week because the pilots misunderstood the controllers' directions. Furthermore, the shortage of pilots had necessitated a reduction in student pilot flight time from 1,100 to 400 hours, and as a result Vietnamese failed to acquire the skills and instincts that come with more practical experience.

Maintenance of helicopters, which required far more service than fixed-wing aircraft, also proved a serious problem for the Vietnamese. A furor arose in February 1971 when a VNAF helicopter carrying Lieutenant General Do Cao Tri and veteran *Newsweek* correspondent François Sully crashed shortly after takeoff from Bien Hoa airfield. The loss of probably the best Vietnamese field commander dealt ARVN a serious blow (see sidebar below). The crash, attributed by U.S. spokesmen to mechanical failure, prompted another *Newsweek* correspondent, Edward Behr, to investigate the airworthiness of the VNAF fleet. At Bien Hoa, Behr found SFC John Keith, who had been a helicopter maintenance man for eight of his eighteen years in the U.S. Army. Keith showed him row after row of Hueys with serious maintenance deficiencies—oil and fuel leaks, engine filters and compressor blades caked with dirt, and missing rivets. Keith and other advisers revealed that Vietnamese never flushed engines with water and solvent, a routine item of maintenance required for every twenty-five hours of operation. Over U.S. objections, many of the helicopters had nevertheless been

---

mer divisional headquarters, in search of a quiet lunch. But when word of their arrival got out, townspeople crowded into the restaurant to welcome their former commander. For forty-five minutes Gen. Thanh bowed and shook hands with the stream of well-wishers; most South Vietnamese senior officers never fraternized with their peasant soldiers or with the rural population.

In III Corps Tactical Zone to the north, Gen. Do Cao Tri struggled to work his corps' ragged divisions, the 5th, 18th, and 25th, into shape. One U.S. general dismissed the 5th Division as "absolutely the worst outfit I've ever seen." And the 25th Division had the ignominious distinction of being considered by one adviser "the worst division in any army anywhere."

Gen. Tri had the personality to achieve the near-impossible. Having survived three assassination attempts, a mid-1960s exile at the instigation of Nguyen Cao Ky, and a barrage of corruption charges, Tri thrived on adversity. Not one to be deterred by Saigon's displeasure, Tri spent months trying to replace two incompetent division commanders, who were favorites of Thieu's. He succeeded. Tri promised to have his three infantry divisions in fighting trim by the end of 1970.

The two generals and their infantry divisions faced their greatest challenge with the Cambodian incursion of May 1970. President Thieu awarded Gen. Tri command of the ARVN operation to clean out enemy bases in the Parrot's Beak and appointed Gen. Thanh to lead four infantry-armor task forces from IV Corps on a sweep north to link up with Gen. Tri's troops. The infantry units selected for the two operations were mustered in part from the improved 5th, 25th, and 9th Divisions.

On the first day of his troops' operation, Thanh flew to the battlefield as usual, knowing that his presence insured a disciplined and speedy advance. Ten miles inside Cambodia, his helicopter collided in midair with a U.S. Cobra. No survivors escaped the fiery crash. Thanh's death cast a pall over the operation. As if to repay his dedication to them, Thanh's troops performed with an unexpected aggressiveness in Cambodia.

As reports of ARVN successes reached Saigon, Thanh's death was overshadowed by the exploits of Tri, who catapulted to the status of national hero. Hard work and careful planning were as much a part of his accomplishment as his inspiring presence on the battlefield. Tri achieved effective results with his use of armor. A sound tactician, he was not satisfied unless he personally directed the battle. More than one hesitant tank commander found the excited three-star general in camouflage jungle suit, baseball cap, and sunglasses dashing through machine-gun fire, shouting "Go fast, man! Go fast." For men starved for leadership, the assurance that Tri's helicopter might set down whenever they were in trouble or stalled worked marvels with their morale. "Tri was a tiger in combat, South Vietnam's George Patton," Gen. Westmoreland later wrote in admiration.

His flamboyant style of command, however, irritated many of his fellow ARVN generals. They cited Tri's actions during the battle for the Chup rubber plantation in Cambodia—Tri had nonchalantly taken a dip in the plantation pool in the midst of the fierce fighting—as evidence that Tri cared more for his own heroics than for sound military judgment. His extravagant lifestyle and growing wealth fueled jealousies and raised suspicions in Saigon. Called "flagrantly corrupt" by two South Vietnamese senators, Tri was accused of being a partner in a money-smuggling ring even as Saigon still buzzed with news of his victories in Cambodia.

Despite controversy over his private life, Tri's renown as South Vietnam's best field commander continued to grow after the Cambodian incursion. Under his direction, ARVN troops repeatedly performed well in their cross-border raids into Cambodia. When the ARVN incursion into enemy strongholds in Laos in 1971 began to flounder, President Thieu turned to Tri. Calling him to Saigon, Thieu ordered him to assume command of the Laotian operation. His new orders in hand, Tri boarded his helicopter. Shortly after leaving Bien Hoa, his helicopter lost power and plummeted to the ground, killing Tri and the other passengers.

"When the ARVN troops were well led they fought as well as anyone's soldiers," recalled Brigadier General George Wear. "They simply needed commanders who would support them properly and who could win their confidence and make them believe that their cause was worth risking their lives for." Generals Tri and Thanh had been two such commanders.

# Maintenance Men

With Vietnamization came a torrent of U.S. equipment, much of it more advanced than anything the South Vietnamese had ever used. The "Huey" helicopter, which the U.S. started giving the RVNAF in May 1969 to replace the older CH–34, was a far more capable piece of equipment, but its very sophistication outstripped the ability of the South Vietnamese to keep it flying. Previously, Americans had borne the responsibility of helicopter maintenance; now it fell to the Vietnamese. Compressed training periods for mechanics and difficulties in translating technical concepts and jargon made maintenance seem an almost insurmountable problem. Nevertheless, the mechanics made measured progress.

Left. *South Vietnamese mechanics adjust the rotor mast of a UH–1.* Above. *Learning by doing. A VNAF mechanic at Binh Thuy air base works on the engine of a Huey.* Right. *Mechanic trainees crowd around the nose of a VNAF Huey to examine the flight instruments.*

rated fit to fly by the Vietnamese maintenance men. One chopper, with a torque so low that the advisers called it a "potential crash just waiting to happen," had been rated unfit to fly early one day. But a Vietnamese technician later blithely gave the chopper a "positive checkout" and certified it as ready to fly. Taking the machine up, Sergeant Keith said, would be "tantamount to suicide."

## Vietnamization's loophole

The VNAF helicopter fleet, considered by the U.S. to be one of the largest, costliest, and most modern helicopter fleets in the world, rapidly deteriorated because of maintenance deficiencies. In late 1971, more than half of its machines were grounded with mechanical failures at any given time. The Vietnamese complained with justification about a shortage of spare parts and pointed out that the United States, with a far larger fleet, could afford to keep three helicopters on the ground for every chopper that was airborne. "If they criticize us, it is because we have less experience than the Americans," explained helicopter pilot Major Tran Duy Ky. "We do not have enough skilled men and we are too busy to maintain our helicopters the way they do."

The passage of time posed a great challenge to Vietnamization. The program's "widest loophole," said General Hinh, "was its failure to provide [South Vietnam] with enough time for an overall improvement." And although the Vietnamese made visible progress, they were being asked, in the opinion of Admiral Salzer, "to undertake a superhuman task of absorbing the full load of military defense of their country with sophisticated equipment—which they needed considering what was coming down from the north—in far too short a time." But laboring as they did under political constraints, U.S. military officials often pulled their punches in assessing the progress of Vietnamization. "When visiting firemen from Washington came through, I told them the ARVN were making great progress," related Lieutenant General Julian J. Ewell, II Field Force commander in 1969–70. "As to the ultimate course of the war, the political decision had been made to pull out and an Army officer is expected to support—not question—political decisions." But privately, Gen. Ewell expressed his doubts, pointing out how comparatively defenseless the Saigon region would become when the heavy concentrations of American troops withdrew altogether and took their helicopters with them.

By the time the RVNAF reached its full 1972 strength of 1.1 million regular forces and militiamen, South Vietnam, according to its rosters, would be Asia's second most muscular power, trailing only China's 2.7 million men under arms. North Vietnam, on the other hand, showed an estimated 877,000 men in its 1970 order of battle—457,000 in the army (215,000 of whom served in South Vietnam, Laos, and Cambodia) and 420,000 in home militia. Another

150,000 Vietcong and Pathet Lao allied with the NVA made the total number of Communist soldiers equal to or slightly more than the RVNAF strength on paper.

Sapped by alarming desertions, rife with leadership problems, and slow to master the complicated machinery of modern warfare, the RVNAF was in fact far less muscular than the figures suggested. And although the battlefields of South Vietnam had grown relatively quiet in 1970 and 1971, thus giving Vietnamization an opportunity to progress, no one believed that North Vietnam was about to give up. In fact intelligence reports in late 1970 indicated that Hanoi was building up its roads and base areas in Laos to improve its strategic and logistical position for the moment that U.S. forces left Vietnam. A senior U.S. adviser asked early in 1971: "What happens if the North Vietnamese are just waiting for us to go home before they come streaming out of the hills?" Top U.S. and South Vietnamese officials, however, had been pondering another question: "What happens if the South Vietnamese go up into the hills after them?"

## The Ho Chi Minh Trail

The first phase of Vietnamization—turning the ground war over to the Vietnamese—was soon to face its first major test as the South Vietnamese struck out on their own to disrupt the Ho Chi Minh Trail complex in Laos. By 1971 the supply route had been improved dramatically.

In 1967 few adequate roads had existed in the Laotian panhandle, and North Vietnamese logistics command 559 Transportation Group (named for the date of its creation in May 1959) still moved some men and materiel along the so-called Ho Chi Minh Trail by foot, by porter, and by bicycle. By 1971, however, well-maintained two-lane roads carried troops and supplies south through the Mu Gia, Ban Karai, and Ban Raving passes in the Annamite (or Truong Son) Mountains to Tchepone and Muong Nong, which were command centers and transshipment points for two key North Vietnamese base areas. Called 604 and 611, these bases lay just across the South Vietnamese border from the northernmost provinces of Quang Tri and Thua Thien. The trail branched off from bases 604 and 611. Men and supplies moved southeast toward the A Shau Valley or south toward other base areas that dotted South Vietnam's entire 1,300-kilometer border with neighboring Cambodia and Laos. At the Laos-Cambodia border, the Ho Chi Minh Trail filtered south into the so-called Sihanouk Trail, by which materiel had been shipped overland from Cambodia. "The trail is any way the enemy can get down to the south," one frustrated American officer said. "The trail is a state of mind, it's a philosophy."

Ninety kilometers wide at some points, the Ho Chi Minh Trail spread out over Laos like a spider web; its strands may have totaled 13,000 kilometers in length. (U.S. intelligence claimed that it had mapped "the entire 3,500 miles [5,645 kilometers] of the trail system—every crossroad and gully." But the North Vietnamese boasted that they had built over 13,000 kilometers of trails.) Group 559 built, maintained, and defended the trail system with 100,000 North Vietnamese and Laotian volunteers and forced laborers to perform construction and upkeep, while as many as 50,000 North Vietnamese troops provided security for the seven base camps, depots, and military posts. Logistical units (called *binh trams*) were composed of transportation, signal, and engineer battalions, as well as one or more artillery battalions. Some twenty way stations linked the heavily guarded base areas, and communication–liaison battalions, fifty of which existed in 1970, guided men and supplies between stations and provided shelter, food, and medical aid. (Freely translated, *binh tram* means "commo–liaison site.")

By 1968 transport of supplies on laborers' backs or on bicycles had ended. Fleets of trucks had replaced the por-ters. Although estimates vary widely, it is believed that between 5,000 and 10,000 trucks moved between hundreds of truck parks in Laos, with an equal number of trucks remaining in reserve in North Vietnam. The trucks traveled at night to make aerial detection more difficult. After dark they left their daytime hiding places to move over the twenty-five- to sixty-kilometer-stretch that constituted one night's leg of the journey.

To keep the trucks running, fuel was pumped south through a pipeline that engineers completed in 1969. The pipeline followed the Ho Chi Minh Trail through the Mu Gia Pass, down to Muong Nong in Laos, and southeast to the A Shau Valley. Running along stream beds or covered over in gullies, the four-inch pipeline, impossible to detect from the air, augmented the North Vietnamese system of sending fuel south in fifty-five-gallon drums on the backs of trucks or floating them downriver like logs. The pipeline's completion not only improved the logistical capability of Group 559, it also made possible the beginnings of conventional, mechanized warfare by North Vietnam. Since the dramatic appearance of PT76 light amphibious tanks at the Special Forces camp at Lang Vei, near Khe Sanh, across from base area 604, on February 8, 1968, no North Vietnamese armor had entered southern battlefields. Since then, U.S. reconnaissance aircraft and photo analysts had occasionally glimpsed a tank on the move through Laos or sighted a telltale tread mark in the dirt. But the overall judgment of U.S. intelligence was that enemy armor posed no threat to South Vietnam.

Senior North Vietnamese General Vo Nguyen Giap aptly assessed the significance of the Ho Chi Minh Trail when he commended the cadres and men of Group 559 for their accomplishments, pointing out their "strategic rear services mission was the most important" of all their tasks. This was borne out by U.S. intelligence, which estimated that between 1966 and 1971, 630,000 NVA troops, 100,000 tons of foodstuffs, 400,000 weapons, and 50,000 tons of ammunition moved from the north along this efficient and resilient life line.

The big push to move supplies along the Ho Chi Minh Trail came during the Laotian dry season from October to March; during the rest of the year the monsoon rains turned

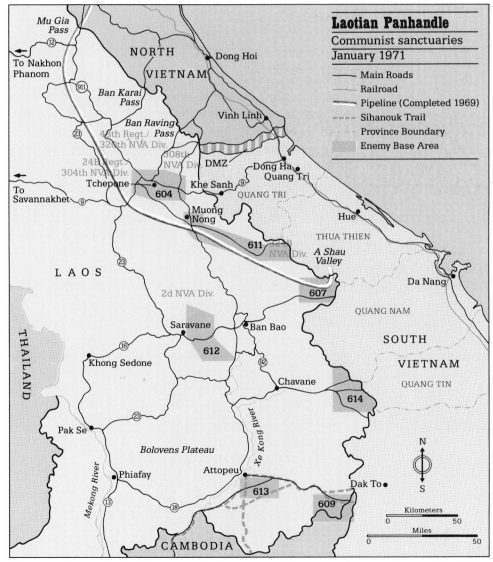

The target of U.S. and South Vietnamese bombing and clandestine raids since 1965, the Ho Chi Minh Trail network had nevertheless thrived and expanded. As this map shows, by 1971 it had developed into a strategic rear service area with an oil pipeline, sophisticated jungle base camps, and several NVA Main Force divisions poised to strike at South Vietnam.

the jungle trails into bogs, all but halting truck traffic. The exigencies of weather dictated that North Vietnamese offensives take place toward the conclusion of the Laotian dry season, when supplies had been moved forward and cached near the battlefields.

## The inevitable target

After Hanoi lost the use of the Cambodian port of Sihanoukville to Lon Nol's coup in 1970, the possibility of a South Vietnamese–U.S. attack against the Ho Chi Minh Trail seemed logical, if not inevitable. In Cambodia the North Vietnamese had abandoned their stores of food and materiel and retreated west beyond the thirty-kilometer limit announced by the Americans during the incursion in May 1970. In Laos, however, Hanoi ruled out retreat and instead upgraded its already formidable defenses, ultimately creating the most effective air defense against airmobility the Americans encountered.

When the dry season arrived in the fall of 1970, twenty antiaircraft battalions marched into Laos to reinforce the *binh trams* around base areas 604 and 611. The battalions' equipment included highly mobile 12.7MM machine guns, 14.5MM antiaircraft machine guns, 23MM cannons, and perhaps 200 pieces of antiaircraft artillery—37MM, 57MM, 85MM, and 100MM guns. The soldiers also arrived with 122MM rockets, mortars, and shoulder-fired B40 rockets. The antiaircraft artillery was constantly shuffled among an estimated 3,000 prepared emplacements.

In the Laotian jungle, there were few potential helicopter landing zones, and the North Vietnamese established 12.7MM firing positions in triangular formations on high ground above the clearings. From such elevated positions, the defenders not only gained complete coverage of a possible landing zone but could also fire on a more horizontal, and hence more accurate, plane as a helicopter descended. Mortars preregistered to zero in on the landing zone could likewise prove lethal if a helicopter touched down for resupply or medical evacuation.

NVA troop strength also increased, as thousands of soldiers began moving down the trail at the beginning of the dry season. By early 1971 total enemy troop strength in the section of Laos opposite Quang Tri Province was estimated at 22,000—7,000 NVA combat troops, 10,000 men in logistic and support units, and 5,000 Pathet Lao, all under a new corps command, the 70th Front. Perhaps more important, eight additional regiments, all supported by artillery, were available as reinforcements to be brought into any battle over a wide area within two weeks.

This build-up alarmed the Americans and South Vietnamese, who believed it might presage an offensive at the end of the Laotian dry season early in 1971 or in the U.S. election year of 1972. A preemptive strike was a tempting idea. Reflecting General Abrams's proclivity for attacking the enemy's "logistics nose," MACV told Washington that

a major disruption of the Communist supply system for one dry season might hamper the North's ability to launch an offensive for one year and possibly longer. "Tchepone and those base areas have got everything—guns, trucks, gasoline," said one high-ranking MACV officer after looking at reconnaissance photographs. "If we went in there and cleaned them out, it would set them back a year, maybe two years. We'd be crazy not to do it."

Since American troops were barred by the Cooper-Church amendment from fighting outside Vietnam, South Vietnamese troops alone would have to carry the battle into Laos. Such an invasion promised important military and political dividends for the Americans: Militarily, it not only would thwart an enemy offensive but also would stand as a test of the first phase of Vietnamization, since a successful foray into the enemy stronghold would confirm the modernization and self-reliance of ARVN ground troops; politically, a success on the scale of the Cambodian incursion was likely to permit a more rapid withdrawal of American combat forces from Vietnam. The lure was irresistible, and MACV and the Vietnamese Joint General Staff went to work on preliminary planning.

The operation was not without political risk for Washington, however. Acknowledging that Laos was "clogged" with men and supplies, Nixon agreed with the military necessity of the operation, but he showed justifiable caution about widening the war after the domestic fire storm he had provoked by the Cambodian incursion. This time he determined to bring all his key cabinet officers and advisers together to ride out the inevitable public storm. By the laborious process by which he often gained consensus, Nixon orchestrated numerous long briefings, each time introducing a new adviser to the plan, and virtually forcing that person to defer to the unanimous wisdom of his colleagues. One great flaw of such a process was that it brooked no opposition, permitting no devil's advocate to question assumptions or military plans; the whole package had to be accepted in toto.* Another flaw was that the process consumed time.

Between the beginning of Nixon's persuasive efforts in mid-December 1970 and the moment of final decision on January 18, 1971, valuable planning time was lost for the South Vietnamese military who were to organize their largest, most complicated, and most important operation of the war. The lack of time for adequate planning, as well as the absence of any questioning about military reality and the capability of ARVN, were soon proved to be crucial drawbacks. The Laotian adventure, Operation Lam Son 719, was to encounter difficulties almost from the start.

---

* President Nixon had been mulling over the problems of properly reporting the history of his administration, and it was during the White House discussions of Lam Son 719 that he installed voice-activated recording equipment in the Oval Office and used it for the first time.

*In the midst of a Communist base area in Laos along the Ho Chi Minh Trail, a cave serves as bomb shelter and living area.*

# Lam Son 719

At dawn on February 8, 1971, South Vietnamese armored personnel carriers, each with a dozen soldiers crouching amid wilting brush camouflage, clanked and rumbled down Route 9, crossing into Laos. The terrain ahead had been raked with artillery fire throughout the night, and the skies overhead began to buzz with American-piloted troop helicopters and shark-nosed Cobras searching for enemy ambush sites. Behind the troops a ragged column of armor, infantrymen, and supply trucks stretched twenty kilometers through Lang Vei to Khe Sanh, the abandoned marine combat base. Khe Sanh had been reactivated as the forward base for Operation Lam Son 719, the long-awaited invasion of Laos in order to cut the Ho Chi Minh Trail.

With the friskiness of schoolboys embarking on adventure, the South Vietnamese bantered as they advanced. "Hey, this is the second time we're going into a foreign country without our passports," said a paratroop veteran of the Cam-

bodian incursion, provoking laughter on all sides. Some soldiers talked, as men often do, about women in the land ahead. But on this D-Day some did not share the confidence that came from progressing without a sign of enemy opposition. Waiting for his unit to move out, Ranger Sergeant Ngo Van Thi pulled his blanket tighter around his shoulders to ward off the morning chill and said, "I've already fought in Cambodia, and now I'm going into Laos . . . I think it will be harder than Cambodia."

That Lam Son 719* would be harder was guaranteed by a red and white painted sign the men passed as they crossed from South Vietnam into Laos. It read: "Warning—No U.S. Personnel Beyond This Point." Neither U.S. ground troops nor advisers were going to enter Laos during the operation, which was expected to extend for three months and involve the best soldiers South Vietnam could put into the field: the ARVN 1st Infantry Division and 1st Armored Brigade from I Corps and a Ranger group. Airborne troops and Marines, whose battalions and brigades constituted the national reserve, were being brought together as divisions for the first time to join in Lam Son 719. The plan, the brain child of General Creighton Abrams, was first to send troops on a quick strike to Tchepone, a trans-shipment point forty-two kilometers inside Laos. Other troops were to man fire support bases inside Laos to protect exposed flanks. All were eventually to withdraw south and southeast through North Vietnamese base area 611, the region in Laos attacked by the 9th Marines two years earlier in Operation Dewey Canyon.

The 16,000 South Vietnamese embarking on Lam Son 719 equaled about one-half the combined Vietnamese-U.S. force that had invaded Cambodia in April the previous year. Later reinforcements would swell the Vietnamese force to 20,000. Although American ground troops and advisers were barred from Laos, U.S. helicopter and airplane pilots were exempt from the ban against fighting there, and, in fact, Lam Son 719 depended heavily on U.S. fire support and logistics. Some 10,000 U.S. combat, engineering, and support troops remained in Quang Tri Province to provide security, logistical and combat support, and to maintain and arm 2,000 fixed-wing aircraft and 600 helicopters. Meanwhile, to mislead Hanoi about the real objectives of the attack, a naval task force carrying U.S. Marines made ready to steam into the Tonkin Gulf.

At the Laotian border American advisers to Vietnamese units halted and, as the first day of Lam Son 719 wore on, one U.S. adviser after another handed over a map case to his counterpart, shook hands, and wished him good luck. In practice, at the battalion and company level, advisers performed the role of fire support coordinators. In the chaos of battle, they took over the radios, calculating dis-

tances, marking targets, calling in artillery, coordinating with other nearby units, and chattering with forward air controllers who were themselves orchestrating aerial ballets of gunships and tactical air support. Lam Son 719 was predicated on air mobility and the might of American firepower to suppress NVA opposition, and South Vietnamese battalion and company commanders were going to have to coordinate fire support by themselves for the first time, articulating the complicated jargon of shorthand figures, facts, and numbers in English or through interpreters flying with forward air controllers. The success of Lam Son 719 depended on many factors—coordination of ground troops, the tenacity of the North Vietnamese, the boldness and efficiency of the plan itself. But at the tactical level the operation was going to succeed or fail in large part because of the leadership of the officers and the skill of the ARVN soldiers.

The troops entering Laos remarked on the lush greenery of the jungle, so different from the ravaged Khe Sanh plateau where chemical defoliants and countless tons of bombs had denuded the red earth. When a convoy of armored vehicles halted, however, the soldiers noted that not a single bird chirped. Perhaps the preparatory artillery strikes had chased away the birds, some suggested. There was virtually no resistance as the troops advanced, and that very absence of opposition was worrisome. A correspondent riding in the armored column reasoned that NVA patrols must surely be following and watching. But "with Cobra gunships firing rockets all around us," he wrote, "we advanced the next day 25 klicks into Laos. There was no return fire and I felt it was an NVA tactic to draw us in deeper."

## Problems of planning

From concept to execution, the plan for Lam Son 719 had taken shape in just a few weeks and in tight security. This had numerous ramifications. Because Communist espionage cells were active within ARVN, the joint planning committee had a strictly limited membership involving only the intelligence and operations staff members of I Corps under Lieutenant General Hoang Xuan Lam, who was to command the operation, and U.S. XXIV Corps, headed by Lieutenant General James W. Sutherland, Jr. Units did not learn they would play parts in Lam Son until January 17, and the Airborne Division that was to lead the operation received no detailed plans until February 2, less than a week before the February 8 D-Day.

In the end, secrecy was breached on all sides. According to one CIA source, Vietnamese Communists had infiltrated the translating and printing shops at I Corps head-

---

Preceding page. *ARVN troops roll down Route 9 toward Laos at the opening of Operation Lam Son 719.*

*The South Vietnamese had named many of their operations *Lam Son*, the birthplace of fifteenth century hero Le Loi, who led a ten-year fight to expel the Chinese from Vietnam. The numerals signify the year 1971 and the Route 9 area.

*American Division troops ride APCs toward Lang Vei as part of Dewey Canyon II, the U.S. operation to clear Route 9 to the Laotian border for the South Vietnamese invasion.*

quarters and filched copies of the plans, probably including sites of proposed helicopter landing zones and firebases. In any event, such espionage was scarcely required to divine the general thrust of the plans.

MACV briefed American reporters off the record on the impending action but then, to enhance security, imposed a rare press embargo on the reporting of troop movements. The embargo, Henry Kissinger wrote later, "proved to be a naive mistake." Communists and other news sources not bound by the embargo published reports of the incursion into Laos, and the very word of the embargo when it reached Washington tipped off news editors that something of that nature was in the offing. The result was that even before the embargo was lifted on February 4, word of the impending operation was on the front pages of newspapers in the States, and their editorial pages were cautioning against the expedition.

"The worst may have happened already," Senator George Aiken of Vermont complained on February 2. "The enemy certainly knows what is happening. I think the American people should have the same privilege." The embargo was lifted on February 4, and newspapers released stories about the build-up of American troops and engineer units who, with Operation Dewey Canyon II, had begun to reopen the base to Khe Sanh and rebuild the roads for a penetration across the Laotian frontier.

U.S. officials attempted to manage the press further by withholding military transportation from the newsmen clamoring to cover the invasion. There was no civilian transport in the area, but military officials invoked an obscure Department of Defense rule against competing with civilian airlines in carrying passengers across international boundaries. That rule had not been invoked in the Cambodian incursion. Reporters could get to the war zone only in the few helicopters flown by Vietnamese, and of those who resorted to this, four photographers were shot down on February 10 (see sidebar, page 88).

The plans for Lam Son 719 were kept closely held for so long that the units involved had too little time for tactical planning and preparation. This was particularly important because many of the units, principally the Airborne troops and Marines, had worked only as separate battalions and brigades and had no experience of maneuvering together or of cooperating in adjoining areas. Commanders and upper level staff members were unaccustomed to working in concert. Except at the highest levels, the U.S. and ARVN staffs did not work together in coordinating plans for the operation. "Planning was rushed, handicapped by security restrictions, and conducted separately and in isolation by Vietnamese and Americans," concluded Brigadier General Sidney B. Berry, assistant commander of the 101st Airborne Division, who took charge of helicopter support. "Planning and coordination for Lam Son 719 were, at the Corps Commanders' level, of unacceptably low quality."

Since the operation lacked a unified system of command and control, coordination posed nearly insurmountable problems. Command posts were located at Khe Sanh, Dong Ha, and Quang Tri, and inevitably there were lapses in communication between them. Problems of communication went beyond the physical location of headquarters. As national reserve units, the elite Airborne and Marine units normally answered to Saigon, the Joint General Staff and President Thieu, but for Lam Son 719 they came under the control of I Corps and were subordinate to overall commander Gen. Lam. Except for the heads of the 1st Division and 1st Armored Brigade in I Corps, no commanding general had allegiance to Lam, and in the highly politicized ARVN, allegiance was as important as rank. In fact Marine commander Lieutenant General Le Nguyen Khang, a strong supporter of Vice President Ky, actually outranked Lam and, moreover, was critical of the Lam Son 719 plan. "We [felt] very unhappy with the poor command," General Khang said later.

Gen. Lam had survived as commander of I Corps for five years because of his administrative and politicking skills. One of Thieu's possible motives in launching Lam Son 719 was to build Lam into a hero, thus enabling him to bring Lam to Saigon as head of the Joint General Staff, replacing General Cao Van Vien who wished to step down. But first Lam needed to conduct an operation of a magnitude and diversity he had never before attempted. Lam Son 719 represented his first great military challenge.

Despite signs of inadequate preparation, in late January and early February, as the planning for Lam Son 719 progressed, U.S. and ARVN commanders and staffs waxed confident. Following a briefing at XXIV Corps headquarters, Colonel Arthur W. Pence, senior adviser to the Airborne Division, summarized the planners' mood:

It was apparent at this time that United States intelligence felt that the operation would be lightly opposed and that a two-day preparation of the area prior to D-Day by tactical air would effectively neutralize the enemy antiaircraft capability although the enemy was credited with having 170 to 200 antiaircraft weapons of mixed caliber in the operational area. The tank threat was considered minimal and the reinforcement capability was listed as 14 days for two divisions from north of the DMZ.

This intelligence outlook was quite inaccurate. As it turned out, the only correct prognosis proved to be about the reinforcements available to the North Vietnamese, although they were already stationed in the south in the A Shau Valley and in base area 612 and did not have to come from the DMZ. Poor weather over Laos in the two days prior to the beginning of Lam Son 719 prevented preparatory air strikes from being carried out, so the enemy's antiaircraft weapons were never attacked.

Tactical aircraft did take to the air, only to be turned back by the weather. At twilight on February 6 one navy pilot mistook the ARVN task force poised at the border for enemy positions. The plane dropped cluster bombs, killing

*At twilight on February 6, a U.S. pilot accidentally bombed ARVN troops poised for the Lam Son 719 strike into Laos. Here a soldier is caught in the blast of a cluster bomb.*

six, wounding fifty-one, and destroying an armored personnel carrier. "It is sad to lose men in this way," said Lieutenant Colonel Bui The Dung of the first ARVN casualties of Lam Son 719. The attack by friendly fire underscored the difficulties ARVN and U.S. support forces would face in coordinating firepower and contributed to a reluctance on the part of ARVN to trust in U.S. tactical air power at close quarters.

The South Vietnamese crossed into Laos along three parallel lines (see map, page 81). The Rangers and 1st Infantry Division moved by helicopter toward landing zones on the northern and southern flanks, while the 4,000-man armor-airborne column (the 1st Armor Brigade and 1st and 8th Airborne Battalions) advanced along Route 9,

*Forward into Laos. On the first day of the invasion, February 8, 1971, ARVN troops prepare to enter Laotian territory via helicopter (left) and on foot (below).*

which lay in the broad Sepone River Valley with mountains rising on both sides. The mission of the armor brigade, a company of seventeen M41 Walker Bulldog tanks plus M113 armored personnel carriers, was to open and secure Route 9 to Ban Dong, about twenty kilometers inside Laos, then to push the final twenty-two kilometers to Tchepone. (The armor brigade was later to be reinforced.)

## Inside Laos

Fear of ambushes in the dense jungle on both sides of the road slowed the advance, as did huge bomb craters, hidden from reconnaissance aircraft by thick grass and bamboo. The first day's progress amounted to only a tedious nine kilometers. "It was like battering down a bamboo tunnel," said Japanese photographer Akihiko Okamura, who had defied the press ban and hidden in one of the armored vehicles. The ARVN 101st Combat Engineer Battal-

ion cleared parts of the road and used its bulldozers to construct detours where the road was totally destroyed. In spite of the engineers' efforts to open the road, throughout Lam Son 719 Route 9 remained virtually impassable to all but tracked vehicles, so the ground line of communication was never completely opened. Since no trucks or jeeps were able to negotiate the terrain, the troops along Route 9 became totally dependent on overtaxed U.S. helicopters for resupply of fuel, ammunition, food, and spare parts.

Heavy rains on the second day turned Route 9 into a red quagmire. The engineers could not work. The armor could not move. On the third day the weather cleared and the column drove to Ban Dong, linking up with another airborne battalion, the 9th, which landed at LZ A Luoi near the close of day. The men set about constructing a camp and patrolling in the vicinity while awaiting orders to continue westward. The main South Vietnamese thrust had reached halfway to Tchepone, opposed only by sporadic sniper fire.

The situation on the flanks was different. At 8:20 on the opening morning, U.S. gunships north of Route 9 made contact with enemy armor, attacking four tracked vehicles, one of which had a 37MM antiaircraft gun in tow. Before noon, gunships spotted more armored vehicles northwest of a hilltop landing zone designated 31, eight kilometers north of Ban Dong. The 3d Airborne Battalion and 3d Airborne Brigade headquarters occupied LZ 31 without any hostile fire and turned it into a firebase with a battery of six 105MM howitzers. The 2d Airborne Battalion had meanwhile reached LZ 30, also located north of Route 9. The 2d Battalion brought in a 105MM and 155MM batteries.

Northwest of LZ 30, enemy 12.7MM machine guns fired on a fleet of helicopters carrying the 21st Ranger Battalion to a landing zone called Ranger South. Three days later, just as the armor column was reaching Ban Dong, the 39th Ranger Battalion deployed to Ranger Base North. With the establishment of this northernmost outpost—little more than a bivouac—the network of four mutually supporting bases on the north flank of Route 9 was in place.

General Lam considered the Ranger bases to be observation and listening posts; the Rangers were to provide early warning to the main column of any enemy force moving south. Light infantry without armor or artillery, the Rangers were expected to delay any NVA advance until heavier firepower could be brought to bear.

South of Route 9, three battalions of the 3d Regiment, 1st Infantry Division, occupied LZs Hotel and Blue against scattered resistance on the first day of Lam Son. Within days other 1st Division battalions flew westward, establishing LZs Delta, Don, and Delta 1, the last just six kilometers southeast of Ban Dong. With the 1st Division manning these five firebases, the southern flank was secured.

While awaiting further orders from I Corps, the South Vietnamese patrolled the areas around their ten Laotian bases—which began to come under mortar and 122MM rocket fire—and encountered increasingly heavy enemy resistance. A patrol from Ranger North killed a reported forty-three North Vietnamese and seized two 37MM anti-aircraft artillery guns. In the southern sector, patrols from the 1st Division's firebases not only ran into enemy soldiers, but they also found major enemy caches that held individual weapons and ammunition, as well as recoilless rifles, petroleum in fifty-five-gallon drums, and huge quantities of food. They also discovered bodies of enemy soldiers killed by U.S. air strikes, twenty-three in one location, fifty in another. American air strikes were so widespread that the discovery of enemy soldiers killed from the air became a common occurrence.

By February 11 the armored column in place at Ban Dong awaited orders from General Lam's I Corps headquarters to continue the offensive. But no orders arrived, and the commanders had little initiative to move aggressively toward Tchepone. Probing Route 9 some two or three kilometers to the west of Firebase A Luoi, APCs and bulldozers repeatedly ran into minefields which, although cleared by ARVN soldiers with mine detectors, were reseeded during the night. Meanwhile Firebase A Luoi began to take mortar and rocket fire during the day as well as at night. The daytime firing became so heavy that after a week the tank patrols could advance no more than a few hundred meters.

In the absence of orders from I Corps headquarters, Lam Son 719 stalled for several critical days. In Saigon on February 14, General Abrams urged General Cao Van Vien to get the South Vietnamese units to Tchepone as quickly as possible. Abrams's plan for Lam Son 719 hinged on taking Tchepone rapidly, but two more days passed without any progress. On February 16 Abrams and XXIV Corps commander General Sutherland met with Generals Vien and Lam at the I Corps forward command post at Dong Ha. Together they decided to extend the 1st Division's line of firebases on the mountaintops south of Route 9 to cover the Airborne's push to Tchepone, estimating that it would take three to five days for the 1st Division to get into position. Three to five days, however, represented a fateful block of time for Operation Lam Son 719. Each day that passed the South Vietnamese were squandering opportunities. The battlefield balance was shifting away from them, and the reactions of the North Vietnamese were daily growing stronger.

## North Vietnam joins the battle

North Vietnam's reaction to the invasion built gradually. In the first days after ARVN crossed into Laos, Hanoi's attention was also drawn to the U.S. naval task force, augmented by two aircraft carriers and escort vessels, cruising in the Tonkin Gulf seventy kilometers off the port city of Vinh. The mission of the force was to feign an attack on Vinh. Each day the 31st Marine Amphibious Unit prac-

ticed aboard the ships for an air assault. The helicopters went through the motions of loading troops, without actually emplaning them, then flew to a point just beyond the twelve-mile territorial limit. Jets from the carrier continually flew overhead as if providing air cover for a landing force. The possibility of an attack on Vinh seemed real enough that Hanoi moved some troops north from the DMZ to the Vinh region.

As the South Vietnamese build-up in Laos continued, however, Hanoi decided that the thrust into Laos was the real threat at hand and committed the 70th Corps Communist troops to battle. The 70th Corps controlled three divisions already in the area, the 304th, 308th, and 320th. (Indeed, an ARVN airborne battalion patrolling in the wake of a B-52 strike discovered the 308th Division command post just two kilometers north of Route 9.) The 2d NVA Division had also moved up from the south to the Tchepone area and began shifting to the east in early February to blunt the ARVN's armored advance. Hanoi continued to respect the U.S.–ARVN diversions by deploying just one regiment—the 64th of the 320th Division—from the DMZ region. By early March, Hanoi had massed 36,000 troops in the Lam Son 719 area, outnumbering ARVN by more than a two-to-one margin.

The North Vietnamese tactics were to mass forces for attack, overwhelming the outnumbered foe. Lam Son 719's isolated firebases presented the NVA with excellent opportunities to encircle them and defeat them one by one. The first step was to cut the firebase's aerial supply lines with antiaircraft fire and to demoralize the men defending the base with round-the-clock mortar, rocket, and artillery barrages. Next the Communist soldiers would storm the base, using a combined infantry-armor force wherever it was possible.

The ARVN's counterpunch was firepower from artillery and supporting aircraft. But their artillery provided them with no great advantage since it had a shorter range than the NVA's 130MM and 122MM guns, and the NVA offered no fixed targets. As for tactical air, helicopter and fixed-wing gunships and jets stayed on the ground in bad weather and, when they flew, had to contend with fierce antiaircraft fire. Although B-52s traveled above the antiaircraft screen and bombed through bad weather, the Stratofortresses required large targets located beyond a safety zone of three kilometers from friendly forces. If the North Vietnamese did not mass until their final attack, or if they stayed close to the ARVN bases, holding their ground by ambushing ARVN patrols (and at the same time cutting the ARVN's ground relief route), they effectively thwarted the B-52 as the protector of a firebase. In fact the closer the NVA came to the ARVN perimeter, the more they disarmed the ARVN's firepower superiority, because experienced commanders even in the best of circumstances hesitated to call in artillery or tactical air support close to their own men.

Concussion-shocked troops stagger from their vehicle, which hit a land mine on Route 9 in Laos west of Firebase A Luoi.

## Ranger bases under siege

The North Vietnamese moved first against the more lightly defended Ranger and Airborne bases north of Route 9. They threw nooses around Ranger Bases North and South and on February 18 began tightening them with artillery and mortar barrages, followed by infantry attacks. Fighting lasted throughout the night, as artillery and tactical air sought the enemy, and flareships patrolled overhead.

The next morning the NVA infantry withdrew from Ranger Base South, while keeping up pressure with artillery fire, and moved against the 39th Battalion at Ranger Base North. Accurate recoilless rifle fire and mortar rounds fell for hours on the base and then the NVA infantry, the 102d Regiment of the 308th Division, all in crisp uniforms and using new automatic weapons, attacked from the east where the Ranger defenses were weakest. With the help of artillery and tactical air support, the Rangers held off the attacks. For a second day the exhausted soldiers fought on after dark.

As the enemy pressure intensified, President Thieu, visiting I Corps headquarters, advised General Lam to proceed cautiously and postpone taking Tchepone. Instead, Thieu suggested more extensive search activities toward the southwest in an effort to cut off Route 914, while awaiting further developments. Lam naturally obeyed and in so

doing surrendered any momentum Lam Son 719 had acquired. By standing still, the South Vietnamese were playing right into enemy hands.

During daylight on February 20 some helicopters braved the antiaircraft fire to bring ammunition to the 39th Battalion at Ranger Base North and evacuate wounded. North Vietnamese gunners brought down a medevac helicopter, and wounded American crewman Specialist 4 Dennis Fujii was stranded at the base after several attempts to rescue him failed. Fujii remained to help treat the Vietnamese wounded as well as to call in many of the tactical air sorties flown that day. A rescue helicopter finally succeeded in picking up Fujii, but it was hit as it lifted out and crash-landed at Ranger South. Tactical air continued to pound enemy positions. "[Ranger North] looked like World War II must have," air force Captain William Cathey, an F-4 pilot with the 40th Tactical Fighter Squadron, said of the apocalyptic scene. "We put a napalm strike within 100 meters of [ARVN] troops. That was tight. We could see them in the trenches."

By late afternoon nearly 2,000 North Vietnamese soldiers had encircled the 39th Battalion, which had dwindled to fewer than 300 able-bodied Rangers. With certain defeat looming, the battalion commander shut down his radio and ordered a retreat toward Ranger Base South six kilometers away. Carrying their wounded,

the men fought their way through the North Vietnamese lines. "The ARVN Rangers were outnumbered six or eight to one," said Lieutenant Colonel Robert F. Molinelli, commander of the 2d Squadron, 17th Air Cavalry, who observed the 39th from above. "For three days we were unable to get supplies to them. When they were low on ammunition, they went out and took NVA rifles and ammunition and fought on. When they decided to move off their hill, they beat their way right through that North Vietnamese regiment, killing them with their own guns and ammunition."

One hundred ninety-nine survivors reached Ranger Base South by nightfall; 107 were still able to fight. Casualties in the three-day fight exceeded 75 percent. Of a total of about 430 Rangers, 178 were killed or missing and 148 had been wounded. The 39th Ranger Battalion was finished as a unit. It had taken a toll of the enemy, however: Reconnaissance photo analysts counted 639 North Vietnamese bodies on the slopes of Ranger Base North.

The North Vietnamese now shifted their attention to Ranger Base South, increasing their artillery fire and turning their long-range 130MM field guns onto the base. The following day the Americans and South Vietnamese organized a huge effort of coordinated firepower and air support in order to evacuate wounded. Once thirteen medical helicopters were airborne and en route to Ranger

*Bombs from B-52 Stratofortresses pound a ridge five kilometers away as soldiers watch from Firebase A Luoi. Despite the bombing, North Vietnamese artillery on the ridge resumed firing twelve hours later.*

Base South, a combination of tactical aircraft, air cavalry gunships, and aerial and ground artillery surrounded the base with a curtain of fire, suppressing suspected enemy positions for nearly an hour while the helicopters landed behind smoke screens and picked up 122 wounded, including Sp4 Fujii.

Four hundred men, including 100 from the 39th Battalion, held Ranger Base South for another two days before General Lam declared their position untenable. The amount of air and artillery support required for each resupply and evacuation flight outweighed the military advantage of the position, and Lam chose not to sacrifice another battalion in a doomed attempt to hold it. He ordered the 21st Battalion to withdraw five kilometers southeast to FSB 30, from which they were evacuated and returned to South Vietnam.

Although the Rangers had been driven from their positions, and the 39th Battalion decimated, the most serious casualties of the battle at Ranger Base North may have been the pride of the Army of South Vietnam, and, by extension, the policy of Vietnamization itself. A number of able-bodied Rangers lost their nerve and tried to climb aboard the last medevacs leaving Ranger Base North. When they were repulsed, they deserted by clinging to the runners and riding back to Vietnam, where they were photographed by television cameras and reporters clustered at Khe Sanh waiting for word of the first major battle of the Laotian campaign. The sight of ARVN soldiers clinging to helicopter skids to escape from Laos and the North Vietnamese became the enduring image of Operation Lam Son 719.

Although Lt. Gen. Sutherland exaggerated in calling the battle "a great victory for the Rangers," the fact that many more men had fought courageously tended to be overlooked. Reporters asked the only American witness, Sp4 Fujii, about healthy Rangers pushing past wounded to get aboard helicopters. Fujii had already told his rescuers that the Rangers had trampled him in their rush for the helicopters. But to the press he denied that it had occurred, adding, "I think the Vietnamese Rangers are some of the most professional and qualified Vietnamese soldiers I ever worked with, and I would like to work with them again." Lt. Col. Molinelli expressed similar sentiments. "Seventeen of their men did panic and they did leave hanging on to helicopter skids," he said. "There were a lot more who did not." In spite of the many protestations, however, the image conveyed by the pictures persisted.

Another casualty of the Ranger base battles, although an indirect one, was ARVN Lieutenant General Do Cao Tri, commander of III Corps and hero of the 1970 Cambodian incursion. The Ranger battles north of Route 9 had been the first major enemy blows against the South Vietnamese invasion and the first challenge for Gen. Lam. He had deployed the lightly armed Rangers to the north to delay NVA reinforcements heading toward Route 9 until heavy firepower could be brought in. By his indecision and poor staff coordination during the battles, however, Lam had glaringly exposed his inadequacies.

Disappointed in Lam's performance, President Thieu summoned Gen. Tri from his III Corps headquarters to Saigon and on February 23 turned over command of Operation Lam Son 719 to the dynamic general. Leaving Saigon to take over, Tri perished in a helicopter crash, and General Lam retained his post.

## Attack on Firebase 31

Located eight kilometers north of A Luoi and virtually astride a Communist north-south supply line on Route 92, Fire Support Base 31 protected the north flank of the main column after the withdrawal of the Rangers, and it now bore the brunt of North Vietnamese attacks. Headquarters for the 3d Airborne Brigade and Colonel Nguyen Van Tho, the base also held the 3d Airborne Battalion. Two of its companies, the 33d and 34th Rifle Companies—the latter reduced by casualties to sixty-five men—defended FSB 31,

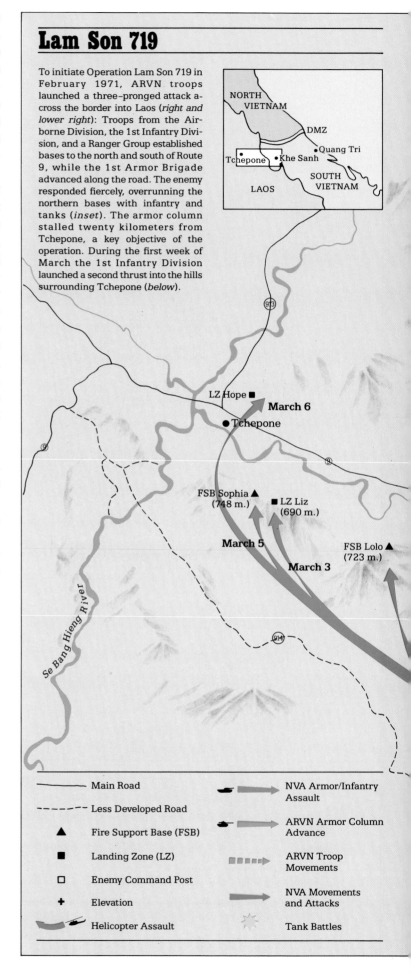

# Lam Son 719

To initiate Operation Lam Son 719 in February 1971, ARVN troops launched a three-pronged attack across the border into Laos (*right and lower right*): Troops from the Airborne Division, the 1st Infantry Division, and a Ranger Group established bases to the north and south of Route 9, while the 1st Armor Brigade advanced along the road. The enemy responded fiercely, overrunning the northern bases with infantry and tanks (*inset*). The armor column stalled twenty kilometers from Tchepone, a key objective of the operation. During the first week of March the 1st Infantry Division launched a second thrust into the hills surrounding Tchepone (*below*).

| | |
|---|---|
| ——— Main Road | NVA Armor/Infantry Assault |
| - - - - - Less Developed Road | ARVN Armor Column Advance |
| ▲ Fire Support Base (FSB) | ARVN Troop Movements |
| ■ Landing Zone (LZ) | |
| ☐ Enemy Command Post | NVA Movements and Attacks |
| + Elevation | |
| Helicopter Assault | Tank Battles |

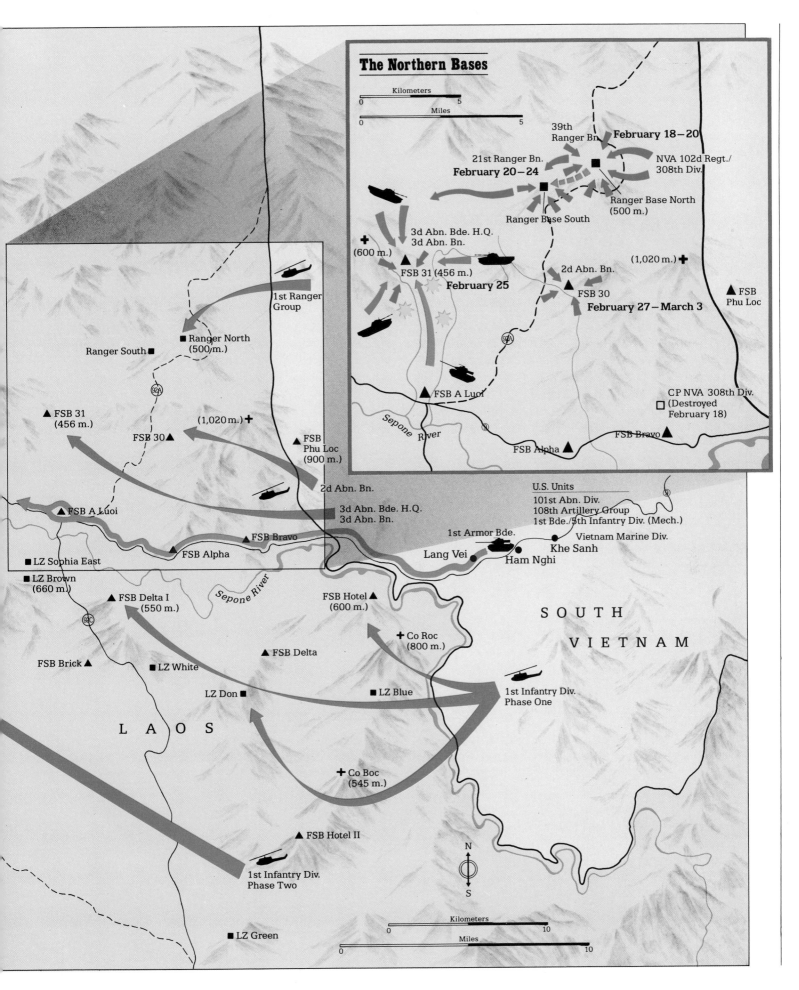

## The Northern Bases

Kilometers
0 ___ 5

Miles
0 ___ 5

39th Ranger Bn.

**February 18–20**

21st Ranger Bn.
**February 20–24**

NVA 102d Regt./
308th Div.

Ranger Base North
(500 m.)

Ranger Base South

3d Abn. Bde. H.Q.
3d Abn. Bn.

FSB 31 (456 m.)
**February 25**

2d Abn. Bn.

(1,020 m.) +

FSB 30
**February 27–March 3**

▲ FSB
Phu Loc

FSB A Luoi ▲

CP NVA 308th Div.
□ (Destroyed
February 18)

*Sepone River*

FSB Bravo ▲

FSB Alpha ▲

1st Ranger
Group

■ Ranger North
(500 m.)
Ranger South ■

▲ FSB 31
(456 m.)

(1,020 m.) +

FSB 30 ▲

▲ FSB
Phu Loc
(900 m.)

2d Abn. Bn.

3d Abn. Bde. H.Q.
3d Abn. Bn.

**U.S. Units**
101st Abn. Div.
108th Artillery Group
1st Bde./5th Infantry Div. (Mech.)

▲ FSB A Luoi

1st Armor Bde.

Vietnam Marine Div.

Khe Sanh

▲ FSB Bravo

Lang Vei
Ham Nghi

FSB Alpha

■ LZ Sophia East

■ LZ Brown
(660 m.)

▲ FSB Delta I
(550 m.)

*Sepone River*

FSB Hotel ▲
(600 m.)

**S O U T H**

**V I E T N A M**

FSB Brick ▲

▲ FSB Delta

■ LZ White

+ Co Roc
(800 m.)

LZ Don ■

■ LZ Blue

1st Infantry Div.
Phase One

**L A O S**

+ Co Boc
(545 m.)

▲ FSB Hotel II

1st Infantry Div.
Phase Two

N

S

■ LZ Green

Kilometers
0 ___ 10

Miles
0 ___ 10

while the battalion's other two companies patrolled the mountain ranges northeast. Another battalion had already been thrown off the mountain range to the northwest, losing over 100 killed, missing, and wounded in less than a day. The mountain range and the valley that ran to FSB 31 belonged to the enemy, and from there the North Vietnamese pounded away at the base with artillery and mortars.

Airborne Division commander Lieutenant General Du Quoc Dong feared that with his men stuck in static firebase positions, their usual aggressiveness had been stifled by General Lam's plan. Dong felt ill-used by Lam. "He remarked on many occasions," said the U.S. adviser, Colonel Arthur Pence, "that General Lam considered the Rangers the first cousins, the Airborne the distant cousins and the 1st ARVN Division the son." Dong also criticized U.S. air support for its inability to supply FSB 31. But enemy antiaircraft fire drove off any helicopters attempting to land. Col. Pence suggested dropping supplies by parachute, but Dong declined, not wanting to risk lowering morale by letting his men know how desperate their plight was. Over four days the number of casualties mounted and evacuation was impossible.

Several of the supporting American helicopter pilots decided to attempt a daring descent into the base to take out the most seriously wounded. Led by Lieutenant Colonel William N. Peachey, commander of the 158th Aviation Battalion, the helicopters braved the antiaircraft fire and flew into FSB 31. When they touched down, however, most able-bodied soldiers stayed in their bunkers, for the arrival of helicopters brought a new round of enemy mortar and artillery fire. With few men to help them into the helicopters, the seriously wounded remained behind, and only some walking wounded made it into the aircraft and escaped FSB 31. The Hueys pulled out the dead in sling loads swinging beneath.

At Col. Pence's suggestion, Dong ordered Colonel Nguyen Trong Luat, commander of the armored task force under Dong's control, to move some tanks of the 17th Armored Squadron north from A Luoi to reinforce FSB 31 against ground attack. By radio Dong ordered Companies 31 and 32, which were patrolling the mountains northeast of the firebase, to link up with the tanks and lead them back. The tanks never arrived at the firebase; the reason why was never suitably explained.

Colonel Pence maintained that Colonel Luat simply ignored Dong's orders and a follow-up order from General Lam. Although the armor was attached to the Airborne Division, and thus under Dong's command, "General Dong

had absolutely no control over the task force commander," said Pence. "General Dong did everything he could do . . . except call the commander in and shoot him." The American senior adviser to the armored brigade told a different story. According to Colonel Raymond Battreall, the armor commander had received conflicting orders from Generals Lam and Dong, and the column of five M41 tanks with accompanying infantry halted as ordered by the Airborne Division commander south of FSB 31. Moreover, in the coming confusion, Battreall said, the inexperienced Airborne Division staff simply forgot about the armored element and neglected to issue any orders. Whatever the reasons, the armor column was still several kilometers southeast of FSB 31 on February 25.

## Conventional warfare

On that day the North Vietnamese sent a rain of artillery fire into the base and followed up with the first large-scale conventional attack of the war. Hanoi was changing the face of the war, abandoning ambushes and hit-and-run attacks and resorting to conventional warfare. The North Vietnamese turned long-range heavy artillery onto their target, brought up tanks powered by ample diesel fuel,

and attacked with infantry regiments of some 2,000 men. Throughout the war, MACV had longed for such large NVA targets to destroy with U.S. firepower. But now that the North Vietnamese were showing their faces, U.S. forces possessed little means to affect events.

A pall of smoke, dust, and haze caused by artillery, air strikes, and napalm hung over FSB 31, rendering the slopes of the 456-meter-high hill invisible to the U.S. forward air controller, who was flying at nearly 4,000 feet to avoid antiaircraft fire. Just after noon, the men of the 31st Company saw enemy tanks south of the base and they called artillery from FSB A Luoi and FSB 30. Directed by the FAC, a flight of tactical aircraft destroyed several of the tanks and drove back the armored thrust.

After another fierce artillery barrage an hour later, North Vietnamese infantry and camouflaged tanks, PT76s and T54s, closed on the base from the northwest and east. The North Vietnamese had FSB 31 surrounded. The South Vietnamese had seen before the thinly armored PT76 amphibious tanks, little more than armored cars. But the sight of Soviet T54s—huge thirty-two-ton battle tanks with 100MM cannons and 12.7MM machine guns—crashing toward them came as an overwhelming shock. The outer defense of FSB 31 consisted of but one ring of concertina wire.

At that moment a U.S. Air Force F-4 Phantom was hit by antiaircraft fire and the pilot and crewmen ejected, parachuting down into the jungle far from the battle. The forward air controller left his station high above FSB 31 to track the airmen and direct their rescue by helicopter. His absence left the remaining aircraft without instructions or guidance, interrupting the air support that was crucial for the beleaguered base. It was an egregious mistake.

With no planes to slow its advance, another column of tanks and infantry attacked from the north. A lone helicopter attacked the column with its M60 machine guns, but NVA soldiers rolled onto their backs and fired up, driving it off. The NVA tanks and infantry breached the defenses and fought their way into the firebase, capturing it within forty minutes. Some of the Airborne troops broke out; most were captured. The victorious tanks spread throughout the base. "The tanks were there, big and ugly," said Lt. Col. Peachey, flying overhead and peering down through the haze. "They were on top of the bunkers, doing 360 degree turns, driving around and around."

Brigade commander Col. Tho and his staff were trapped in a collapsed bunker. They raised FSB A Luoi on the radio and reported that North Vietnamese soldiers were tearing the top off the bunker. They asked for artillery fire on their own positions, and it came but apparently without effect. The men surrendered, and shortly after their capture they made statements over the North Vietnamese radio denouncing Lam Son 719.

*ARVN soldiers rush wounded comrades to a medevac helicopter, which has landed near an armor unit at FSB A Luoi.*

Two members of a helicopter recovery team at Firebase A Luoi turn their backs to dust whipped up as a Huey "slick" hoists a light observation helicopter, which has been shot down by NVA antiaircraft fire. Although ground troops were forbidden from entering Laos, American pilots flew in support of Lam Son 719.

General Dong ordered a counterattack by 31 and 32 Companies, supported by the armored task force located to the southeast. But communication was poor, and conflicting reports about the disposition of friendly and enemy troops left the situation hopelessly confused. The weather also worsened, precluding further air support. Fire Support Base 31 remained in North Vietnamese hands, at a cost to them of an estimated 250 KIAs and eleven PT76 and T54 tanks destroyed. The Airborne suffered 155 killed and over 100 captured and had lost its battery of 105MM howitzers. The 3d Battalion was decimated. The Airborne survivors felt particularly bitter toward the armor unit that had failed to come to their rescue.

Fire Support Base 30 lasted less than a week longer. Although enemy tanks could not ascend the precipitous slopes to the mountaintop base, the tanks' cannons added direct fire to the indirect fire falling on the base from artillery and mortars. B–52 strikes and fixed-wing gunships helped the 2d Airborne Battalion to hold the base for a time. By March 3, however, all the base's artillery—six 105MM and six 155MM howitzers—had been damaged, and the 2d Battalion received orders to destroy its guns and evacuate the base.

A few days earlier, the tanks of the 17th Armored Squadron had finally joined the battle north of Route 9, fighting the North Vietnamese to little better than a standstill in the first toe-to-toe armored battles of the Indochina War. In the five days between February 25—the day FSB 31 fell—and March 1, the relief column, consisting of five M41 tanks, numerous APCs, the 8th Airborne Battalion, and remnants of the 3d Battalion, barely outgunned the NVA tanks and infantry in three major battles. With the help of U.S. air strikes, the ARVN destroyed seventeen PT76 and six T54 tanks and killed a reported 1,130 soldiers in the process. The ARVN lost twenty-five APCs, as well as three of the five M41 tanks. ARVN also lost over 200 killed and wounded.

Two days later in the same vicinity, the reinforced tank column encountered a battalion of North Vietnamese soldiers without armor and, aided by B–52 strikes, virtually wiped it out, recording nearly 400 killed. In the week of battle, the ARVN armor had performed well, killing the equivalent of a regiment of North Vietnamese soldiers. But it had not arrived in time to prevent the fall of the firebases, and now the ring of armor to the north of FSB A Luoi was all that stood between the North Vietnamese and the main ARVN column dug in on Route 9.

## On to Tchepone

With the main armored column mired at A Luoi for three weeks and ARVN losses mounting, President Thieu and General Lam decided to launch an airborne assault to take Tchepone, now more a political and psychological symbol than a valuable military target. South Vietnamese and U.S. leaders, as well as correspondents, had focused on Tchepone as one of the main objectives of Lam Son 719. Now the goal seemed to be merely to set foot in it rather than to destroy the North Vietnamese logistical system. If his forces could "occupy" Tchepone, Thieu would have a political excuse for curtailing the Lam Son 719 operation and withdrawing his forces without total loss of face. Disturbing information later reached Washington about Thieu's intentions: that he had originally ordered his commanders to halt the operation when ARVN casualties topped 3,000 and that he had always wished to pull out in any case at the moment of "victory"—presumably the taking of Tchepone—in order to parade at the head of his troops, thus accumulating political capital for the fall elections.

A small town on Route 9, Tchepone had been abandoned long ago by its civilian population. It was a clutter of ruins and bomb craters. Surrounding forests and mountains, especially to the west, held caches of war materiel, and enemy lines of communication existed to the east and west, by-passing the town proper. Tchepone itself had no military significance.

The operation to take Tchepone nevertheless began on March 3. Largely because of its familiarity with, and obedience to, General Lam, the 1st ARVN Division was chosen instead of the weakened Airborne to make the assault. Two brigades of the Marine Division reserve moved into Firebases Delta and Hotel, releasing 1st Division troops to move westward. This brought the reserve not only for Lam Son 719 but for the entire nation down to one Marine brigade. The 1st Division moved west, establishing against strong enemy resistance a string of three bases named Lolo, Liz, and Sophia on the escarpment south of the Tchepone River and Route 9. (Lolo and Sophia were firebases, Liz only a landing zone.) Eleven helicopters were shot down and forty-four others were hit as they brought one battalion into Firebase Lolo. "They put in five hours of airstrikes and Cobras on that hillside," said one pilot of a downed chopper. "Then we went in and it sounded like a million people opened up on us." At Firebase Sophia, only four-and-one-half kilometers from Tchepone, two battalions of the 2d Regiment set up eight 105MM howitzers, which put the town easily within range.

On March 6 an armada of 120 Huey helicopters, protected on all sides by Cobra gunships and fighter planes, lifted the 2d and 3d Battalions of the 2d Regiment from Khe Sanh to Tchepone—the largest, longest helicopter assault of the war. Losing only 1 helicopter to antiaircraft fire en route, the fleet set down the troops amid sporadic gunfire at LZ Hope, four kilometers northeast of Tchepone. Thanks to intensive B–52 and tactical air strikes, little resistance came on the ground. For two days the two battalions prowled the deserted Tchepone region, including the shambles of the town itself, finding little but bodies of enemy soldiers killed in air strikes. The NVA response to the assault on Tchepone was to increase fire against

ARVN firebases, notably Lolo and A Luoi.

On March 9 the battalions and the 2d Regiment command post set out on foot to climb the ridge to Firebase Sophia. Cautious about ambushes, the troops maintained radio silence so as not to disclose their location and moved their positions every two hours during the night. They arrived safely at the firebase the following day, and the ARVN "occupation" of Tchepone, a principal terrain objective of Operation Lam Son 719, was complete.

## Disengagement begins

Their goal achieved, President Thieu and General Lam ordered South Vietnam's withdrawal from Laos beginning on March 9. During the remainder of March, ARVN forces were to fall back toward Vietnam, destroying base areas and supplies in their paths. General Abrams urged Thieu to reconsider. He suggested that instead of retreating, Thieu send the ARVN 2d Division from I Corps Tactical Zone as reinforcement into Laos to accomplish the mission's original objective—the disruption of the enemy's supply system until the rainy season halted all movement on the trails.

Finding the reasons for withdrawal compelling, Thieu declined. The terrain, which the enemy knew, and the weather, which hampered air support, both favored the North Vietnamese. Their air defenses showed no signs of weakening. Despite U.S. countermeasures, antiaircraft fire remained devastating. The North Vietnamese had also moved SAM missiles into Laos west of the Ban Raving Pass, and these represented a new threat to air support. Though discounted before the invasion, NVA armor was proving decisive. The NVA's ability to maneuver tanks over hidden forest trails, while the ARVN was confined to congested one-way roads, gave the enemy another advantage. In addition, the North Vietnamese were clever at employing the tanks as highly mobile field guns, even using them to conduct ambushes and then escape through a seemingly impenetrable forest. It was the NVA capacity to reinforce that proved most significant. One month into the operation, North Vietnamese forces already out-

numbered ARVN two to one, and more regiments were on the move toward the Route 9 area. Yet ARVN had reached its limit, as the one Marine brigade in national reserve dramatized. South Vietnam might have sent another division, as Abrams urged, but that would have left its area of operations in South Vietnam exposed to enemy troops or sappers already in I Corps Tactical Zone.

As events soon demonstrated, the advantages held by the North Vietnamese translated equally well into attacking a withdrawing army as thwarting an invading one. When it became apparent to the North Vietnamese that withdrawal was underway, they concentrated on choking off resupply and evacuation helicopters, on attacking increasingly undermanned firebases, and on ambushing forces retreating on the ground. The North Vietnamese suffered great losses, especially to tactical air strikes and B–52s, but as usual they considered the sacrifice of men secondary to the attainment of their political and military goals—in this case manhandling South Vietnam's best divisions while at the same time seeming to throw them out of Laos. Only a well-trained, coordinated, and disciplined army can effect an orderly retreat. In the case of the army of South Vietnam, withdrawal quickly became a rout. The ordeals of the 4th Battalion, 1st Regiment, 1st Division, and the 147th Marine Brigade epitomize the most trying aspects of the withdrawal.

On March 11 the 1st and 2d Regiments began pulling

*At FSB Sophia, the westernmost ARVN encampment inside Laos, soldiers peer from behind a battery of 105MM howitzers as B–52s make a strike on a ridge overlooking Tchepone.*

back from the westernmost bases, Sophia, Liz, and Lolo, and leapfrogging into other bases to the east. Both were to fan out along Route 914, searching for enemy base areas. After the 2d Regiment had left Firebase Sophia, U.S. fighters bombed the base, destroying the eight abandoned 105MM howitzers to keep them from falling into enemy hands. At Firebase Lolo the 1st Regiment found itself surrounded by the North Vietnamese. With all air supply and the possibility of evacuation cut off, the 1st Regiment planned a breakout on foot, with the 4th Battalion holding the base in a rear-guard action.

Most of the regiment did manage to escape, and then the 4th Battalion, rejecting NVA calls to surrender, fought its way out. For two days the battalion kept on the run, with the enemy in close pursuit. Near the Sepone River, the North Vietnamese intercepted the battalion, and the resulting firefight lasted most of the day. The battalion commander and most of the officers died in the battle. The survivors escaped and worked their way toward Route 9, where on the following afternoon U.S. helicopters and tactical aircraft mounted a daring rescue. Two helicopters took fire and crashed and one fighter plane, hit by the enemy, exploded. The choppers managed to pull out the remnants of the 4th Battalion—just thirty-two men. The following day another fifty stragglers reached safety. In fulfilling its rear-guard mission for the regiment, the battalion had sacrificed more than three-quarters of its men.

At Fire Support Base Delta the 147th Marine Brigade faced its own trial by fire. Having moved up from the A Shau Valley, two regiments of the North Vietnamese 324th Division—the 29th and 803d—surrounded Delta, while the division's 812th Regiment attacked the 258th Marine Brigade at Firebase Hotel in the Co Roc Highlands. With ten antiaircraft guns positioned in the hills around Delta, the North Vietnamese closed down air access to the base while pounding it steadily with 130MM artillery. NVA infantry, called "suicide troops" by the South Vietnamese, reached the defense perimeter and dug in. At dawn on March 21, an intensive barrage of mortars and direct fire from tanks signaled an attack, but with artillery fire, tactical air support, and a B–52 strike (which a prisoner later revealed had caught his battalion squarely, killing 400 men), the marines held the base, though at a cost of more than 300 killed and wounded.

Ammunition began to run out, however, and the next day the NVA overran the base. They launched the assault from positions inside the marine perimeter, supported by ten flame-throwing tanks. NVA infantrymen rushed over the bodies of their slain comrades to charge into the base. The marines knocked out four tanks, then fell back. Trying to break out, the three battalions ran into NVA ambushes. The troops scattered. One survivor recounted:

The last attack came at about 8:00 P.M. They shelled us first and then came the tanks moving up into our positions. The whole brigade ran down the hill like ants. We jumped on each other to get out of that place. No man had time to look for his commanding officer. It was quick, quick, quick or we would die . . . . When I was far from the hill, with about 20 other marines, there was a first lieutenant with us. We moved like ghosts, terrified of being ambushed by the North Vietnamese. We stopped moving many times when there was firing—not daring to breathe . . . . Our group bumped into a North Vietnamese unit, and we ran again like ants. And the lieutenant, he whispered to us, "Disperse, disperse, don't stick together or we will all be killed." After each firing, there were fewer and fewer of us.

A marine who escaped Delta described the agony of the Vietnamese leaving their wounded comrades.

They lay there crying, knowing the B–52 bombs would fall on them. They asked buddies to shoot them, but none of us could bring himself to do that. So the wounded cried out for grenades, first one man, then another, then more. I could not bear it. We ran out at 8:00 P.M. and about midnight we heard the bombs explode behind us. No more bodies! They all became dust.

# Laos: A Class by Itself

From the first day of Lam Son 719 the U.S. servicemen flying over Laos encountered ferocious North Vietnamese air defense. For the helicopter pilots ferrying troops and supplies, flying Cobra gunships and medevac helicopters, and scouting the enemy in defenseless light observation helicopters (LOHs, or "Loaches"), Laos was an entirely new kind of warfare. The enemy had prepared the ground better than ever before to defend against American airmobility. "We're fighting a conventional war out there," a Huey crewman said of the Laos incursion. "Choppers ... [are] not built to tangle with those defenses." Antiaircraft artillery lined the valley leading to Tchepone, and 12.7MM machine guns were deployed with overlapping fields of fire on high ground a kilometer or so from every potential landing zone. A helicopter dodging fire from one direction found itself careening toward another machine gun position.

In Vietnam and Cambodia, U.S. pilots had encountered only limited 12.7MM fire, whereas in Laos 12.7MM fire scored the vast majority of helicopter hits and "kills." In spite of the heavy concentration of larger caliber weapons and antiaircraft artillery—23MM, 37MM, and 57MM "flak" guns—pilots still found the 12.7MM machine gun to be the most dangerous. The 12.7MM tracer round "looks like a basketball" coming past, one shaken flier reported.

Helicopters returned to Khe Sanh with their Plexiglas fronts blasted in, their sides and blades punctured with bullet and shrapnel holes, their seats splattered with blood. It was a sobering experience for the cocky and highly decorated pilots and crewmen of the 101st Airborne Division (Airmobile) and the other air cavalry units assigned to the operation. "This is two, maybe three times worse than Cambodia," Warrant Officer Clarence J. Romero, a Loach pilot, wrote in his diary after three days of flying in Lam Son 719. "Laos is in a class by itself .... It's only a matter of time before I get killed." (Romero survived, leaving combat after three weeks with a shrapnel wound in the shoulder.) On the same day, Major Burt Allen brought in his helicopter pierced with bullet holes. "I've been flying for six months, took my first hit yesterday, and since then have taken thirteen," he said. "We had a hundred percenter, seven choppers hit out of seven." The NVA antiaircraft defenses in Laos were considered by many to be the heaviest in all of Indochina, surpassing even the home defenses of North Vietnam.

Equipped for the first time in the field with a formidable array of firepower, the NVA adapted new tactics to defend its logistics network in Laos. In South Vietnam enemy soldiers had often allowed U.S. helicopters and planes to pass overhead without firing on them, for fear of revealing their positions. In Laos, however, the NVA shot at virtually every target, though they usually let the escort of Cobra gunships and Loaches pass before firing on the troop-carrying helicopters. Their thick concentrations of weapons gave the NVA the confidence to slug it out with the sky cavalry. In addition to being placed around potential landing zones, antiaircraft guns were positioned along the escarpments north and south of Route 9, which offered the best navigational route through the mountains. In the frequent bad weather, the valley was the only route to the forward bases, and the helicopters had to run a gauntlet of fire.

Even the normally safe zone of high altitude disappeared in Laos. "They hit us at 2,500 feet," Warrant Officer Harold Smith reported after his Huey limped back to Khe Sanh dripping fuel. "In Vietnam I've never even been fired at above 1,500 feet." To counter this, pilots adopted "nap of the earth" tactics, flying just above tree level. But near landing zones or firebases, no tactic seemed to work. "Up in those hills, they have 360 degree vision," said Captain Wayne Baker. "They just sit there waiting for you, and when they open up, all you can do is break for the border."

Pilots quickly learned to avoid the areas of greatest threat in the highlands. Every day they traded information on enemy gun positions, evasion tactics, and flying routes. Communication was not always effective, however, and cooperation between U.S. and ARVN pilots, also flying in support of Lam Son 719, was often shaky. Early in the operation, pilots' lack of familiarity with the terrain cost the lives of the I Corps operations and logistics officers and of four news photographers—old Vietnam hands Larry Burrows of *Life* and Henri Huet of AP, as well as UPI's Kent Potter and Keisaburo Shimamoto of *Newsweek.* All were on a flight of four VNAF helicopters flying to Ranger Base South. "They picked the wrong bend in the river and turned north before they should have," recounted Lieutenant Colonel Robert F. Molinelli, commander of the 2d Squadron, 17th Cavalry, who was airborne and within sight at the time. "They were heading right for the heaviest concentration of 37MM guns in that part of Laos. They were in a flight of four Hueys, at 1,500 feet, in line and at eighty knots. We saw them coming and were calling them on all frequencies to warn them away. The first [with the ARVN colonels] blew up in midair, and the fourth [with the newsmen] took a hit in the mast and lost a blade."

Machine guns and antiaircraft artillery were not the only weapons taking a heavy toll on the helicopters. Mortar fire, dispersing shrapnel in a wide circumference, proved especially dangerous to helicopters setting down on a landing zone. Early in Lam Son 719 a group of troop-carrying "slick ships" was landing at one of the northern firebases when mortar shells began raining down on the clearing. "When they burst on the east side of the landing zone, we flew up to the west side; when they started falling on the west side, we flew back to the east side," recounted First Lieutenant Clifford C. Whiting, his helicopter pocked with twenty-five shrapnel holes after the mission. As the choppers hovered for several long seconds, the South Vietnamese refused to disembark. "We were sitting ducks," said another pilot. "Finally we had to push and kick them [the ARVNs] out." The American pilots expressed resentment that ARVN troops often made no effort to pin down enemy troops or to suppress mortar fire and antiaircraft fire near the landing zones. In fact, with no American soldiers or advisers on the ground, there were few personnel experienced enough to explain a unit's needs to the pilots or to coordinate loading and unloading.

Later, during the retreat from Laos, the extraction of troops proved as difficult as had their insertion. With the enemy in close pursuit, some South Vietnamese troops were hard pressed to break contact with the enemy and create a safe pickup zone. Each time units paused long enough to clear even a rudimentary landing zone, the NVA poured mortar fire into their positions. U.S. planes and helicopters of the 158th Aviation Battalion, led by Lieutenant Colonel William N. Peachey, conducted a daring rescue of one such battalion—the 2d Airborne—which was trapped north of FSB Alpha. After having been pushed off Firebase 30 during the first week of March, the unit had been fighting the enemy for two weeks. On the nineteenth, Peachey attempted to rescue them but was frustrated by enemy troops who were within fifty meters of the landing zone all day. The battered unit, with its fifty-seven wounded men, moved dur-

ing the night to what was hoped to be a safer landing zone.

The next morning Cobras and tactical aircraft under Peachey's command blasted the jungle beside and behind the troops, enabling the soldiers to get far enough ahead of the enemy to stomp down the eight-foot-high elephant grass into an LZ for the orbiting choppers. Fearful of drawing mortar fire, however, the ARVN soldiers repeatedly refused to release smoke grenades to mark their location, and in the haze of smoke from gunship fire and burning grass, the helicopters could not find the troops. Finally, Peachey brought his own command helicopter down to drop smoke grenades, but on his way out enemy riflemen hit the helicopter, wounding Peachey in the shoulder. Debris struck his face, knocking him unconscious. His copilot struggled to pull the helicopter out of the LZ.

Peachey regained his senses at about 1,000 feet. Every light on the control panel glared red—most of the chopper's systems were down. Neither Peachey's controls nor his mike worked. He shook the copilot's arm and shouted, "Land the damn thing or we're gonna crash!" "No, no," the copilot yelled back, "we can make it to Khe Sanh." "You're gonna land this goddam thing or I'm gonna blow your head off!" Peachey shouted. The copilot

obeyed. He pushed the helicopter down, making a rough landing just as the hydraulic fluids ran out. The two pilots spent only minutes on the ground before another helicopter picked them and the ARVN soldiers up. All made it safely back to Khe Sanh.

The heavy losses inflicted on U.S. helicopters during Lam Son 719 brought into question the viability of air cavalry in a conventional conflict. Commanders often overused and misused helicopters, too often expecting them to fight the infantryman's battle. Yet few disagreed with Brigadier General William J. Maddox, Jr., director of U.S. Army Aviation, when he reminded critics that without the 100,000 sorties flown by helicopters, the battle in Laos would indeed have been a fight "tree by tree along Highway 9." Still, airmobility exacted a steep price. Fifty-five U.S. pilots and crewmen lost their lives, 178 were wounded, and 34 were listed as missing in action. Many more helicopters were hit but managed to fly back to Khe Sanh. Overall, the U.S. listed 108 helicopters lost and 618 damaged. Even so, many aviators felt that not all losses were reported so that the picture of helicopters' survivability would be rosier. Said one colonel: "If they can cut the tail number out of the wreckage and glue a new chopper onto it, they'll never admit that the aircraft was lost."

*A North Vietnamese 12.7MM machine-gun team fires on U.S. aircraft at Ranger Base North during Lam Son 719.*

Many of the 147th Brigade stragglers found their way to friendly positions. During the withdrawal many soldiers at the firebases looked for any opportunity to escape the battlefield, and they tried to clamber aboard overcrowded helicopters. To reduce the number of trips through anti-aircraft fire, Brig. Gen. Berry ordered his pilots to bring out as many Vietnamese as possible in each flight. Seeing helicopters filled to overflowing, and afraid of being abandoned, the soldiers panicked. "They would do absolutely anything to get out of Laos," said Lt. Col. Peachey, who flew throughout most of Lam Son 719:

The healthy would run over the dead and wounded. We would hover at six or seven feet and the crew chief and gunner would lay on their bellies and pull people up. If you got on the ground, they would turn the helicopter over. A later tactic was to run and jump on the shoulders of people and grab on to the skids. The helicopters would go up to 3,000 or 4,000 feet, and after five or ten minutes, they'd get tired and turn loose. I can still see the bodies coming down through the sky.

The armored brigade and Airborne troops withdrawing along Route 9 fought through ambushes and steady harassment, losing many of their vehicles. U.S. planes destroyed the damaged and abandoned vehicles to prevent the North Vietnamese from making use of them. "Route 9 was cluttered full of junk," said marine Lieutenant Colonel Robert Darron, flying in a FAC plane. "Tanks and trucks and all kinds of things . . . stretched about a mile." About nine kilometers west of that site, Darron also spotted twenty enemy armored vehicles, led by T54 tanks, rolling down Route 9 in pursuit of the ARVN column. U.S. planes bombed the tanks, but North Vietnamese gunners firing the 12.7MM machine guns on the tanks claimed one F-100 Supersabre and its pilot.

To avoid more ambushes, the task force, with 100 armored vehicles and the 1st and 8th Airborne Battalions, left Route 9 and crashed through dense jungle searching for a way back. Finally the column crossed the Sepone River and returned to Vietnam on March 23. By March 25, forty-five days after they had entered the country, most South Vietnamese troops had quit Laos.

As the South Vietnamese retreated toward Khe Sanh, NVA tanks appeared in five locations on the Laotian side of the border but were driven back by gunships and fighters. The North Vietnamese pursuit had a momentum that seemed to carry across the border. Khe Sanh itself had come under increasing attack from artillery and sappers, so units hurriedly packed up to leave (see photo essay, page 92). ARVN launched two small face-saving raids into a border region called the Laotian Salient that jutted into Vietnam. By the time the second raid concluded on April 6, Khe Sanh had again been abandoned, and Operation Lam Son 719 was over.

No sooner had the operation ended than Saigon and Hanoi traded boasts of great victories, each presenting opposing versions of the campaign. Reviewing his Airborne troops at Dong Ha, President Thieu told them, "This is the biggest victory ever . . . a moral, political and psychological Dien Bien Phu," in which the South Vietnamese had killed more than 13,000 North Vietnamese at a cost of fewer than 6,000 ARVN killed and wounded.

In its own account of Lam Son 719, published shortly after the battle, Hanoi trumpeted "the heaviest defeat ever" for "Nixon and Company," and ridiculed the cooperation between the Americans and ARVN, especially during the withdrawal. Hanoi alleged that the helicopter pilots had "plastered the choppers' skids with grease to prevent the Saigon soldiers from hanging onto them, leaving the poor devils in the lurch! A fine picture of Vietnamization indeed!" The North Vietnamese claimed that they had killed, wounded, and captured 16,400 men, including 200 Americans, in the "Route 9–Southern Laos victory." According to U.S. XXIV Corps figures, Saigon had lost more than 9,000 killed, wounded, and captured, a casualty rate of nearly 50 percent. U.S. support forces, both helicopter crews in Laos and ground troops in Vietnam, had lost 253 killed and missing and 1,149 wounded, for a total of 1,402 American casualties.

For all of the casualties, ARVN had accomplished some of its objectives by interrupting the enemy logistical build-up in Laos and halting the flow of materiel into South Vietnam. According to Lt. Gen. Sutherland, Lam Son 719 had forestalled an enemy offensive for at least six months, or until the beginning of the next rainy season in Laos, which, as a rule, would provide another few months' breathing space. Yet at best the invasion had scored only short-term gains. Within a week of the climactic battles at Firebase Delta, reconnaissance aircraft reported North Vietnamese traffic moving freely down the trail, and a month later activity had resumed around Tchepone. Furthermore, the North Vietnamese continued to upgrade their conventional combat forces in Laos and consolidated their hold on the panhandle. Hanoi knew that the ARVN had spent itself and was unlikely to invade Laos again. With American bombing declining, North Vietnam felt more secure than ever in its Laotian sanctuary. Even though it would require time to restore war materiel, Hanoi could do so virtually unimpeded by the ARVN or U.S. forces.

South Vietnam, meanwhile, reverberated from the shock of Lam Son 719. Thieu banned U.S. news magazines *Time* and *Newsweek* and several opposition newspapers whose coverage of the operation conflicted with Thieu's version of events. He also kept the hard-hit Airborne and Marine Divisions in the north, rather than returning them to their bases around Saigon, where their bloodcurdling stories were bound to circulate among the public and their families. These units were filled out with many sons of upper-class South Vietnamese. Now these influential families were grief stricken, and because dead and wounded had been left in Laos, many families had no bodies to venerate. According to a Vietnamese commentator, the families were thus "condemned to live in perpetual sorrow and doubt. It was a violation of beliefs and familial piety that Vietnamese sentiment would never forget and forgive."

Many in South Vietnam, including those in the military, found fault with the Lam Son 719 plan and with its execution. The use of fixed firebases, in slavish imitation of American tactics in South Vietnam, came in for severe criticism. Firebases in territory already prepared by the enemy merely presented him with fixed targets to hammer with artillery. Critics said that firebases should have been moved frequently to thwart artillery attacks and that ARVN failed to perform aggressive patrolling required for firebase security. The helicopter, designed to free infantry from the "tyranny of terrain," became itself tyrannized by flying through antiaircraft fire to ARVN's fixed positions.

The inexperienced ARVN generals, mired in parochial disputes and disagreeing over military strategy, seemed beset by inertia. A strong North Vietnamese reaction had been expected, and intelligence, though it missed the threat of armor, had correctly predicted (albeit from the wrong direction) NVA reinforcement within two weeks. Armed with this information, the South Vietnamese nevertheless allowed opportunities to slip away through indecision. General Lam in particular proved himself unequal to his post and responsibilities. "I remember seeing him one morning towards the end of the operation when things were worms in Laos . . . ," said Lt. Col. Darron of the XXIV Corps headquarters staff. "He was laying back, kind of in a crucified position, leaning back against his bunker . . . looking up in the sky with his eyes closed, and he was obviously under a terrible, terrible strain. Frankly, I think he was just in over his head."

Many junior officers and men in the ranks were understandably bitter about their superiors' failings. One Vietnamese Marine lieutenant spoke for many when he told adviser Major William Dabney of the U.S. Marines, "It is my perception that the Americans were using us [troops] as training aids for the senior staff."

## The future of Vietnamization

The performance of Saigon's troops, who were slated to take over all ground combat responsibility in the summer of 1971 at the completion of Vietnamization's Phase I, received mixed reviews. A lasting impression of ARVN in Lam Son 719 came from the panic of disorganized retreat. But in fact many of the South Vietnamese had performed well in individual battles; MACV took some heart from the ARVN performance. Citing XXIV Corps figures of more than 14,000 enemy killed, the MACV Command Overview said, "The results were obvious: the NVA had taken still another beating." General Abrams passed on his enthusiasm to Washington, and President Nixon credited the South Vietnamese with having tied down some of the enemy's best divisions and with having disrupted his supply lines for six weeks. "General Abrams . . . says that some [ARVN] units did not do so well," said Nixon, "but 18 out of 22 battalions conducted themselves with high morale, with great confidence, and they are able to defend themselves man for man against the North Vietnamese."

Those closer to the scene than President Nixon or even General Abrams tended to disagree with that assessment. They said the South Vietnamese knew they had suffered a defeat and that their morale might prove difficult to restore. Maj. Dabney, who flew over Laos as an airborne coordinator, contrasted the Vietnamese Marines before and after the operation. "These were brave men, well led, well supplied, who had a certain élan and a certain confidence in themselves when they went in," Dabney said. "When they came out, they'd been whipped. They knew they'd been whipped and they acted like they'd been whipped."

Although, as President Nixon said, ARVN soldiers might have been able to handle NVA regulars, the South Vietnamese succumbed to a numerically superior, conventional army, one with armor and artillery. After Lam Son 719 Saigon and MACV had to confront the probability of further conventional warfare. It was not until 1970 that plans were approved for a combined arms school where officers would learn to employ jointly infantry, armor, and artillery. Now this program took on pressing importance; soon MACV and RVNAF planning groups began to collaborate on *The Combined Arms Doctrinal Handbook*, which was to become a key element in RVNAF training. Shortly after the conclusion of Lam Son 719, General Abrams requested the urgent shipment to Vietnam of a battalion of fifty-four M48 tanks, more sophisticated than the M41, to counter the NVA's Soviet-supplied armor. MACV and RVNAF planners hurriedly devised an abbreviated training program of six months (as opposed to the norm of one year) for Vietnamese tank crews.

For the United States, Lam Son 719 raised questions about Phase II of Vietnamization in which South Vietnam was to develop air and naval support systems and artillery, logistical, and maintenance systems to replace those that since 1965 had been supplied by the United States. Although no timetable was established for the completion of Phase II, U.S. planners admitted that it would take longer than Phase I had because of the complex training involved. The Laos operation had been possible only because of the enormous air support and logistical effort mounted by the United States. While the war continued and peace negotiations remained stalled, the U.S. would need to maintain that level of support even as it gradually pulled out of the war on the ground.

# End of a Mission

Lam Son 719, the South Vietnamese invasion of Laos, reached its conclusion in late March 1971 when the withdrawal from Laos became a headlong retreat. As the departing South Vietnamese marched homeward, the enemy turned Route 9 into a deadly corridor of fire. When the weary RVNAF soldiers arrived at Khe Sanh and Ham Nghi, some were confident that they had fought well. For others, all that mattered had been getting out of Laos alive. "Only the madmen would stay and politely wait for the next helicopter," said one ARVN sergeant who had escaped Laos by clinging to the skids of a helicopter. Khe Sanh proved to be no longer a safe haven; artillery fire fell on the base, raising fears that the enemy might follow the departing troops into South Vietnam.

Left. *South Vietnamese soldiers dash for cover as a 122MM rocket slams into the helicopter landing pad at Ham Nghi on March 20, 1971.* Above. *A stream of wounded ARVN soldiers, medevacked by U.S. pilots, arrives at Khe Sanh.*

At Khe Sanh on March 15 the distant battlefield in Laos suddenly seemed very close when artillery rounds slammed into the base, wounding five South Vietnamese and three Americans. U.S. troops providing support for Lam Son 719—including the 101st Airborne Division; the 1st Brigade, 5th Division (Mechanized); and the 11th Brigade, 23d Infantry Division—began to suffer casualties daily as the enemy stepped up its bombardment. Hastily dug foxholes and bunkers supplanted tents, and Khe Sanh began to resemble the besieged combat base of 1968, when 6,000 U.S. Marines had withstood seventy-seven days of relentless shelling during the Tet offensive.

*No safe haven. Above. Explosions ripped through the night for three hours after NVA sappers detonated a main ammunition dump at Khe Sanh, March 23, 1971. Right. GIs seek cover behind low earthworks as incoming rounds tear into Khe Sanh.*

"Sappers inside the wire!" The cry that was every soldier's nightmare rang out in the darkness at Khe Sanh on the night of March 23, sending men scrambling for weapons and helmets and stumbling out of their bunkers into the confusion. As many as forty NVA sappers had penetrated the base. Tossing grenades and satchel charges into the bunkers, they made for the airstrip and destroyed several helicopters and set two main ammunition dumps ablaze. The sappers left three Americans dead and fourteen wounded; fourteen North Vietnamese died in the attack and one was taken prisoner. The sapper attack underscored the vulnerability of the sprawling base, so the eastward movement of equipment and troops was accelerated. On April 7, with the last South Vietnamese troops back inside their own country, Khe Sanh was again abandoned, as it had been in 1968.

*Aftermath of the sapper attack. Right. A U.S. Army combat photographer takes pictures of the remains of an NVA sapper, cut down on the runway at Khe Sanh the night of March 23. Inset. An American soldier awaits news of his best friend, who was wounded in the predawn attack. His buddy died later that day.*

# Diplomacy and Politics

While the battles of Lam Son 719 were being fought across the cratered panhandle of Laos, in the Hotel Majestic on Avenue Kleber in Paris, not far from the Arc de Triomphe, the peace talks languished. After four years of negotiations and 100 meetings, the participants had agreed on nothing more important than the shape of the negotiating table.

But National Security Adviser Henry Kissinger maintained hopes for diplomatic progress with the North Vietnamese. He persistently encouraged President Nixon to keep some sort of offer before Hanoi. Nixon, for his part, remained skeptical of the value of negotiations, thinking they might be considered a sign of weakness, and in particular the president never liked the form of the sessions at the Majestic. Nixon believed the talks did nothing but provide the North Vietnamese with the chance to stand before America's press and undermine his domestic support. As a result, Kissinger observed, "He constantly sought

ways to diminish [the talks'] importance." Given the neglect of the Americans and the intransigence of the North Vietnamese, the discussions had degenerated into a periodic exchange of statements for consumption by the press.

In an effort to force some sort of shift in the North's negotiating stance and to establish a less public forum for discussions, Kissinger had proposed in 1969 that the U.S. attempt secret talks with the North Vietnamese. Two considerations prompted the national security adviser: He considered America to be in the strongest position it had achieved in the war; and he believed if Hanoi were ready to talk it would do so only in secret.

On January 14, 1970, orders went from Henry Kissinger to Major General Vernon "Dick" Walters, a World War II intelligence officer who had since spent many years as U.S. Army attaché to a number of countries and occasionally served as presidential interpreter. Gen. Walters had recently been made the military attaché to the U.S. Embassy in Paris. Walters, using the code name of "André,"

was to make contact with Xuan Thuy, head of the North Vietnamese negotiating team, and suggest Thuy meet privately with Kissinger. After some wary back-and-forth exchanges, Thuy told Walters that Le Duc Tho, a member of the Politburo and a former head of COSVN, would come to Paris for talks with Kissinger.

On February 20, 1970, a cold Friday morning, after reporting routinely to the White House, National Security Adviser Kissinger slipped out of his office at about 9:45 and stepped into his limousine, which headed east along the Potomac. At the end of a forty-five-minute drive, his long, black car stopped on an isolated stretch of cement taxiway at Andrews Air Force Base, where he furtively boarded one of the Boeing 707 jets of the presidential fleet. The plane flew him to Avord, a French military air base 100 miles south of Paris, where in the darkness the pilot hoped the American aircraft would blend in with the outwardly similar Boeing-made tanker aircraft of the French nuclear strike force based at the airfield.

General Walters was there to hustle Kissinger into a small executive jet aircraft of French registry, in which they departed for the small Villacoublay airport outside Paris. Meanwhile, the big presidential jet continued to a U.S. base in Wiesbaden, Germany, where the crew spent

### The House on Rue Darthe

While the formal Vietnam peace talks in Paris limped along without results, the North Vietnamese and Americans resorted to secret negotiations at 11, rue Darthe in a Parisian suburb *(far left)*.

Participants in the official and the almost equally fruitless secret negotiations were *(left)* Henry Kissinger, President Nixon's national security adviser, and *(opposite, left to right)* Xuan Thuy, official head of the North Vietnamese delegation; Madame Nguyen Thi Binh, PRG representative at the official meetings; and Le Duc Tho, North Vietnamese Politburo member and Hanoi's secret negotiator.

the night. Once in Paris, Walters drove the national security adviser to his apartment in a rented Citroën. There Kissinger was introduced to the housekeeper as Walters's old army friend, General Harold A. Kirschman. (Walters thought it necessary for the initials to be correct.) Next day the general drove Kissinger to a small house in a suburb of Paris, Choisy-le-Roi. There, in a worn setting that contrasted with the opulence of the Hotel Majestic, Kissinger held the first of what were to be fourteen secret meetings at 11, rue Darthe with North Vietnamese representatives.

It became apparent that Le Duc Tho, a member of the secretariat of the North Vietnamese Politburo responsible for organization and negotiations, was empowered to negotiate, the only North Vietnamese in Paris who truly held that authority. The silver-haired Tho was dignified, invariably composed, impeccable in manners, and skillful. Kissinger found him to be an impressive but exceedingly frustrating individual. "Le Duc Tho's profession," Kissinger wrote later, "was revolution, his vocation guerrilla warfare." His purpose was plainly to wear down his American antagonist.

Time after time Kissinger made that clandestine journey to the house in Choisy-le-Roi, but after a year he had made no more progress than had the negotiators in the formal talks at the Majestic. Then the launching of Operation Lam Son 719 seemed to doom the talks. But little more than a month later, the national security adviser later wrote, he felt he could relax the American position. The Lam Son fighting was over. The U.S. and U.S.S.R. had reached breakthrough agreements in strategic arms limitation talks. So Kissinger proposed a resumption of the secret talks and the North Vietnamese agreed.

## Mixed signals

On May 31 in the house at 11, rue Darthe, Kissinger presented a seven-point proposal to the North Vietnamese that offered at least two important American concessions. The United States was willing to set a date for the complete withdrawal of American fighting forces from South Vietnam. The U.S. also was willing to withdraw its forces without requiring North Vietnamese withdrawal at the same time. This latter proposal was not so much a concession as an offer that brought the American negotiating position into line with American actions, since American forces were already withdrawing irrespective of North Vietnamese deployments. But most important, it separated the military issues from the political for solution; plans for

a government for South Vietnam would be decided after the fighting ceased.

Xuan Thuy, who directed the North Vietnamese side of the negotiations while his "special adviser," Le Duc Tho, was temporarily in Hanoi, rejected the American proposal because it did not include the removal of President Thieu. But Kissinger felt that they had treated his offers "with more care than usual." In many instances he had referred to the "never-never land," or "fairy tale atmosphere" of the secret talks, but he came out of the May 31 meeting believing that "serious negotiations seemed in the offing for the first time." He and Xuan Thuy agreed to another meeting twenty-six days later, and this time Le Duc Tho was to be present again.

The secret meeting in May had given Kissinger the impression that the Communists were interested in talking further, and he was correct. The North Vietnamese were willing to negotiate because they saw the South Vietnamese presidential election, slated for October, as a new opportunity to satisfy their demand for a political settlement that excluded Thieu. They viewed one of the presidential candidates, Duong Van Minh, as an acceptable leader of South Vietnam. Although "Big" Minh had close ties with the United States, he was a "peace candidate" and favored U.S. neutrality in the elections.

At that next meeting at the house on rue Darthe on June 26, Le Duc Tho led the American negotiators into the dining room (instead of the living room), where a table had been covered with green baize. The Americans sensed that the table meant serious business was at hand.

In the afternoon, after a tea break, the North Vietnamese stopped the normal exchange of prepared statements and presented a set of nine conditions for a settlement. For the first time they offered to release all U.S. POWs by the end of 1971, simultaneously with the withdrawal of all American troops from Indochina. They stipulated that cease-fires in the various Indochina countries should be settled by those countries and the United States, not by Hanoi and Washington. Most important, they did not ask directly for the removal of President Thieu from power but simply for the U.S. to stop supporting Thieu and Ky so there could be a new administration in Saigon "standing for peace, independence, neutrality and democracy." Kissinger was elated. He saw that the document could serve as the basis of an agreement or, at the least, further discussions. Each point seemed negotiable. An aide to Kissinger observed that his boss left Paris with "his first taste of peace."

Four days later, however, Kissinger received a surprise. At the official Paris plenary sessions, Madame Nguyen Thi Binh, representative of the Provisional Revolutionary Government, established as the government of the National Liberation Front earlier that month, presented a seven-point peace proposal. The new document repeated several of the private offers, but it left out the points on inter-

national supervision and respect for the 1954 and 1962 Geneva agreements while introducing several new items bound to complicate the simpler private document. Madame Binh's proposal included a call for reunification, South Vietnamese diplomatic neutrality, an end to "Vietnamization," dismantling of military bases, inclusion of the PRG in the South's government before any elections, and a release of all political prisoners.

Some found the proposal to be a hard-line document calling for President Thieu's immediate removal and for a date for total withdrawal, but others saw it simply as a plea to the United States to withdraw support for Thieu before the October election. To confuse matters further, in an interview with the *New York Times* on July 6, Le Duc Tho indicated that the matter of military withdrawals could be separated from a political settlement as the United States had secretly suggested; simply put, separation meant a cease-fire would precede the lengthy negotiations. In private with Kissinger, Tho had taken the opposite position.

Pondering the two differing North Vietnamese positions, Kissinger concluded that Le Duc Tho's interview and Madame Binh's public proposal were propaganda ploys. He viewed them as efforts to suggest to the American people (who remained unaware of the secret talks) that the Communists were flexible and willing to settle, while the Nixon administration was insincere in trying to negotiate an end to the war.

To the administration's dismay, many journalists presented Madame Binh's proposal as a major peace initiative, one that offered a breakthrough in the Paris negotiations. Through his peripatetic middleman, General Walters, Kissinger inquired of Le Duc Tho which Hanoi proposal was really on the table, Madame Binh's public seven-point paper or the nine points that had been laid out in the private negotiations? Le Duc Tho said that the representatives of North Vietnam intended to negotiate from the privately presented nine points. To preserve the secret channel of negotiations, the Americans decided to refrain from exposing what they considered a propaganda maneuver.

Subsequent secret negotiations seemed at first to justify that American restraint. In discussing the first eight points, both sides found several possible areas of agreement. The ninth point, Hanoi's insistence that Washington withdraw its support of President Thieu, proved to be the brick wall. President Nixon and Kissinger believed that the GVN would disintegrate without a strong man like Thieu in charge. Kissinger presented various verbal constructions (all approved by Nixon) that might get around this issue, such as an American pledge of neutrality and an open election. But the Communists insisted on a clear-cut American disavowal of Thieu. Kissinger was increasingly convinced that the previous concessions "were only come-ons to induce us to overthrow Thieu." The deadlock persisted through the summer. Hanoi would not accept an administration with Thieu at its head, and the U.S. refused to make peace at the cost of abandoning and over-throwing an allied government. On September 13 the secret talks adjourned but, Kissinger noted, "with the understanding that either side could reopen the channel if it had something new to say."

## One man, one vote, one candidate

Try as he might to celebrate Lam Son 719 as a victory, President Thieu was confronted with the reality that the Laotian incursion had cost him political capital with the military rather than winning him the support he had hoped for. The president had only six months to reforge support and orchestrate an election victory.

Thieu's victory in the 1967 presidential election was built on a plurality of only 34.8 percent. Thieu's critics repeatedly charged that this had given him no real mandate for his autocratic rule. The president decided to silence his critics by achieving a landslide victory. He was determined to employ whatever means at his disposal to influence voters and block opposition.

The situation in 1971, however, did not guarantee Thieu an easy victory. He was beleaguered by the country's economic problems, by the increasingly organized opposition of the militant An Quang Buddhist faction, by the nation's war weariness, and by the nagging problem of continuing corruption within his government.

Another destabilizing factor was that unlike the previous election, when he divided and conquered seven opponents, this time he had two major competitors. His vice president, Nguyen Cao Ky, actually had little chance of winning the presidency, but his support lay among the same constituency that backed Thieu—the military and conservative anti-Communists—and the splitting of that vote would take support from Thieu. Lt. Gen. Duong Van "Big" Minh was a more powerful contender than Ky. Minh had returned to Saigon in October 1968 after four years of exile in Japan and Thailand. He was still a hero to the Vietnamese for his role in toppling former President Ngo Dinh Diem in November 1963 and had served as South Vietnam's president from November 1963 through January 1964 before being removed in a coup. A coalition of non-Communists, anti-Thieu forces—including Buddhists, southern Catholics, intellectuals, and politicians, calling themselves members of the "Third Force" in Vietnam—formed around Minh's bid for the presidency. Even the National Liberation Front for the first time urged followers to work within the system by voting for Minh in the fall election. Minh's appeal stemmed primarily from his advocacy of a coalition government that would include representatives of the Communist Provisional Revolutionary Government of the NLF.

Ky, in an effort to seize political ground between Thieu's uncompromising anticommunism and Minh's coalition for peace, abandoned his earlier advocacy of an invasion of North Vietnam and took the position that military victory for the South was now impossible. He called for recognition of the NLF (or PRG) as a political party and a negotiated settlement with the North. This was a remarkable transformation for the flamboyant pilot who had led the Vietnamese Air Force on its first bombing raid of the North in February 1965 and declared that day "the most beautiful" of his life.

## Too much Thieu

As an incumbent, Thieu held enormous advantages in the election: He controlled the military and the police, as well as a government apparatus that allowed him to distribute favors and win support from important constituencies. Thieu was a master at using these prerogatives to his advantage. In March 1971, for example, when the Lam Son venture into Laotian territory was beginning to falter and his support in the army to waver, Thieu excused civil servants and members of South Vietnam's armed forces from having to pay taxes.

Anxious to win big, Thieu concentrated first on eliminating Ky from the contest so that he could face Minh alone. In January 1971 Thieu supporters in the South Vietnamese Senate put forward an electoral law that included a provision requiring all presidential candidates to obtain nominations from at least forty members of the National Assembly or from a minimum of 100 of the nation's 554 city and provincial councilors appointed to advise the government. Thieu claimed that provision served only to limit the number of candidates and allow the winner a clear majority, but it was obvious to observers that Nguyen Cao Ky would be among those unable to acquire the necessary number of signatures.

The Senate defeated the controversial provision, but Thieu put intense pressure on the House to override the Senate's decision. (If the South Vietnamese Senate rejected a bill, the House could overrule the decision by a two-thirds vote. If not amended by Thieu, the bill became law in thirty days.) In a stormy two-day session in early June, in which one anti-Thieu deputy brandished first a revolver, then a grenade, and vowed to kill himself, Thieu's bill passed in its entirety. Ky was thus apparently blocked from standing for election. Later in the month Thieu "streamlined" his cabinet by removing ministers associated with Ky, effectively isolating the vice president and further doing in his candidacy.

The U.S. government declared a position of neutrality in the election, but behind the scenes the U.S. Mission devised various ways of furthering Thieu's candidacy. According to Henry Kissinger, he and the president "considered support for the political structure in Saigon not a favor done to Thieu but an imperative of our national interest." The Nixon administration was not about to "toss Thieu to the wolves."

That "imperative" translated into a stance that went far beyond mere favoritism and into meddling. Telegrams sent in mid-1971 to Washington from the head of the CIA's Saigon bureau, Theodore Shackley, show that the CIA provided money for Thieu to bribe legislators so they would vote for the restrictive electoral bill and refrain from endorsing the vice president.

Other forms of U.S. support were more subtle. On February 12, 1971, a story in the *New York Times* reported that the U.S. pacification agency, CORDS, passed on to the Thieu government the results of its secret Pacification Attitude Analysis System survey. According to one CORDS employee, Richard Winslow, part of the survey was to study "people's feelings toward the 1971 election so that Thieu would know where his strong points were and where he'd come out ahead in a given area."

## Give the president a legal opponent

Other Americans were concerned about Washington meddling in behalf of Thieu. During the spring of 1971, lower-level political officers at the U.S. Embassy predicted that Ky's removal from the race might prompt Big Minh to withdraw his candidacy. Said an embassy report of March 31: "[S]uch a situation would intensify Vietnamese cynicism toward the political system, undercut Thieu's legitimacy and invite plotting against him. The political instability that would ensue could represent a serious threat to American policy objectives."

By June, when he signed the electoral bill into law, Thieu had obtained the backing of 452 of the 554 city and province councilors, four times the number he needed to qualify as a candidate, and that of 102 legislators. When Minh submitted the signatures of 44 legislators and Ky the signatures of 102 councilors to the electoral commission on July 29, the Supreme Court ruled 40 of Ky's endorsements invalid. Big Minh condemned Thieu's use of "dishonest tricks" to eliminate Ky and threatened to withdraw from the race himself.

On August 12 Minh and several province chiefs submitted to the U.S. deputy ambassador, Samuel Berger, evidence of Thieu's election rigging. The documentation consisted of copies of a ten-page sheaf of instructions from Thieu to his province chiefs detailing a secret plan to assure his reelection. Phase I of the effort constituted a hamlet-level study of voters to help cadres working the campaign to "know [their] target." Province chiefs were asked to provide duplicate registration cards to pro-GVN voters so they could vote more than once, to buy off or transfer opposition leaders, to send others to jail for Communist sympathies, or to find a "scar" (a past misdeed or indiscretion) with which to blackmail them.

Minh's allegations shook the highest officials at the em-

bassy. On August 17 a cable from Ambassador Berger warned the White House that if Thieu decided "to go through with a one-man sham election, he will become subject to growing opposition which would soon require repressive measures. . . . The outlook therefore would be for growing political instability." Ambassador Ellsworth Bunker flew to Washington to consult with President Nixon and on his return met with Minh at the general's home to urge him to remain in the race. This encouragement soon took on a substantive form. According to Minh and several of his associates, Bunker sent everyone but Minh from the room. The ambassador, according to the general, said he understood the difficulties Minh had and offered him financial assistance. Angered by what he took to be the offer of a bribe to remain in the race, General Minh withdrew the next morning, August 20. "I cannot put up with a disgusting farce that strips away all the people's hope of a democratic regime and bars reconciliation of the Vietnamese people," he announced.

Bunker's public demeanor did not waver in the face of Minh's action, and he quickly produced an explanation for the former general's withdrawal. "I think he rather expected us to run the election for him," he told reporters, and claimed he was not disappointed by Minh's withdrawal. However, the ambassador continued to lobby for a contested election. The day Minh withdrew he paid a visit to Nguyen Cao Ky to tell the vice president the Supreme Court appeared likely to reverse its decision to bar his candidacy and to urge him to reenter the race. Ky said that the American ambassador offered him financial support and told him a "one-man show will not be a good example for the rest of the world." As Ambassador Bunker had predicted, the South Vietnamese Supreme Court reversed itself the following day. "It was a political decision," one of the justices admitted. "[I]t was clear that we had to do something to give the President a legal opponent." The reversal was to no avail. Ky quit the race on August 23 and denounced the Supreme Court as the "supreme beauty parlor" that had attempted to cosmetize the race by placing his name back on the ballot.

## A vote against communism

On the day Ky resigned, President Thieu, in an effort to solidify his support among the military, met with ten of his generals, remnants of the Armed Forces Council that had installed him in office in 1966. Thieu wanted to sound out their reactions to the withdrawal of Ky and Minh from the race. Most of the generals preferred to follow the lead of the chief of the JGS, General Cao Van Vien, and stay neutral. Thieu received outright support from only three or four generals. Meanwhile, Thieu sent Tran Thien Khiem, his prime minister and minister of the interior, around the country to sound out the commanding officers of some of the major army divisions. Khiem received assurances that

*President Thieu addresses Marines and Airborne troops at Dong Ha immediately after their return from Lam Son 719 in March 1971. The operation was planned to cement political support from the military; instead the near disaster forced Thieu to woo them anew before the October election.*

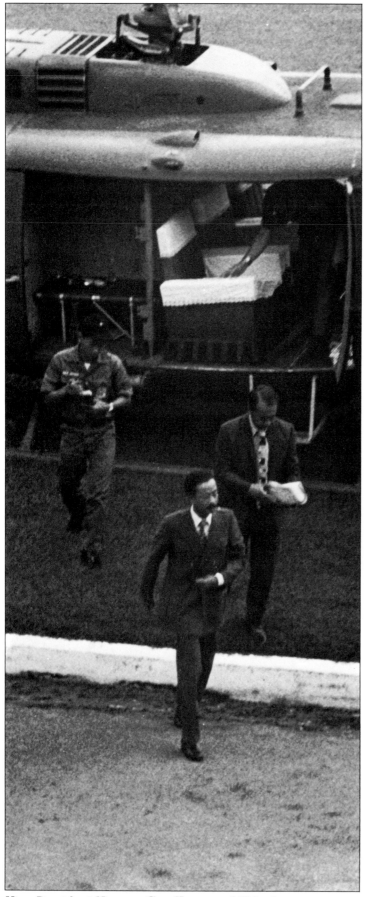

*Vice President Nguyen Cao Ky, one of Thieu's opponents in the 1971 election, leaves his personal helicopter for a press conference in Saigon.*

all of them supported the president, though none considered it politically expedient to say so publicly. Thieu could go ahead with his plans for an uncontested election knowing that at least for the time being the military would not oppose him.

On the evening of September 2, President Thieu went on television and radio to give his first lengthy public statement following the withdrawal of Big Minh on August 20. In the absence of an opponent, he tried to salvage a semblance of democracy by describing the election as a referendum on his government. The president said, "the coming election will be an opportunity for the people to express, by their votes, their confidence or lack of confidence toward my position and my policies." Later in the month he told voters they could vote against his government by mutilating or throwing away their ballots. A torn or marked ballot was one way to cast a dissenting vote. Another was to put an empty envelope into the voting box. Thieu told reporters, "They can draw a mustache on my face or mark out my eyes. If I don't tell them how to do it, many people will know anyway."

In Saigon the approaching "election" touched off a series of public protests. At least two Vietnamese war veterans burned themselves to death. Sunday, September 19, two weeks before the election, university students battled with Saigon police on two separate occasions. The most violent of the demonstrations came after dusk at the Minh Mang University compound in Cholon, the Chinese section of the capital, where about 100 students had hoisted placards and banners. After chanting anti-Thieu and anti-American slogans, the students threw gasoline bombs into the street and then charged from the compound to burn a Vietnamese police jeep and throw fire bombs at an empty American army bus. They also stopped a Vietnamese army jeep, beat the driver, overturned the vehicle, and set it afire. The police finally dispersed the students with a barrage of tear gas canisters. By the end of September, riot police in combat uniforms were patrolling the capital. Ky formed a coalition that staged its first and only rally on October 1 and urged the voters to boycott the election. That evening police used tear gas to break up an anti-Thieu Buddhist demonstration of 300 people.

## An uncertain mandate

Still, most South Vietnamese planned to vote. Some feared possible reprisals if they failed to do so. "I will go to vote to have my voting card stamped and notched," said a Saigon woman. "You are really in trouble if you cannot show your voting card when you are checked by the police." A Saigon cabbie told a reporter, "These are my election stubs from the past five elections. These assure the police that I am a good citizen and they assure me I will keep my driver's license." Other citizens, among them some junior army officers, said they intended to vote for Thieu not because they were for him but because they wanted to cast a "vote against communism."

Election day was marred by violence. The Vietcong chose to send rockets into Saigon, Can Tho, Bien Hoa, and Tay Ninh for the first time since December 1970, killing or wounding thirty civilians. In the northern city of Hue, two large anti-Thieu demonstrations were mounted by 3,000 students who attacked the police with fire bombs. After the students were dispersed by tear gas, the police closed the University of Hue for the rest of the day to prevent the students from regrouping. Still, according to the official figures, 87.9 percent of the more than 6.3 million registered voters turned out at polling stations, and Thieu received 94.3 percent of the votes—about 6 million.

In spite of his arrant disregard of democratic electoral rules, Thieu had gained the votes of a vast majority of his countrymen and had the government and military well in hand. The South Vietnamese people seemed willing to accept four more years of his administration. For Thieu the victory brought the consolidation of his control after years of careful political maneuvering. But he had alienated large segments of the population, thereby creating potentially more political instability than was evident before the election. His capture of 94.3 percent of the vote symbolized a grasp of power rather than popularity. President Thieu's answer to discontent appeared to be to shift toward even greater repression.

## Secret talks revealed

After Thieu was safely elected, Washington, through the redoubtable General Walters, secretly presented the North Vietnamese with a new negotiating proposal on October 3 along with a request for another clandestine meeting. The offer called for an electoral commission—an independent body representing all political forces in South Vietnam—to organize yet another election in South Vietnam. In the American scenario, Thieu would resign a month before the polls opened. The Americans additionally suggested a new withdrawal formula that called for the departure of U.S. troops within seven months of an agreement, allowing for only a small residual U.S. force to provide "technical advice, logistics, and observance of the ceasefire." For their part, the Communists were to release all American POWs.

But for the DRV the time for talk was now past. Seeing no chance to bargain further for a U.S. hand in Thieu's downfall, the North Vietnamese had no intention of continuing negotiations. Nor were they about to give up the POWs, perhaps their main bargaining chip, before all U.S. troops had left Indochina. Ignoring the fact that the North had itself institutionalized single-candidate elections, DRV Vice-Foreign Minister Nguyen Co Thach later maintained that when "the United States refused to let Thieu face an honest election in 1971 . . . we realized that

the biggest goal of Nixon and Kissinger was the maintenance of the Saigon government, and not the sharing of power." The DRV representatives did initially agree to Walters's request for another secret meeting between Kissinger and Le Duc Tho on November 17, but three days before the encounter the Communists sent word that Tho was too ill to attend. Kissinger saw no point in talking only to Xuan Thuy, who had no real power to negotiate. Six months were to pass after the diplomatic "illness" before talks between Tho and Kissinger resumed in May 1972.

While the secret talks were in abeyance, the Communist seven-point peace proposal remained on the table in Paris. Knowing it to be a sham, the U.S. had avoided any comment. Nixon's critics severely reproached him for this. Some asked why Nixon had not responded to the Communist peace proposal of July 1 by offering a date for the final withdrawal of U.S. troops in exchange for a cease-fire and the return of the POWs.

Nixon answered those critics on the evening of January 25, 1972, when he revealed the secret negotiation during a nationwide radio and television broadcast. He told the listeners that "after 10 months of no progress" in the Paris peace talks, he had followed Kissinger's advice and decided to use private channels to inject some progress into

*General Duong Van "Big" Minh, Thieu's strongest opponent in the election, speaks with a reporter in July 1971 during the campaign.*

## Thieu's Urban Opposition

Violence flared in Saigon during the two weeks before the October 3, 1971, presidential election. Previously, many students, intellectuals, workers, Buddhists, and others had protested his policies, including his uncompromising positions on the war and communism; some of them had ended up in prison, where they faced the possibility of inhumane treatment at the hands of their jailers. After it became apparent that Thieu would be unopposed in the 1971 election, some members of the opposition took to the streets. Groups of primarily Buddhist students burned vehicles and battled with police to protest military training and Thieu's unopposed reelection bid. Some veterans' groups, holding peaceful marches, added their dissent, as did a group of deputies from the National Assembly, but fighting in Saigon was limited to several brawls involving up to 200 students in the weeks immediately before and after the election. On election day in the capital city, a massive police presence discouraged street demonstrations, and more than 6 million South Vietnamese turned out to vote for Thieu.

Top. *In front of the National Assembly on September 19, one of eighteen anti-Thieu deputies holds a banner stating, "Oct. 3 election is a means of establishing a dictatorial and foreign-directed regime." Inset. The National Assembly deputies' demonstration ended when tear gas dispersed the protesters.*

Top. *In August protesting students from Minh Mang University pelt police with rocks from behind a barricade in Cholon where they have set a fire. Below. One of two students wounded by police at Saigon's Van Hanh University on September 19 is carried away from the riot. At the Buddhist university, protesters fire-bombed a police jeep and several motorcycles.*

the negotiations. With the knowledge and approval of President Thieu, Nixon revealed he had sent Kissinger to Paris as his "personal representative" for a series of twelve secret meetings with Le Duc Tho and Xuan Thuy.

The president justified his decision to negotiate secretly: "Privately, both sides can be more flexible in offering new approaches and also private discussions allow both sides to talk frankly, to take positions free from the pressure of public debate." He mentioned the recent impasse in negotiations and defended his decision to disclose the secret talks: "Just as secret negotiations can sometimes break a public deadlock, public disclosure may help break a secret deadlock...."

Kissinger, supporting the president's decision to reveal the secret talks, was bitter over the discrepancies between the DRV's secret nine-point plan and its public offers. When asked if the United States was betraying a sacred trust in revealing the secret process, Kissinger replied: "Look, we kept it secret as long as the secret channel was in tandem with the public channel.... For the first time [the North Vietnamese] used the secret talks to create confusion, and we cannot permit that."

The disclosures had the effect of pushing aside the public perception of Kissinger's posture of stony intransigence to reveal a statesman who had earnestly been seeking peace. His revelations temporarily silenced the critics and boosted the president's political fortunes early in that election year. A Harris poll showed that Nixon held a four-point lead over the then most popular Democratic aspirant in the 1972 presidential race, Senator Edmund S. Muskie of Maine.

Beyond the flurry of public approval at the dramatic announcement of meaningful peace talks, serious questions remained. Some 125 plenary sessions at the Paris peace talks had served up little more than revolutionary hyperbole on the one side, countered by bombastic sermons on democracy and self-determination on the other. As the public now learned, the only talks that had any chance of ending the Vietnam War had been going on secretly, yet they, too, had reached stalemate. Neither side seemed ready to budge; certainly not to back down. Only by seizing some advantage to use as a bludgeon would one side be likely to force the other to capitulate.

In disclosing the process of the secret talks, the Nixon administration hoped to stir up world opinion and put on Hanoi the onus for the deadlock. The day after Nixon's speech, Washington restated its commitment to negotiations by sending a private message to Hanoi indicating willingness to resume talks. This achieved nothing. Within a few days Minister Xuan Thuy withdrew all the Communist peace proposals that had been offered in Paris, saying with some finality: "You should realize the difference of the conditions in 1971 and the present conditions in 1972." For the Communists the difference was their growing strength, the improvement of their tactical position,

and the realization that Thieu was, for the time being, firmly in control of the country. The Communists hoped they could still win on the battlefield in South Vietnam what had eluded them at the green baize table in Paris.

## A fragile security

Stalemate in Paris did not greatly perturb newly reelected President Thieu. He had reinstituted elections of local officials in the villages. Almost every village under GVN control had held some form of election, and many were governed by their own choice of village chief and village council for the first time since the 1950s. To retired U.S. Marine Colonel Robert Heinl, it hardly seemed as if the Communists held any advantages. He toured South Vietnam as a newsman in late 1971 and was so impressed with what he saw that he wrote: "If successful pacification is the yardstick, the war in Vietnam is already settled. We have won." He went on to warn that the future of pacification was uncertain, for it depended on "one large imponderable"—the enemy. The Communists still were troublesome in areas such as Military Regions 1 and 2, Kien Phong Province southwest of Saigon, and the Mekong Delta provinces of Dinh Tuong, Vinh Binh, and Vinh Long. According to American advisers, the problem was that military occupation of the countryside and the waning popularity of the Vietcong had not resulted in greater allegiance to the government of Nguyen Van Thieu.

Another American observer with far more impressive credentials saw the dark side to the appearance of pacification progress. He was John Paul Vann, one of the Americans most knowledgeable about Vietnam (see sidebar, page 157). The retired lieutenant colonel of infantry had battled with Pentagon leaders in the early 1960s about the American role in the war and resigned on principle. He returned to South Vietnam as a minor AID official, but through his connections and dynamic personality, by 1972 Vann had become perhaps the single most influential American civilian in the country as senior adviser to Military Region 2.

Vann knew most of the Vietnamese leaders and had lived among them from the time ten years before when he arrived in Vietnam as an army adviser. The Vietnamese knew his dedication to their nation and, in turn, they gave him their respect and confidence, treating him as one of their own. As a result, Vann, although unable to speak Vietnamese, had insights that few Americans could match. With this perceptiveness, Vann had pointed out the flaws in pacification—flaws that had plagued the entire U.S. effort in Vietnam. All the statistics attesting to its success did not necessarily give an accurate picture. "Military occupation is only the first step to pacification," said Vann, "and if the government never gets beyond that then it won't be viable. In order to survive, [the government is] going to have to change."

In September 1971 a senior adviser in Binh Dinh Province pointed out that "nowhere in the HES [Hamlet Evaluation Survey used by CORDS to measure pacification] is it asked if RF/PF are carrying out their missions." He complained that the Regional and Popular Forces in his area just were not doing their jobs. They "receive good intelligence and utilize it effectively; when they know the enemy is coming to a hamlet they simply avoid them by withdrawing or defending in the wrong direction." A CORDS study of the same province also found the territorial forces to be "poorly disciplined, ill-led, and lacking in inter-unit cooperation." While the GVN had military superiority in the province it remained politically weak.

The seeming tranquility of a region could be deceptive, because the lack of Vietcong activity did not always mean that the insurgents had been eliminated. Many Vietcong were "going legal," as journalist Robert Shaplen pointed out, returning to their law-abiding activities while continuing to report to their local Communist leaders and awaiting a signal to rejoin their military units. Military people called the phenomenon "going to ground."

In some cases the enemy and local officials had learned to tolerate one another. The deputy province adviser in the Mekong Delta province of Vinh Binh, for example, described a hamlet in which the Communists and local government forces had reached a tacit agreement to avoid each other. From their base right next to the rice fields, the VC made forays to collect taxes and propagandize the villagers who were also members of the government self-defense force and whose children dutifully sang the South Vietnamese national anthem each day. The VC could make life and death decisions concerning the villagers, but since no incidents were reported to the GVN, the hamlet was labeled "secure" with only "sporadic enemy activity"—the second highest rating.

The Vietcong infrastructure (VCI), made up of hard-

## Contest for Loyalty

*The struggle for the loyalties of the South Vietnamese. Near right. Communist political cadres hold classes for "Young Volunteers against U.S. aggressors, for national salvation" during the summer of 1971. Far right. The GVN endeavored to enlist supporters by involving them in the electoral process after reinstituting elections for some local offices.*

core political cadres, the "true believers," remained intact in many areas and was still a force to be reckoned with. The Phoenix Program, designed to eliminate the Vietcong infrastructure of senior cadres and Communist party members, achieved mixed results. Although CORDS officials pointed out that Phoenix (called *Phung Hoang*—a mythical bird that brings tidings of peace—by the Vietnamese) had eliminated 21,000 members of the VCI in 1970 and 18,000 in 1971, fewer than 3 percent of those were cadres who operated above the district level; three out of four were from the lowest level of the VCI in hamlets and villages, and the majority were not Communist party members.

The Chieu Hoi (or "Open Arms") program, designed to help eliminate the VCI, could sometimes even be counterproductive. The program encouraged Vietcong to rally to the GVN by offering pardons, money, and training to those who defected. Only 20 percent of the ralliers were political cadres, however, and of those, only 5 percent were senior cadres. The number of so-called defectors—47,000 in 1969, 33,000 in 1970, and 20,000 in 1971—was somewhat deceptive because a significant number of them were not members of the VC or NVA but merely people seeking the cash rewards offered. And by 1971, according to a Rand Corporation study, many Communist agents pretended to defect in order to infiltrate the Chieu Hoi centers and ultimately to gain assignment to ARVN units. At a propitious moment in the future, their job would be to try and persuade their fellow soldiers to defect or desert to the Communist side.

The appearance of stability was misleading. Security in the South remained so fragile that it almost seemed to invite an assault. When that assault would come, and the nature of it, was the subject of much discussion and the object of years of planning in the North.

# Rebuilding the North

In December 1971 North Vietnamese Politburo member Truong Chinh gripped the dais before the members of the Third Congress of the Vietnam Fatherland Front assembled in Hanoi. He demanded in ringing, if familiar, revolutionary polemic that the people of Vietnam once again make contributions "in blood and bones" to smash the U.S. aggressors and their "henchmen." Chinh was announcing the Politburo's decision to launch a major offensive with the northern army, newly mechanized with the latest weapons from its Communist allies. For Chinh it was an abrupt about-face. Within Hanoi's inner circle he had long been the major opponent of large, costly attacks. But in a demonstration of solidarity and singleness of purpose within the nine-man Politburo, Chinh had been selected as the official advocate of the offensive.

This speech culminated nearly three years of political infighting and maneuvering among the

Politburo members and several satellite personalities. The two principal factions were represented by Chinh and army General Vo Nguyen Giap. The two had conducted a written and verbal feud for twenty years over how to fight the DRV's war for independence. Chinh and his followers embraced the Chinese Communist style of waging war—a long, low-intensity fight that keeps the opponent off balance but that demands the least sacrifice of lives and national treasure from the attacker. His political enemy through the years, General Giap, admired the Russians' tactics of big offensives requiring massive amounts of men and material but which might also bring a quick end to war. Siding with Giap in the struggle was Le Duan, first secretary of the party who had replaced Chinh when the latter was demoted in 1956.

Chinh had fought his way back to prominence after being demoted from the post of Communist party secretary-general in 1956 for his role in the suppression of land reform protests in North Vietnam. The riots were put down by army troops who, under orders from Chinh, shot and killed a large number of peasants. By the time of Ho Chi Minh's death in 1969, Chinh's status had sufficiently recovered to allow him to join in the struggle for party leadership. The intraparty competition centered around Giap's and Chinh's dispute over whether the Soviet or Chinese philosophy for the conduct of the war applied best to the DRV's situation.

Truong Chinh, in the wake of the Communists' heavy 1968 losses, gathered majority support for a return to guerrilla warfare and temporarily dominated. But the wily Le Duan, party hawk and chief advocate of the 1968 Tet offensive, eventually regained his premier role in the Politburo, although he seemed to be a chastened man and, at least temporarily, was "dovish" in the discussion of a renewed offensive. In fact, he had no intention of rejecting either Soviet aid or the Soviets' conventional style of warfare.

In May 1971, after the "victory" of Lam Son 719, Le Duan and Giap saw the chance to push for a new offensive. When the Political Bureau of the Party Central Committee and the

committee's Military Commission met to discuss how to use their newfound knowledge about the mobility and strength of their army, Le Duan told the members that the fight in Laos showed that the NVA now had the tactical ability to react very quickly to opportunities presented by the changing situation in South Vietnam. But to exploit these opportunities, the North needed a change in strategy and an end to the old Maoist-inspired, three-stage warfare. With Le Duan favoring an intensified war, and with the added urging of Giap, the DRV leaders agreed to mount a mechanized attack with the regular army in the spring dry season of 1972. Since the Politburo, most of whose members had been together since 1940, stands or falls as one man, Chinh, as the main opponent of the offensive, was assigned to speak in its support.

North Vietnam had already spent years of rebuilding and planning for a new military offensive. After the U.S. attacks on North Vietnam stopped on the last day of October 1968, the Communists took stock of the damage that the years of bombing had done to their nation. The few

Preceding page. *A section of Haiphong lies in ruins, destroyed by U.S. bombers. With the bombing's end in 1968, the DRV began quickly to rebuild.*

large factories the North had been able to build had been obliterated. Many port facilities and petroleum storage areas had been destroyed. The production of coal, North Vietnam's major export before 1965, had been cut by more than half, and electrical capacity had fallen by two-thirds. For a country in the very early stages of industrial development, these losses were a major blow. The cities of the North had become half-deserted, coming alive only at night or on the weekends when the displaced slipped back to visit. Hanoi's population, for instance, fell from 1 million to less than half that figure.

Taking advantage of the respite from U.S. bombs, the DRV's leaders, with Chinh in ascendancy, decided to delay any major military confrontation in the South and concentrate on rebuilding their industrial and economic base. As Le Duan explained in early 1970 on the North Vietnamese party's fortieth anniversary, "Not daring to carry out military struggle when it is needed, or, conversely, going ahead with the military struggle when the conditions are not ripe, are both serious errors." Until much of the military damage wrought by the years of warfare and bombing could be repaired, conditions would not be ripe.

As the city most often visited by Western journalists, Hanoi put on a new face. New homes went up, the central market and some factories reopened, and the Polytechnic Institute resumed classes. Meanwhile, efforts to build and protect North Vietnam's new light industries, dedicated to war and consumer needs, redoubled.

But if construction proceeded apace, progress was uneven in other areas of the economy. Crop harvests, for instance, increased sluggishly. From a 1968 yield of 4 million metric tons, rice production had grown to only about 5 million metric tons by 1972. To feed its population of 22 million, North Vietnam needed almost another million tons of unhusked rice from the field. As one westerner pointed out, "Agriculture . . . depends on fertilizers . . . which depends on factories which do not exist."

With several exceptions, the Communists did little rebuilding of industries that might be primary targets in the case of renewed bombing. In many cases, small factories that had been built into caves during the bombing were simply moved a few meters to the outdoors and reassembled beneath hastily constructed bamboo huts. The workers remained close enough to the caves to return to them if bombing resumed.

Since the North Vietnamese relied on the Soviet Union and China to provide most armaments, they had little need to build heavy munitions factories. The North had a ready supply of weapons; providing transportation for them was the more important task. Reconstruction of roads and railroads progressed rapidly, and all major airfields were repaired and then expanded to handle a growing Mig force. Haiphong, North Vietnam's most important port, was completely repaired and was soon in heavy use.

Relations between the DRV and its two allies, China and the Soviet Union, were marked by difficult moments. The most serious turbulence came in the summer of 1971 when the United States announced that President Nixon would visit China sometime before May 1972. The announce-

Left. *Exhorted by a megaphone-wielding leader, North Vietnamese peasants march out to repair roads in November 1968.*

## The North Rebuilds

Above. The Deo Nai coal mine north of Haiphong achieved an annual production of 5 million tons of coal, the nation's major export. The bombing halt between 1968 and 1972 allowed the mine—and other industry in the North—to redouble its efforts to rebuild its own economy and support the war in the South.

Left. North Vietnamese workers assemble agricultural equipment needed to replace the manpower absorbed by the expanding northern army.

A train passes through the Lao Cai phosphate mine, which provided raw materials for fertilizer. Since Lao Cai fell within the no-bombing buffer zone along the Chinese border, and was thus protected from American air raids, phosphate mining continued there throughout the war.

ment that the staunch anti-Communist president would journey to Peking startled the world, but nowhere was the surprise greater than in Hanoi. Only a few months earlier, during the South Vietnamese raid into Laos, China had announced that "the Chinese people are determined to take all necessary measures; not flinching even from the greatest national sacrifices, to give all-out support and assistance to the Vietnamese and other Indochinese peoples for the thorough defeat of the U.S. aggressors." In their surprise and dismay at the U.S. announcement, the North Vietnamese quickly accused the U.S. of attempting to divide the Communist world by "perfidious maneuvers" in a "false offensive" for peace in Vietnam and then lapsed into silence about the U.S.-China rapprochement.

This petulant silence rewarded the DRV, however. China tried to allay North Vietnam's fears of abandonment by sending Deputy Premier Li Hsien-nien to Hanoi to assure the DRV of continued Chinese support and to offer even more economic and military aid for 1972. For Hanoi, this was a pleasing reversal of the usual spectacle of its leaders journeying to Peking with their hands out.

## Aid without strings

Perceiving the bitterness among the DRV's leaders over China's "betrayal," the Soviet Union attempted to widen the rift between Hanoi and Peking. As soon as the Chinese delegates departed from Hanoi, a large Soviet delegation headed by Soviet President Nicolai V. Podgorny descended on Hanoi and announced stepped-up support from Moscow. On December 21, 1971, the Kremlin reported that it had signed an agreement guaranteeing Hanoi "additional aid without reimbursement" in order to strengthen the defense of North Vietnam.

How much the Soviets and the Chinese gave was not clear. Disputes arose continually among U.S. agencies trying to calculate actual levels of aid being delivered. The most common figure in 1972 estimated Soviet aid—both economic and military—at about $500 million a year and Chinese aid at about $200 million.

The CIA had a good idea of how many ships were unloaded in Haiphong and what they carried but knew far less about what came in by land routes. The agency frequently warned that the margin for error in many of the figures it supplied might be great, but pressure exerted by the White House and other U.S. agencies for U.S. dollar estimates of Soviet and Chinese aid forced the agency to produce bottom-line figures despite the agency's warnings about inaccuracy. As it turned out, the figures were often quite wrong. By the time estimates of the aid supplied by Communist allies were recast in the 1980s, the numbers quoted by the Pentagon reversed the earlier picture: Of the $1.5 billion in military aid sent to North Vietnam by the Soviets and Chinese between 1970–72, two-thirds came from China.

## The road to Hanoi

The supply channels were more evident than the value of what moved through them. Basically two different routes were used: through China by rail and over water through North Vietnam's ports. In 1971 and 1972, the port of Haiphong became exceptionally important to the North Vietnamese. A Western diplomat reported in March 1972 that as many as forty ships were being unloaded in Haiphong every month. The rail routes remained the most difficult to monitor. Supplies from both the Soviet Union and China traveled over two Chinese railroads. One, in Yunnan Province, funneled supplies into the north-central region of the DRV. The other, in Kwangsi Province, carried material from Nanning to Psingsiang on the border of China and then into the northeast corner of Vietnam.

Across these land and sea routes came the supplies needed for a modern, conventional army. Gone forever was the time when a string of bicycle-pushing porters kept the NVA army in action. The Russians and Chinese sent a flood of weaponry: a thousand T54A and T59 medium and PT76 (T63 PRC) light amphibious tanks; hundreds of antiaircraft missiles; a range of fast-firing, track-mounted cannon for backing up the missiles; and antitank missiles to complement new regiments of heavy-caliber, long-range artillery (see picture essay, page 130).

The Soviets gave two particularly impressive supporting weapons to the NVA. Most important on the battlefield was the 130MM field gun. Extremely accurate, it fired seven rounds per minute at a range of up to seventeen miles. Towed by a tracked vehicle, the 130MM could traverse almost any terrain, including jungle mountain trails. Simultaneously, the SA-7 "Strela" antiaircraft missile made its combat debut. Carried by a single man and fired from the shoulder, the weapon incorporated an infrared homing system that proved very effective against slow-moving aircraft and helicopters.

## Soviet tactics

These new weapons required the services of highly trained personnel. To encourage troops to volunteer for the new corps of specialists, the NVA leadership proffered promotions and party memberships as rewards. Twenty-five thousand Vietnamese received training abroad, 80 percent of them in the Soviet Union and eastern Europe. More than 3,000 North Vietnamese tank crews received four to five months' training at the Russian armor school in Odessa. There the troops learned basically sound but uninnovative tactics: pin down the enemy with artillery fire, shift the fire to the enemy's rear to cut off reinforcements, and, finally, overrun the objective with waves of tanks and infantry.

Spearheads of fast-moving tanks trailing columns of infantry in armored vehicles, both supported by self-pro-

*Soviet President Nicolai V. Podgorny embraces DRV Politburo member Le Duan in October 1971 after he announced increased Soviet support for the North's war effort.*

pelled artillery and antiaircraft guns, became the DRV's style of warfare. While they could have a devastating impact these tactics were vulnerable: All that mobility demanded extremely precise coordination of the tanks, infantry, artillery, and logistics.

The North Vietnamese military planners tied their scheme of attack to prepositioned caches of supplies: gas stations and armories for the new motorized army built all along the routes to battle. As the tanks moved toward the fighting they filled up at each of the prearranged stations, thereby keeping fuel levels high at all times, ready for combat. Once the attackers moved out of friendly territory, they planned to establish transshipment points at abandoned ARVN outposts where supplies were to be immediately unloaded and distributed to combat units. This dispensed with the need for huge supply dumps and large convoys close behind the attacking force. The North Vietnamese Army also prepared an extraordinary concentration of antiaircraft guns and missiles to protect its transfer sites and supply corridors.

The new warfare called for a general with the skills of a tank commander, a man who not only recognized tactical flaws in enemy positions but who also dared to exploit them quickly with his mobile force of tanks and guns. Some Western observers later noted North Vietnam's adoption of mechanized warfare left Giap out of his medium. "Giap is not Patton," observed a MACV officer, referring to America's most renowned practitioner of tank warfare. But he did not have to be. Giap, as the allies were wont to forget, was not the only general in the North Vietnamese military. While the DRV still relied on Giap's organizational strengths, the actual conduct of the war had for some time rested in other hands.

## A new kind of war

In the wake of Lam Son 719, as the NVA counted its dead and began to reorganize disrupted supply lines, the army also evaluated its performance. In all its years of fighting, the North's success had always sprung from meticulous planning, diligent attention to logistics, and surprise. Now, even though it cost some 13,000 lives, the NVA recorded

Lam Son 719 as a victory against an attack by the best troops the South could field, and it had achieved the win with quick reaction and maneuver, its enemy's strong suit.

The North Vietnamese, it was discovered by the CIA, were surprised that they could move so quickly and that their unorthodoxy could achieve such success. As so often happened in Hanoi, the various Politburo strategists began to write about their findings and ideas in public journals. A series of articles by General Vo Nguyen Giap and others by a commentator using the name Chin Tang, which means "Victor" (believed by the CIA to be the pseudonym for General Van Tien Dung, the NVA chief of staff and the real mastermind of North Vietnamese strategy), argued the virtues of mechanized warfare, challenging the idea that the NVA had to move gradually from one stage of guerrilla warfare to the next.

Hanoi's leaders had officially begun to consider an offensive during the Nineteenth Plenum of the Central Committee of the party in early 1971. Party leaders observed that 1972, an election year for the U.S., was the time to deal with Richard Nixon, as they had dealt with Lyndon Johnson in 1968. Hanoi's leaders planned to discredit Washington's Vietnamization policies and embarrass the president. In March 1971, supply units in border areas of North Vietnam, Laos, and Cambodia were ordered to prepare for a military campaign that might "last a year" and "decide the war," according to captured North Vietnamese Army documents.

With its border sanctuaries in Laos and Cambodia, the Communists held great geographic advantage. The South needed to patrol a border of more than 600 miles, and ARVN forces remained thinly deployed at firebases and border camps along the entire length. The NVA moved unhampered along this border, from where it could concentrate forces without interruption and attack at will.

Hanoi had exploited the disadvantages of the South's position. The ARVN divisions were overextended almost to the breaking point in order to fill the areas vacated by the departing American forces. There was no way for Saigon to strengthen this posture without additional combat forces, which meant more men, equipment, and money—and it was now obvious to the North that the U.S. had put limits on its aid.

Le Duan, more than any other man, assumed responsibility for the key planning decisions of the 1972 offensive. The hero of Dien Bien Phu and the man given credit in the West for the stunning Tet offensive, Giap—his very name "short and dry as a slap in the face," wrote Italian journalist Oriana Fallaci—had been pushed aside. While he was the figurehead "genius" of North Vietnam's military struggle, Giap was considered to be chiefly a logistician. The Politburo had relegated him to the job of working out operational details of their concepts. The chief of staff, General Van Tien Dung, in relative anonymity, now "ran" the army.

## "Disintegrate enemy units"

With the strategy, composition, and date (spring 1972) of the attack settled, the organizers still needed to answer two tactical questions: where to strike and what goals to strive for. The possible goals included breaking the back of ARVN, deposing Thieu, and demonstrating to the U.S. the hopelessness of supporting the South and the failure of Vietnamization. The Communists assumed a range of political, military, and diplomatic options and did not assign to their offensive any single objective. "It doesn't matter whether the war is promptly ended or prolonged," stated a party journal in 1972. "Both are opportunities to sow the seeds; all we have to do is to wait for the time to harvest the crop."

As for where to attack, geography dictated as the main conduit, the demilitarized zone. Even though improved roads and the petroleum pipelines snaked their way deeper into the South than ever before through Laos and Cambodia, the best place through which to apply—and supply—military leverage remained the DMZ dividing North and South Vietnam. Hanoi's lines of communications would be shortest there, and in the South's MR 1 the NVA could concentrate its forces against a weak new ARVN unit that had been formed to take over from departing U.S. units. To replace two strong U.S. divisions, the nascent 3d ARVN Division was spread dangerously thin along the northern border.

"Since the enemy is weakest in the northern part of South Vietnam, violent attacks by friendly forces on this part will disintegrate enemy units there and force the enemy to narrow his defensive lines, making it impossible for him to have enough troops to deploy everywhere," said a Communist B-5 Front (northern South Vietnam) communiqué, written in early spring. "Therefore, regardless of whether the war is ended soon . . . or not, we will have the capability of gaining a decisive victory."

In addition to the cross-DMZ thrust, the NVA decided to launch attacks in two other areas as well: a strike into the highlands, in order to cut the country in two, and a move south out of Cambodia to threaten Saigon. "We were told that this was the one time in 1,000 years that the situation would be favorable for us," an NVA officer recalled. "If this attack were not successful, it would be . . . years before we could launch another big offensive."

## Spying on the DRV

Some of the NVA preparations for its big offensive were evident to U.S. and South Vietnamese intelligence. The details were buried, though, in mountains of captured papers, prisoner reports, and electronic intercepts gathered by various monitoring agencies. It was difficult to sort the meaningful from the useless. Analysts sifted through the incredible welter of information looking for patterns, pieces of interlocking information, tidbits that might help to determine enemy capabilities and predict enemy intentions in South Vietnam.

Each agency dealing with Communist activity had its own special methods for making assessments or predictions. Foremost in the examination and weighing of intelligence was the CIA. Its daily reports, combining all available intelligence, were among President Nixon's first reading each day, and its periodic National Intelligence Estimates served as a basis for foreign policy planning. But the CIA's methods for arriving at supposedly authoritative conclusions were, as in all bureaucracies, flawed by procedural pitfalls and human failings.

CIA analysts always asked two questions when predicting enemy intentions: Is there a precedent for the event predicted? and Does it make sense for the enemy to go through with it? In the case of information that seeped into U.S. intelligence agencies in late 1971 and early 1972 concerning a potential offensive, the answers were "maybe" and "no."

As to precedent, the Communists had mounted an offensive in 1968 during Tet, but it had come from inside South Vietnam and relied mainly on Vietcong troops. Catastrophic losses in that effort had drained the Vietcong of any future offensive potential. In 1972 the weapon of the Communists was the North's regular army, which had been used mostly in supporting roles during the Tet offensive. Without the Vietcong to support them from inside South Vietnam, it was considered unlikely that the NVA would launch a major offensive alone.

Would an offensive across the DMZ make sense? The CIA's answer was no. The NVA had never been involved in an overt invasion of South Vietnam even though it had been involved in extensive infiltration over the years through the DMZ, Laos, and Cambodia. The NVA was believed to possess few of the tanks and little of the heavy artillery essential for such a conventional assault. In any event, U.S. air power should be able to exact a terrible toll. Furthermore, the DRV still denied that its troops were involved in South Vietnam. Any obvious invasion across the DMZ, behind which the NVA appeared assembling, would be a gross violation of the Geneva accords.

## Cassandras and Pollyannas

In November and December of 1971, CIA analysts at headquarters in Langley, Virginia, were deeply concerned but incapable of agreement about North Vietnamese intentions for the spring dry season.

Specialists on Cambodia had watched tens of thousands of VC and NVA troops, soldiers who had formed the advisory force to the budding Khmer Liberation Army, moving out of Cambodia. They were headed toward the area of South Vietnam they had quit in 1970 when they were sent to support the Cambodian Communist forces.

This abandonment of the advisory role left Hanoi with a large army that could strike at the southern part of South Vietnam with little warning.

While the specialists on Cambodia monitored the reassembly of the Communists' 1st, 5th, 7th, and 9th Divisions and those units' trek to the east, other CIA analysts also discovered evidence of unusual activity in North Vietnam. Articles on the advantages of mechanized warfare that had been appearing in the North Vietnamese press caught the attention of some Americans, as did reports of stepped-up recruitment and growing infiltration of men and materiel to the South. Not only were the infiltrators more numerous, they were moving south in October and November, unseasonably early; this meant that the NVA was taking advantage of the earliest possible moment after the monsoon season to push troops down the Ho Chi Minh Trail. This was the same kind of early movement that preceded the NVA's big offensives in 1965 and 1968.

These early warning signs were detected at the lower levels of the CIA but were not included in the agency's official reporting to the president and other select officials. The NVA had installed a sort of informational safety valve when planning the offensive. To insure secrecy, headquarters in Hanoi did not pass information about the overall nature of the offensive to any lower command. Troops in Cambodia, for example, had no idea of the orders for their comrades in arms assembled along the DMZ and vice versa. Therefore, an agent the CIA relied on in the headquarters of the southern Communist command had little idea of the overall size and direction of NVA activities; he too was in the dark. So the lower-level CIA reports were inherently myopic.

Apart from the agent's reports there was another reason for the CIA's reluctance to report its controversial findings: Analysts in the intelligence agency disagreed about how to interpret the available evidence. The growing split produced "Cassandras on one side and Pollyannas on the other," according to George Allen, a senior CIA official who began dealing in Vietnamese affairs in the early 1960s. Some of those at the lower levels in the CIA thought they saw clearly that a mechanized assault was in the offing but others disagreed. Since the agency could not develop anything like a clear consensus, it declined to predict a major offensive. "We did expect a major attack on Kontum," Allen explained. "We thought there would be another one of some size in [MR 1]—out of Laos probably . . . but [the CIA wasn't] expecting it to involve any significant quantities of heavy artillery and armor." CIA decision makers decided to rely on the information from their imperfectly informed agent in Cambodia and to accept the conservative analysis. Shortly before the NVA invasion, the CIA sent to the president and other senior government leaders a memorandum stating that a series of high points—attacks—by the enemy was coming, but there would be no major assault in 1972.

# Listening to the NVA

While the CIA analyzed the intelligence information from around the world, an even more secretive organization, the National Security Agency, collected much of the raw data on which analyses were based. Ninety thousand men and women, military and civilian, worked for NSA in many places around the world to search out electronic and photographic intelligence. One of NSA's installations, manned by the U.S. Air Force's 6908 Security Squadron located at Nakhon Phanom, Thailand, employed electronic intercept specialists to keep track of traffic on the Ho Chi Minh Trail. The unit monitored the shipment of military goods along the NVA's many supply routes by listening to North Vietnamese radio conversations.

Air force Staff Sergeant Edward Eskelson headed one of the crews that normally monitored the frequencies between twenty-five and forty-five megahertz, those used by the NVA transportation battalions and their attached air defense units positioned along the trail. In December one of the operators, turning his radio dial through the frequencies, picked up NVA radio traffic in the twenty to twenty-two megahertz range. Eskelson and his men recognized it as military transmissions but did not realize it issued from enemy tanks rumbling down the trail toward South Vietnam. Eskelson reported the radio contact to NSA but received no order to keep monitoring the active frequency. Had he done so, the U.S. might have discovered that between December and April the NVA was driving a large share of its 1,000 new tanks to the South. Signs of this heavy tank movement might have confirmed the minority CIA opinion that the NVA was moving to a new type of warfare. Three months later the sergeant and his crew received orders to monitor the radio frequency being used by the enemy armor, but then it was too late. The NVA tanks were already on the battlefield.

Aware that enemy activity was building, though sadly deficient in knowledge as to its size and nature, MACV attempted its own effort to determine the threat's scope. Saigon headquarters sent small long-range teams of three or

*As U.S. and GVN intelligence tried to anticipate their next moves in spring 1972, the NVA brought its new equipment into position for attack. Above. ZSU-57s move into battle near Loc Ninh to provide antiaircraft cover for NVA armored formations. Right. Artillerymen train with 122MM howitzers, which will be used to support attacking tanks.*

four men into the Mu Gia and Ban Karai pass areas of Laos to check visually on the traffic pushing down from North Vietnam. At first the teams were lifted in by helicopters, but mortality among the teams was so high that MACV resorted to HALO (High Altitude Low Opening) jumps. In a HALO operation, the reconnaissance team would be flown to a jump area at night in a special black-painted C-130 Hercules transport flying at an altitude of 20,000 feet to escape detection from the ground. Team members jumped at the high altitude but, to reduce the chances of their descent being seen, delayed opening their parachutes until only a few hundred feet above the ground. A captain assigned to one of those Studies and Observations Group (SOG) teams parachuted into the middle of a heavily built-up area during the summer of 1971. "We came up to the road system southwest of Tchepone about four or five klicks," recalled Captain James Butler. "It was one of the biggest truck, tank, and people parks I have ever seen." It was obvious to the team that traffic south along the trail had grown heavy in vol-

ume. Butler's report and that of other SOG teams added to the evidence being assembled in Saigon.

Lacking any clear-cut assessment from the CIA, the military shaped a scenario of its own, although this effort suffered, as did the CIA's, from an absence of consensus. MACV found it possible, though, to deduce that the enemy was preparing to mount a major offensive, probably in February, and it would concentrate on the central highlands and northernmost provinces of South Vietnam. While others were doubtful, General Abrams was convinced and stoutly supported this assessment in a series of weekly intelligence evaluation updates (labeled WIEUs, pronounced woos). On one occasion, Abrams seized a pointer from the hand of a navy intelligence officer in mid-briefing, called for a series of graphics to be flashed on the slide screen, and rattled off detail after detail while popping the screen with the pointer at each item. "He raised his voice and got red in the face," one officer remembers. Some staff officers disagreed with the estimate, "but he stuck with his arguments."

Near the end of January, MACV put its evaluation on paper: "Recent assessments indicate the strong possibility of an enemy offensive in western MR 2 [central highlands] around mid-February ... Hanoi's search for a dramatic tactical success might focus on this region, where RVNAF units are more dispersed and of poorer quality than those in MR 1 [northern provinces near the DMZ]." The evaluation went on to say that informal discussion with representatives of other intelligence agencies about the enemy plans and capabilities indicated the MACV assessment matched the others. There was "considerable unanimity."

The South Vietnamese suffered severe intelligence problems of their own. With limited means, they found it difficult to confirm reports from the field. For example, a report by a ground patrol that it had spotted a concentration of enemy tanks along the Cambodian border was dismissed when an aerial photo reconnaissance failed to produce more evidence. The South Vietnamese military also shared its own preconceptions about the enemy intent. Because of the Geneva agreements and the 1968 U.S. understanding with the NVA (not to violate the DMZ in exchange for a halt to bombing in the North), senior officers did not think the NVA would dare attack in force across the DMZ. They knew of activity in the DMZ and just north of it but assumed it related only to artillery emplacements and supply dumps needed to support NVA operations in Laos. As one JGS colonel observed, "No one had the correct information."

To compound ARVN's problems of preparedness was a habit some South Vietnamese commanders had picked up from their French and American predecessors. It was almost a certainty that any intelligence estimate that was written according to prescribed staff procedures and format would be too long to read. Tactical commanders, already overwhelmed by paperwork, usually responded "only to simplified, condensed pieces of intelligence," explained ARVN's senior intelligence officer. "They were interested only in short, clear-cut answers."

## "The offensive never happened"

However flawed their information was, by early February of 1972, the Americans and South Vietnamese were aware that an offensive from the North was likely, if not imminent. With memories of 1968 still strong in their minds, both military and civilian officials expected that the strike would come during or near the Tet holidays. They made no secret of their expectations, and by mid-February speculation of fighting to come was prevalent in the press. The Tet holidays came and went. As they had criticized the military for not anticipating the Tet offensive of 1968, the media now ridiculed them for predicting a 1972 offensive that had not materialized. In its March 24 issue, *Life* magazine said in an editorial:

Remember all the predictions about this year's big Tet offensive? "The enemy has advertised an offensive as they have advertised no other offensive in Vietnam," said Defense Secretary Mel Laird in January. Army Chief of Staff Westmoreland predicted it would take place in February, and Pentagon speculation was that it would be timed to embarrass the President on the eve of his trip to Peking. Well, Tet and the President's trip are past, and the offensive never happened.

For their part, the American and South Vietnamese officials also let the passing of the Tet holiday in peaceful calm cause them to relax and to turn their efforts back to the concerns of pacification, Vietnamization, and the American withdrawal.

The failure of the NVA to strike when it was expected to strike did at least give the senior South Vietnamese and Americans stationed along the northern border welcome time to strengthen their positions and improve their troops' posture. All along many of them had been somewhat skeptical of the alarms being sounded in Saigon. They shared MACV's belief that some sort of attack was coming but that the first signs of enemy movement would leave them considerable time to prepare. I Corps commander Lieutenant General Hoang Xuan Lam, for instance, knew of the logistical build-up and troop concentrations north of the border, but he also remained positive the NVA would not risk offending world opinion by attacking through the supposedly sacrosanct DMZ. Thus he felt he had nothing to worry about until the enemy divisions began moving into Laos in order to hook around the west end of the DMZ into South Vietnam. Then, he predicted, the enemy attack would come along Route 9—due east into the heart of Quang Tri Province. I Corps senior advisers agreed with Lam (and with MACV) that all the indicators and intelligence pointed to an attack from the west. Meanwhile, the NVA divisions remained in place north of the DMZ.

In early March a U.S. civilian province adviser summed up his frustrations:

On again, off again, gonna come, didn't come—it has been a virtual merry-go-round this month of pending action that never materialized. It is very hard to actually ascertain the enemy's present intention.

Then noting that the ARVN forces had been on alert for attacks during much of February, he continued:

We feel that if [NVA] intelligence collection is any good at all he certainly realized the stern posture that the local forces assumed and perhaps he was dissuaded from [an attack] at this time.

The advisers and South Vietnamese began to chafe under the demands of standing in readiness. It diverted them from the problems of Vietnamization and the need to prepare for the departure of American ground troops. The most demanding problem was the poor quality of the new ARVN division near the DMZ that had been formed in

# NSA in Vietnam: The Secretive Service

At Kadena Air Force Base, Okinawa, Sergeant Tom Bernard pulled on his flight gear and joined a group of intelligence analysts climbing into the long, silver fuselage of a high-flying RC–135. This military version of the Boeing 707 was jam-packed with the latest electronic and communications eavesdropping gear. Bernard served in the U.S. Air Force, but he worked for the National Security Agency, an extremely secretive organization that scans the world with electronic, microwave, telephonic, and photographic equipment in search of information about friends and enemies.

Among the NSA's other employees were thousands of airmen, marines, soldiers, and sailors—among the brightest and best educated enlisted personnel—assigned to intelligence gathering on ships, aircraft, and land stations in many parts of the world. Each day some of the information they collected found its way, distilled, into a daily intelligence summary compiled by the CIA for the president. As one of those intelligence collectors, Sgt. Bernard's task consisted of listening during the long flights to the chatter over enemy communications in Asia—conversations between pilots, messages to and from air control centers, signals from air defense sites, and even the status reports of units moving through jungles and rear areas.

Often the Okinawa-based RC–135 made first for Hong Kong, where it intruded into Chinese airspace to check air defense responses. After triggering the Chinese radar, the U.S. crewmen would monitor the communications of the Chinese trying to deal with their overflight. Then the aircraft, flying at about 35,000 feet, moved on to orbit over Laos near the Chinese border or one of the other prearranged sites around Indochina.

Beside the RC–135s, NSA used redesigned EB–66s, ancient EC–47s and EC–121s, potbellied EC–130s, high-altitude U–2s, and SR–71s, which flew at a speed of Mach 3+, as well as low- and high-orbit space satellites. These sources were supplemented by information collected at ground listening posts such as those at Nakhon Phanom and Udorn, Thailand. At Udorn huge Wullenweber antennas worked around the clock. "This is a circular antenna array, several football fields in diameter ... capable of picking up signals from 360 degrees," one expert related. "They're very sensitive. We can pick up hundreds of signals simultaneously ... [even] voices speaking over short-range radio communications thousands of miles away." Men who worked with the Wullenweber called it an "elephant cage" because of its size. It actually looked like the framework of an oil storage tank. With its sensitive capabilities, operators were able to plot the direction of any signal. The information collected then went to a central command post where sign-readers could picture enemy locations and movements.

The main object of the Thailand activities became the North Vietnamese General Directorate of Rear Services (GDRS), which controlled the NVA rear echelons and directed the Ho Chi Minh Trail. The GDRS operated a series of battalions, each of which held responsibility for a section of the trail. These units assured that supplies, weapons, and troops moved quickly through their areas and also provided air defense. They regularly radioed or telephoned progress reports to the GDRS upper echelons in North Vietnam in primitive code. The messages dealt with strength, morale, promotions, health reports, and bomb damage assessments, and a large number concerned U.S. and South Vietnamese soldiers taken prisoner—whether the POWs were alive or dead and whether they should be sent along or shot.

As the NVA also began to use more and more telephone lines, small specially trained CIA units slipped behind enemy positions to put taps on the wires. The taps then transmitted the NVA conversations automatically to aircraft orbiting overhead, and the planes relayed them to the U.S. collection centers.

The lowest levels of intercept and decoding took place at several well-guarded American bases in Vietnam: Phu Bai, Da Nang, Pleiku, Tan Son Nhut, and Cam Ranh Bay. There, analysts looked especially for transmissions from enemy ground units in combat or about to enter combat. As soon as an aircraft or ground unit located one of these units through direction finding, they plotted its position on huge maps and then often called for artillery or air strikes to destroy the transmitting site and perhaps some of the enemy force.

By late in the war, it had become Communist practice to regularly move their major headquarters in order to frustrate the U.S. intelligence-gathering operation. As another counterintelligence technique, the central complex of the NVA Military Region Tri-Thien-Hue, located in Laos near the border between North and South Vietnam, strung a vast complex of antennas all over the jungle. When it came time to transmit orders, NVA technicians moved the signal transmission from one set of antennas to another. "The signal goes out over a several mile area from these different antennas," explained an analyst. "First it will be nine miles in one direction, and then twelve miles in another, and fifteen in another."

If a message arrived in a code that Americans could not decipher quickly, it passed on to progressively more sophisticated code-breaking centers until broken. Sometimes messages went all the way to the NSA headquarters and decoding complex near Baltimore.

Notwithstanding its sophistication and excellent collection capabilities, NSA suffered from two problems. First, the mass of information became so great it was often difficult to grasp what was important and to route intelligence to those who might benefit from it. Second, information sometimes reached the unit needing it too late to be of use. Occasionally analysts established unofficial but direct pipelines to officers in the field in order to pass along the enemy positions before NVA troops moved. At one point during the enemy Easter offensive in MR 1, this backdoor process worked so effectively that an NVA regimental commander's message was cut off in midsentence by an artillery barrage called in on the location of the commander's transmission. The Communist officer did not return to the air.

1971 to make up for departing U.S. forces. Formation of the 3d Division brought into bold relief all of the ARVN's most critical shortcomings—lack of competent leadership, inadequately trained men, insufficient supplies, and poor distribution. MACV advised the South Vietnamese against creating another division since the U.S. could not provide the necessary rifles, tanks, artillery, and trucks. The JGS decided to go ahead, forming the 3d Division officially on October 1, even though its soldiers lacked much equipment. What the 3d did accumulate came from the warehouse stocks or "donated" gear, some of it obsolete and in poor repair, handed over by other units in ARVN.

## A new division

To create the 3d Division, the 1st—ARVN's best division—gave over its 2d Regiment, and the 11th Armored Cavalry came from the I Corps reserve. These two regiments were well organized and trained, but the 3d Division's other two regiments—the 56th and 57th—were made up of recaptured deserters and soldiers who had been released from jail, as well as men from the regional and provincial forces with only a few weeks of training. Commanding the regiments were cast-off officers and NCOs from other units, and rounding them out was a new crop of draftees from the ever-dwindling pool of manpower left to the South Vietnamese military.

Normally such a ragtag outfit as the 3d Division would have benefited from a sprinkling of Americans to advise, prod, and encourage the new unit as it formed. But because of the U.S. troop withdrawal, there were too few advisers to be sent into the field with each ARVN battalion and company as had been the case in years past. For a time the 2d Regiment had no advisers at all. The American junior officers and enlisted men who earlier fought the enemy shoulder to shoulder with their ARVN comrades were gone. "ARVN [always] knew they could count on us [as long as] our guys were down in the trenches with them," explained Lieutenant Colonel William Camper, senior adviser to the 3d Division's 2d and 56th Regiments. But the days when Americans would share the Vietnamese trenches had passed. Now American advisers served mainly at the upper staff levels at regiment, brigade, and division headquarters. The absence of junior-ranking Americans in the field also eliminated the senior advisers' contact with the smaller units. The generals, colonels, and other staff officers back at headquarters were now largely unable to verify locations of units or accurately assess battlefield reports. Without such information, the Americans could not provide timely advice or help to the smaller formations in the event of emergencies.

To address these many problems, the South Vietnamese high command took two important steps. It appointed as commander of the new division the best man available, newly promoted Brigadier General Vu Van Giai, deputy

commander of the 1st Division. Also, the JGS assigned the division to the area next to the DMZ, considered a "safe" area even though it abutted North Vietnam, because the Americans and South Vietnamese still believed that the North Vietnamese would not overtly attack through the zone. As the least critical area in MR 1, the region southeast of the DMZ offered the best site to train a new unit. Should the enemy choose to test the province's defenses, two Vietnamese Marine brigades held the line in the west of Quang Tri. "No one disagreed . . . with the idea that this was the place to form them," said Colonel Raymond R. Battreall, U.S. Army Advisory Group chief of staff and armor adviser.

Gen. Giai took command when the 3d Division, named "Ben Hai" for the river separating the North and the South, assembled on October 1. Giai, a pale slim man, was strict and tough. Toward U.S. advisers his manners were pleasant, but he demanded complete obedience when dealing with his ARVN subordinates. A native of North Vietnam, a Catholic, and an infantryman, Giai soon came into conflict with I Corps commander, Lt. Gen. Lam, a Buddhist and an armor officer from central Vietnam. Lam, masterful in his dealings with people, skillfully manipulated the various factions in MR 1, but he had shown in Lam Son 719 he was a general in rank only. Realizing his weaknesses, Lam concentrated on administration and left tactical matters to his division commanders. This was a workable solution only so long as the division commanders encountered no major difficulties.

## Lam wasn't listening

To Lam's discomfort, Giai discovered problems almost from the start. As soon as he had taken command, the general surveyed the disposition of firebases and strong points in the division's area and expressed dismay. He disliked the large, fixed positions he had inherited from the Americans. Having perhaps learned from ARVN's failings in Lam Son 719, Giai preferred to use small units to set up temporary bases that could be relocated quickly to prevent destruction by heavy weapons. Concentrated troops offered the enemy inviting targets.

Giai brought his headaches to Lam. His units were in poor defensive positions; at least two experienced North Vietnamese divisions faced him across the DMZ; and unlike most of the senior generals, Giai did not believe the NVA would necessarily respect the sanctity of the DMZ. Furthermore, Giai was accelerating his training schedule in order to bring the green 56th and 57th Regiments up to combat readiness.

But Lam was not moved. He ignored Giai's protestations and requests for help and took pains to keep Giai's complaints from reaching Saigon and the JGS. Nor did Lam and his staff perform the duties of a corps headquarters, a key link in the chain of command stretching from

Saigon down to the 3d Division. When unrealistic requests came from Saigon ordering the 3d Division to perform tasks clearly beyond its capability, Lam, dismissing Giai's complaints, merely repeated the JGS orders. Also Lam failed to inform Saigon of the poor preparedness of the 3d Division troops and defensive positions, thus allowing his superiors to believe the 3d was prepared for any eventuality. As a mere brigadier general far down the chain of command, Giai had no recourse. "[He] was very pessimistic," said a friend of his. "No one believed him, Lam wasn't listening; [Giai was] caught in a situation that he could do little about."

In the weeks before Easter 1972, Giai threw his troops into a heavy training program. As part of this training, the division commander decided to rotate two of his regiments to familiarize them with more of the division's front and to prevent the men from growing too comfortable in any particular firebase. When Easter weekend came, Giai planned to exchange the 56th Regiment in the camps around Firebase Charlie 2 along the central DMZ with the 2d Regiment manning the outposts supporting the big American-built artillery base at Camp Carroll in the west. Giai's idea was worthwhile, but the plans went awry.

Because of a shortage of trucks to move the units simultaneously, each troop-laden vehicle shuttled between the bases, picking up troops at one post, dropping them off at the next, and then reloading. Soon after this movement began at dawn on March 30, Holy Thursday, the two units found themselves hopelessly intermixed and disorganized. Pushing the convoys through fog and occasional rain squalls, the two regiments endeavored to switch their soldiers among the camps and fortifications along the DMZ. In order to exchange headquarters sites, at 11:30 A.M. the commands of both regiments shut down their radios. For the duration of the move—an hour or two—the regimental commanders were out of touch with their already disoriented outfits. It also cut off Giai's contact with the bulk of two of his three infantry regiments.

With its communications fragmented, its units entangled, and the weather bad enough to prevent most aircraft from flying, the 3d Division offered the massed NVA forces to the north an irresistible target.

*Lieutenant General Hoang Xuan Lam (left), the corpulent commander of I Corps, was politically astute but a poor soldier. Before the Communists' spring 1972 offensive, he clashed with the commander of his new 3d Division, the authoritarian but clear-thinking Brigadier General Vu Van Giai (right). Their arguments worsened as the battle wore on.*

# The North's New Weapons

Hanoi's change in strategy and its decision to invade South Vietnam produced a need for the tanks, heavy artillery, and other impedimenta of a modern army. From the U.S.S.R. and China came a flood of supplies that gave the NVA mobility, versatility in tactics, and great striking power. Since the North was still largely a nation of farmers, the weapons needed to be simple, rugged, easy to use, and, above all, cheap. For these requirements the fighting man was to pay a price. The Soviet- and Chinese-made machinery of war was often crudely manufactured, which meant many repairs and a short service life. The primitive equipment also stretched the physical endurance of the crews and was itself sometimes dangerous to the operators. All these elements contributed to heavy losses of men and machines. Despite these drawbacks, the new equipment gave an added dimension of effectiveness to the NVA's war machine.

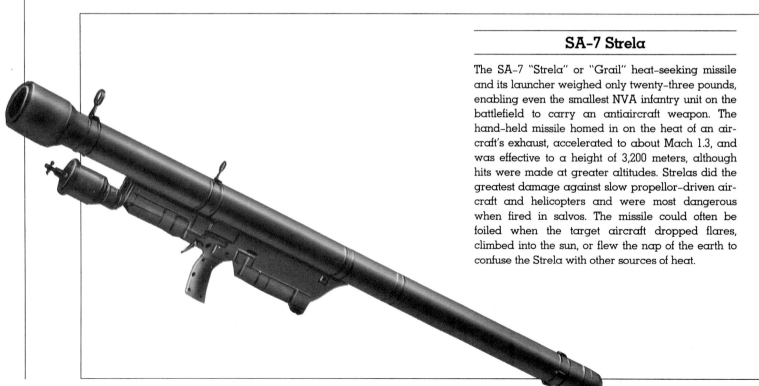

## SA-7 Strela

The SA-7 "Strela" or "Grail" heat-seeking missile and its launcher weighed only twenty-three pounds, enabling even the smallest NVA infantry unit on the battlefield to carry an antiaircraft weapon. The hand-held missile homed in on the heat of an aircraft's exhaust, accelerated to about Mach 1.3, and was effective to a height of 3,200 meters, although hits were made at greater altitudes. Strelas did the greatest damage against slow propellor–driven aircraft and helicopters and were most dangerous when fired in salvos. The missile could often be foiled when the target aircraft dropped flares, climbed into the sun, or flew the nap of the earth to confuse the Strela with other sources of heat.

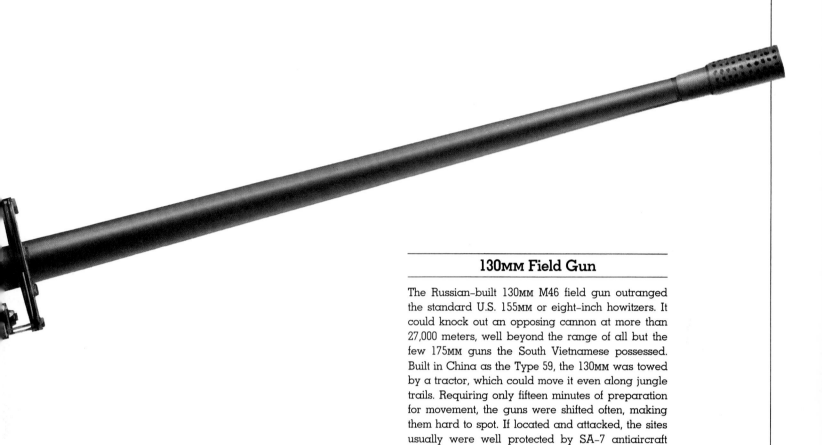

## 130mm Field Gun

The Russian-built 130mm M46 field gun outranged the standard U.S. 155mm or eight-inch howitzers. It could knock out an opposing cannon at more than 27,000 meters, well beyond the range of all but the few 175mm guns the South Vietnamese possessed. Built in China as the Type 59, the 130mm was towed by a tractor, which could move it even along jungle trails. Requiring only fifteen minutes of preparation for movement, the guns were shifted often, making them hard to spot. If located and attacked, the sites usually were well protected by SA-7 antiaircraft missiles.

## AT-3 Sagger

The AT-3 "Sagger" antitank missile could knock out the heaviest tanks in South Vietnam. A two-man team carried a control box, which one of the men slung on his back, and up to four "suitcases," each containing a twenty-five-pound missile. The weapon could be set up in five minutes. Guided visually by its gunner, the missile was attached to the control box by two thin wires that reeled out behind after firing. Sighting in on a flare on the missile's tail, the gunner used a joystick to pass signals to the missile. Jet nozzles kept the Sagger on course. The 3,000-meter range was limited by the gunner's eyesight, which made the effective range actually about 1,000 meters.

## ZSU-57

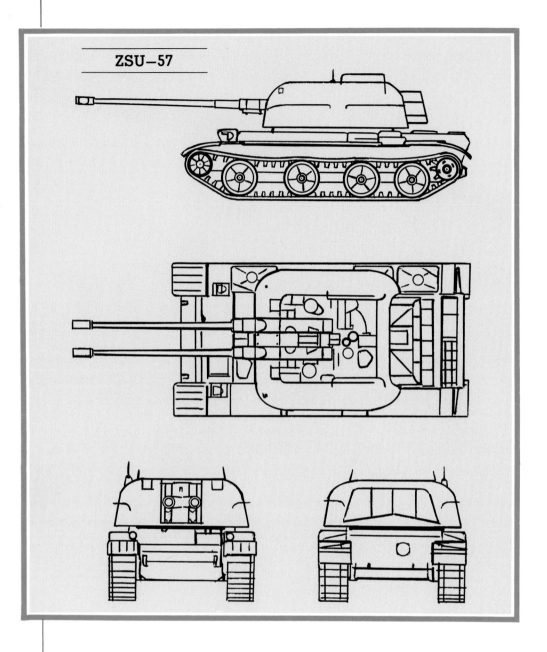

## ZSU-57

The ZSU-57-2 was used to add an antiaircraft capacity to the NVA's mobile armored columns. Two 57MM cannon were mounted on a lightened T54 hull and a chassis with only four road wheels per track. The vehicle could maintain the same thirty-mile-per-hour speed as the tanks. Since it had no radar the ZSU-57 was relatively ineffective in an antiaircraft role when assigned to mobile convoy defense; however, it was used successfully as a direct-fire weapon against the South Vietnamese infantry and other ground targets. The six-man crew could sustain fire of seventy rounds per minute on visual targets within four kilometers.

## T54 Tank

The Soviet-made T54A tank was assigned to NVA infantry divisions and 100-tank armored regiments. With a 100MM gun, thick armor, and a driving range of 325 kilometers, the T54 gave the NVA great mobility, presented a small target, and was much cheaper than its western equivalent. The T54 had its drawbacks: It caught fire easily, had a short (150–500 hour) engine life, provided only a cramped space for its four-man crew, and its gun remained difficult to load. But its disadvantages were outweighed by its ability to assault entrenchments, terrorize ARVN troops, and lend direct support to attacking NVA light infantry.

## PT76 Tank

The NVA used tactics that employed the PT76, one of the few fully amphibious tanks in the world. These lightly armored, fourteen-ton vehicles made the initial reconnaissance probes in an attack, and some were used as the first elements to make river crossings where its machine gun and 76MM cannon could wreck havoc on lightly armed troops. The 240-horsepower diesel engine ran hydraulic jets that propelled the tank through water at seven miles per hour. Its disadvantages: The PT76 was hard to keep on course while swimming and it sank easily in rough water. The NVA also used the Chinese Type 63 amphibious tank, which was based on the PT76 but was armed with an 85MM gun.

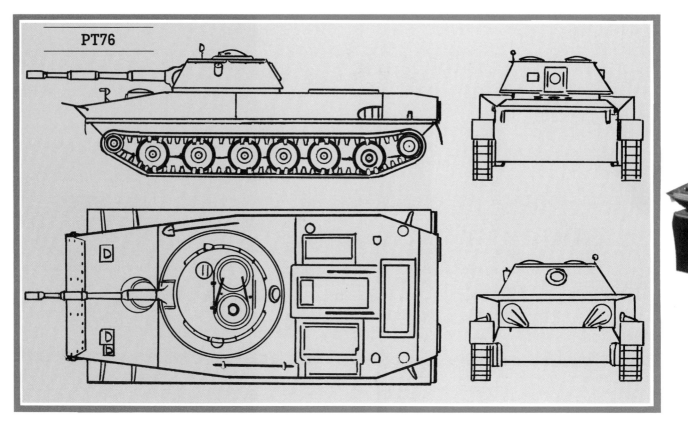

PT76

## BTR50 Troop Carrier

North Vietnam also fielded some armored personnel carriers (APCs) such as this BTR50. Based on a PT76 chassis, the amphibious vehicle traveled on land at a top speed of twenty-seven miles per hour. Along with two crewmen and twenty troops, the BTR50 could carry a heavy machine gun. Roof hatches insured that dismounting the vehicle under fire was a dangerous operation, and thin armor offered little protection to the troops inside.

# Easter Invasion

Exactly at noon on Holy Thursday an incoming artillery round hit the 3d Division's headquarters at Ai Tu Combat Base just north of Quang Tri. There was something new in the sound; the split second between the sharp crack of the incoming shell and its explosion meant it came from one of the new high-velocity, 130MM howitzers emplaced by the NVA along the DMZ. A mortar or rocket round would have given the defenders a few seconds to judge the flight of the incoming fire and leap for cover. The new weapon provided no such warning. The first shell was followed by a barrage over a wide front, and soon the drumfire of Communist artillery was reaching outposts and bases along the thirty-kilometer ARVN defensive line below the DMZ. The shelling went on for six days.

The enemy smothered the allied positions with perfectly targeted fire. The rounds fell so fast that the ARVN gunners abandoned their artillery pieces for refuge in bunkers or on the backsides

of hills. It did little good for them to shoot back since many of the NVA guns stood at least 2,000 meters beyond the ranges of the ARVN 105MM and 155MM howitzers.

Under cover of the artillery barrage, 30,000 North Vietnamese troops and more than 200 tanks, the equivalent of three divisions, charged across the demilitarized zone that had been established sixteen years before in Geneva. The North had cast prudence aside and in so doing had confounded American and South Vietnamese assumptions that the enemy would not risk so overtly violating the DMZ.

Supported by regiments of tanks and artillery, the North Vietnamese flooding through the DMZ followed Russian-style mobile tactics and patterns of assault. Antiaircraft weapons, many of heavy caliber mounted on tracked vehicles, moved forward in successive lines to protect command posts, logistics and fuel sites, and troop assembly areas from those few aircraft that could attack through holes in the rainy, low-ceiling weather.

Under this pounding, sizable units of the mixed and disorganized regiments of the ARVN 3d Division, driven from their guns within the first forty-eight hours, began falling back from their positions. As the South Vietnamese troops, armored personnel carriers, trucks, and light tanks jammed the roads, NVA units appeared in fields just beyond the range of ARVN small-arms fire. During the next three days the ARVN and NVA forces conducted a desperate race toward the bridges at Dong Ha and Cam Lo, bridges across the rivers of the same names that could carry the ARVN to safety or, if not destroyed, the NVA to victory (see map, page 151).

As critical as the situation appeared on this Easter weekend, it was only one aspect of ARVN's plight. The NVA had initially struck from the north, but that attack was to be only the first of three. It was designed to rivet allied attention to MR 1 while farther south the Communists moved into attack position. As the U.S. and GVN reacted to the attack across the DMZ, two southern prongs, each with a core of three 10,000-man regular divisions, planned their separate advances, out of Cambodia toward Saigon in early April and by midmonth into the central highlands. Ultimately the three attacks would employ the equivalent of over fourteen divisions, the greatest offensive

Preceding page. *NVA soldiers mount the ramparts of an ARVN firebase in Quang Tri Province, early in the Easter offensive.*

since 300,000 Chinese "volunteers" swept across the Yalu River into Korea during the winter of 1950–51.

## The bridge at Dong Ha

At 3d Division headquarters at Ai Tu, just within range of the 130MM guns firing from the DMZ, a mixed group of Americans, including naval gunfire and air force liaison teams, tried to help ARVN plan a defense. U.S. Marine Corps Lieutenant Colonel Gerald Turley, on an inspection tour when the offensive struck, found himself the highest-ranking American at Ai Tu's tactical operations center (TOC). He took charge of coordinating the limited air and naval gunfire that could be summoned from U.S. ships cruising offshore. If this could slow the enemy just a bit, the retreating South Vietnamese might have time to cross the critical bridges, set up defensive lines behind the Cua Viet and Cam Lo rivers, and hold off the invaders at the first natural line of defense south of the DMZ.

Through the three holy days preceding Easter Sunday, the battle raged for control of the ARVN camps and outposts south of the DMZ. On Easter morning, April 2, two NVA columns of tanks—both amphibious PT76s and T54 main battle tanks—and supporting infantry troops approached the Highway 1 bridge at Dong Ha fourteen kilometers below the DMZ. Highway 1 was the most direct path to Quang Tri City and Hue, the old imperial capital of Vietnam. In the NVA's path stood the 3d Battalion of the

258th Vietnamese Marine Brigade, whose American adviser was marine Captain John Ripley, and the 20th Tank Regiment advised by army Major James Smock. Both units had rushed from camps south of Quang Tri (the green tank unit straight from its final training exercise) to help establish the Cua Viet–Cam Lo line and shore up the crumbling ARVN 3d Division. The ARVN tanks mounted the heights west of the town of Dong Ha and fired their 90MM cannons at the approaching NVA, slowing the enemy columns with a number of direct hits. The marines deployed on the south side of the Highway 1 bridge and an adjacent railroad bridge. A lone enemy T54 tank that had dared to run ahead of the main column came rolling onto the north end of the highway bridge as the marines took position. One Vietnamese sergeant and another marine bravely grabbed light antitank weapons (LAWs) and rushed onto the bridge and fired. After a few near misses, the sergeant hit the tank, apparently jamming the turret. The tank backed off the bridge and fled north.

## Bridge-breaking

At General Lam's forward I Corps headquarters in Hue, far from the fighting, ARVN staff officers, grandly dreaming of eventual counterattacks, ordered the marine companies and army tanks to hold the bridges. But the leaders of the two units at the river knew that it was absurd to expect they could hold off more than 10,000 NVA soldiers and the tank force rushing at them. If the bridges were not destroyed, the overwhelming NVA force would capture the two structures and smash the small force of defenders. Then the heavy enemy tanks could cross the river, and any chance of establishing a defensive line along the Cua Viet would be gone. From the south bank of the river, Highway 1 was open to the Communists all the way to Hue. U.S. advisers Ripley and Smock called Col. Turley at Ai Tu on a radio frequency used exclusively by the Americans and explained the worsening situation. Turley, at the 3d Division's tactical operations center, had heard the orders from I Corps (supported by MACV and the JGS) to hold the bridges. But emboldened by the new information from the scene, he pleaded with the Vietnamese to destroy the bridges—to no avail. Finally Turley, who had never before wrestled with such responsibility, made a decision, although he was careful in his phrasing. "Smock," he radioed the U.S. adviser, "I can't give [this] kind of approval, but the bridge must be destroyed."

Ripley and Smock took explosives and clambered into the bridge girders braving enemy small-arms fire and occasional mortar and artillery shelling. Ripley, hung from a support and "hand-walked" several meters hanging twenty feet above the river until he reached some key structural crosspieces. Smock labored with boxes of TNT and C–4 explosives, shoving them piece after piece to Ripley who wired them to the bridge supports as enemy riflemen fired at them from across the river.

After many tense minutes beneath the highway bridge, the pair moved to the railroad bridge about fifty meters downstream and also wired it for destruction. Then they scrambled back to the embankment. The first attempt to detonate the explosives failed. The enemy columns were again moving toward them. Ripley climbed out, rewired the explosives, and replaced faulty electrical detonators with time detonators. The charges again failed to go off. Two VNAF A–1s tried to slow the NVA tanks, but as the second aircraft made its attack, one of the hand-held SA–7 Strela's missiles shot out of the enemy column and smashed the aircraft. The sacrifice, however, gave Ripley time to try again. This time he succeeded. The bridges blew up and dropped into the river.

*Soldiers of the 20th ARVN Regiment man positions on the heights near Dong Ha as a B–52 strike answers the Communist advance.*

Now the Communist tanks had to detour to the bridge at Cam Lo, twelve kilometers and at least half a day away. While each kilometer took its toll in wear on the vulnerable treads of the tanks, the detour gave time for the South Vietnamese artillery and allied air support to find the range of the lumbering tanks.

## Intrigue at Camp Carroll

The situation at Cam Lo looked much better for the South Vietnamese than it had at Dong Ha. Camp Carroll, situated a few kilometers southwest of the river town, boasted the largest artillery concentration in MR 1. Its guns, including four 175MMs, controlled the routes toward the remaining bridge at Cam Lo. These large guns outranged even the NVA's Russian-built 130MM artillery. Almost half the 56th ARVN Regiment, some 1,500 men who had made it intact to the right post despite the invasion day chaos, provided security for the base under the command of Lieutenant Colonel Pham Van Dinh, hero of the battle for Hue during the 1968 Tet offensive.

In the four years since his feats at Hue, Dinh, "the young lion," had turned into a pudgy officer deeply involved in the political interplay of I Corps. Preoccupied with his extracurricular activities, Dinh had passed effective command of the 56th to his executive officer, Lieutenant Colonel Vinh Phong, a man who, according to Lieutenant Colonel William Camper, the regiment's senior U.S. adviser, was "strongly anti-U.S. and not friendly to the advisers." This was soon to have profound consequences for Col. Camper and the entire regiment.

The sprawling firebase had endured three days of shelling, but as Easter Sunday dawned Camp Carroll, in Camper's opinion, remained strong enough to survive at least another week. Unknown to Camper, however, Dinh, Phong, and other members of the 56th Regiment's staff had been talking to the NVA by radio, a common practice throughout the war. ARVN troops seldom used codes or secure lines, and the NVA employed captured radios to monitor South Vietnamese conversations. Thus able to communicate, men of the two sides would frequently exchange polemics or taunting remarks. But this time, according to Col. Camper, the conversations between the 56th's staff and the NVA were anything but banter. At 2:30 P.M. on Easter Sunday, April 2, the ARVN officers held a meeting closed to the Americans. Shortly after Dinh came to Camper at his bunker and told him that a cabal of disaffected ARVN officers had forced him to negotiate a surrender of the camp complete with its artillery, ammunition, and American advisers. After being told by 3d Division headquarters that no reserves could be spared for Camp Carroll, Dinh said, in an interview aired on Communist radio after the fight, he believed "we would die if we remained in the base and we would also die in large numbers" if they tried to retreat. As a result, "The commanders

of the various units reported to me that most of the soldiers did not want to resist the liberation forces anymore." The white flag was to go up in an hour. Col. Dinh offered to join Camper in a suicide pact to preserve their "honor." When the American declined, Dinh suggested that they mix in with the surrendering soldiers and escape into the high grass. Camper turned down that offer too.

Instead Camper gathered his assistant, Major Joseph Brown, and two Vietnamese radiomen, set his bunker on fire, and began cutting through the camp wire to head south toward the next outpost. Behind them the ARVN troops stacked their weapons for surrender. As they worked to escape, Camper called Lt. Col. Turley at Ai Tu headquarters on the advisers' radio network to tell him of the situation. The pilot of a CH-47 Chinook, flying with an escort of two Cobra gunships to deliver ammunition several kilometers south, overheard the trapped officer's report and volunteered to try to rescue the four men. The helicopter and two gunships dipped below a hundred feet and flew toward besieged Camp Carroll.

Informed by Turley of the helicopters' approach, Camper, Brown, and the two Vietnamese hurried back through the wire to the base's helipad. On the way Camper found numbers of ARVN soldiers who had kept their weapons and who wanted to continue the fight. He took them along and ordered them to hold the surrendering ARVN at bay. Altogether the colonel assembled thirty-three men before the Chinook popped up out of the valley and over the wire of the camp to land. The Cobra gunships buzzed the edge of the base, and their rapid fire forced the approaching NVA troops to keep their heads down. On the landing strip the big troop carrier loaded the group and lurched up and over the wire, absorbing a farewell small-arms fusillade from the NVA. The limping Chinook, rejoined by the Cobras, carried Camper, Brown, and the ARVN soldiers to what remained of the South Vietnamese lines. Camp Carroll was now in enemy hands, as were Col. Dinh and all but thirty-three of his troops. Eventually, one of the heavy American-built 175MM guns, the first captured by the NVA, was put on display in Hanoi. On April 3, Radio Hanoi carried an appeal from Col. Dinh urging all ARVN soldiers to lay down their arms and surrender to the NVA.

## A patchwork defense

With the surrender of Camp Carroll, the bridge at Cam Lo fell into North Vietnamese hands. Because Camp Carroll and its artillery occupied a key strategic position in the South Vietnamese defense line, the loss was catastrophic. The camp sat astride the junction of the ARVN east-west defensive line, stretching along the DMZ to the sea, and a north-south line that protected against invasion from Laos. With the capture, the NVA had knocked a huge hole in the corner of the ARVN positions and effectively turned two ARVN flanks, the end of the east-west line and the top of the north-south line. As the northern soldiers poured through the gap, the ARVN troops in positions on each side of Camp Carroll had to retreat or be surrounded. Within the next two days, the entire line of defense lurched rearward some ten kilometers, half the distance to Highway 1.

At I Corps headquarters in Hue, the staff shuddered over what had happened. "Until Carroll was lost we didn't get too excited," said the deputy senior adviser, Brigadier General Thomas W. Bowen. "It blew our minds—we lost a whole regiment. Lam wanted to go shoot everyone concerned." Lam, however, was the man chiefly to blame by insisting on continued concentration of large forces in vulnerable firebases.

The day that Camp Carroll fell, MACV and the U.S. First Regional Assistance Command (FRAC), supporting the South Vietnamese I Corps, decided to evacuate all unessential American personnel—enlisted clerks, administrators, and noncombat personnel—from Ai Tu. They were to move out of Communist artillery range to Quang Tri, Hue, or Da Nang. As the evacuation began, enemy shells were flying in and the departing rear-echelon Americans

began to panic. "The soldiers began to fight among themselves about who was going to get on which copter," Lt. Col. Turley recalled. "Guys were running out with their stereo sets—no weapons just their stereos—it was the most disorganized, mass hysteria that you could imagine." After the 100 or so nonessential Americans had left, some fifty combat advisers remained to share the fighting with the South Vietnamese.

ARVN soldiers were scattered all over the landscape. Gamely, ARVN officers put together a patchwork defense, contacting what units they could by radio or by driving over the fields and back roads to find stragglers. When they spotted soldiers they stopped and tried to calm them and then moved them into defensive positions. On April 4 the ARVN line extended from the coast along the Cua Viet River, southwest from Dong Ha and west of Ai Tu to the Thach Han River. As the South Vietnamese began to destroy NVA tanks with their light antitank weapons, their resistance stiffened. For three weeks the NVA offensive in Quang Tri Province ground to a halt as the South Vietnamese held their own. But the halt was temporary.

Saigon's confusion, built mostly of ignorance of actual events along the DMZ, was shared in Washington. It was

*NVA soldiers clamber over Camp Carroll bunkers after ARVN surrendered the base on April 2. Taking the camp virtually intact, the Communists collected a great deal of war materiel, including an M42 "Duster" with twin 40MM cannons (front).*

difficult for the president and his national security adviser to grasp the quickly deteriorating situation in South Vietnam. As early as March 31, Good Friday, Secretary of Defense Melvin Laird advised that the fighting constituted a major attack, but Henry Kissinger recalls that for some reason the Pentagon continued to issue "soothing" accounts. General Abrams reported from MACV that the situation was not yet "critical." Abrams's assessment was less than acute, possibly because both he and Ambassador Ellsworth Bunker were out of South Vietnam at the beginning of the attack.

Kissinger later speculated that high civilians in the Defense Department (he did not name them) concealed or sugar-coated information about the severity of the attack, because they were opposed to a strong American response and were aware of Nixon's threat, often repeated since his election, to react strongly to any North Vietnamese offensive. In any event, conflicting reports induced anger at the White House. Kissinger thought Abrams "testy" and "pedantic" in responding to his constant demands for more information from the battlefield, and Nixon considered the military's assessments unimaginative and lacking in aggressiveness.

Not until the fourth day, Easter Sunday, April 2, did Kissinger feel he was given a reasonably accurate picture of the fight in South Vietnam: It was possible that ARVN might collapse in a matter of days, even hours. He knew the U.S. needed to move quickly to prevent calamity. Kissinger and Nixon agreed that they "had to carry the war to North Vietnam." Defeating the NVA offensive was essential if the U.S. was to hold a workable bargaining position in the coming summit meeting with Soviet Premier Leonid Brezhnev. Nixon could not go to Moscow in the wake of a military defeat inflicted largely by Soviet-supplied weapons.

Late on April 4 the president decided on a devastating bombardment of the North. He abandoned financial limits that had been imposed on the planning of air strikes and authorized air strikes in the North all the way up to the eighteenth parallel.

Nixon made those decisions in defiance of advice from civilians in the Departments of Defense and State, as well as the systems analysts on Kissinger's staff, who urged that if Vietnamization was to be truly tested the South Vietnamese should be required to resist the invasion without extra aid. But the president was not to be persuaded.

Three men met in the White House on April 6 to begin dealing with the specifics of a counteroffensive: President Nixon, Kissinger, and U.S. Air Force General John W. Vogt. The general received command of the 7th Air Force and a new mandate. According to General Vogt, the president told him, "I want you to get down there and use whatever air you need to turn this thing around . . . stop this offensive." American ground troops were not going to be reintroduced into South Vietnam, so American air

power had to make the difference.

That same day, with approval from President Nixon, American fighter-bombers struck military targets sixty miles north of the DMZ, breaking the restraints that had been imposed by the White House on the military since 1968. Simultaneously, from bases around the globe, many American ships and squadrons of aircraft went on alert and began moving toward Southeast Asia. Within sixty days the U.S. forces available for use in Vietnam would increase by 100 B–52s, hundreds of tactical warplanes, and 4 additional aircraft carriers. The 7th Fleet increased from 84 to 138 ships.

In some cases Strategic Air Command B–52s were transferred from other pursuits and were flying bombing missions over South Vietnam less than three days after being alerted in the United States. In the first sixty days, the number of bombing raids by attack and heavy bombing aircraft over North and South Vietnam increased threefold to 2,200 per month.

## It was a warning

On April 10 the president raised his ante and moved the bombing line even farther north. Twelve B–52s struck supply dumps near the port of Vinh, about 150 miles north of the DMZ. It was the first use of B–52s in North Vietnam by the Nixon administration. "It was a warning that things might get out of hand if the offensive did not stop," said Kissinger. On April 12 Nixon told Kissinger he had decided in favor of a bombing campaign that included strikes around Hanoi and Haiphong.

The high commands of the air force and navy were elated by the lifting of many of the restrictions that had leashed their power for so long. The no-bombing zones around Hanoi and Haiphong were narrowed to ten and five miles, respectively, and could be lifted altogether for strikes at special targets, such as a two-day B–52 raid in mid-April on fuel storage depots near the cities.

Nixon had ordered an air offensive in MR 1 in the South as well, but ground-hugging clouds delayed attempts to assault the enemy attackers. At one point Kissinger sarcastically suggested to Admiral Moorer that if his planes could not fly "maybe they could taxi north [to the DMZ]." By the second week after the enemy moved across the DMZ, air attacks began to hit the NVA's mobilized army, causing heavy losses. Before long the NVA could not assemble its men for a daytime attack without being attacked from the air. Entire units of enemy soldiers were destroyed by the intensive bombing.

Ultimately President Nixon approved the bombing of most of the sites in North Vietnam that had been on a lengthy target list drawn up by the JCS before the bombing halt in 1968. The growing air campaign against the North, which acquired the code name "Operation Linebacker," had three principal objectives: to isolate North

*The start of an Operation Linebacker bombing mission to Haiphong in May 1972. An A-6A Intruder of Attack Squadron 165 moves onto the catapult of one of the six U.S. carriers assembled to retaliate for the NVA Easter offensive.*

Vietnam from outside help by destroying harbors, railroads, and bridges; to destroy stockpiles of war supplies and food; and to strike hard at supplies and equipment moving toward the battlefield in the South. Before Operation Linebacker finished on October 22, planes had flown 40,000 sorties and dropped more than 155,000 tons of bombs.

The objective of isolating North Vietnam from its Chinese and Soviet sources of supply involved President Nixon in his riskiest move of the Vietnam War. But he and Kissinger were desperate for an achievement that would strengthen America's bargaining hand in the face of growing apprehensions about the South Vietnamese military position. So Kissinger ordered his aides to bring up-to-date a three-year-old plan called "Duck Hook," aimed at stopping ship traffic by mining North Vietnam's harbors. In contemplating such a step, Washington knew that it must move carefully in diplomatic channels to assure Russia and China that it intended no attack on their ships and citizens, that the counteroffensive was aimed strictly at the North Vietnamese, and that the U.S. had resorted to this course only as a result of the unprovoked invasion of the South. Otherwise, the harbor mining would endanger not only efforts at détente with Moscow and Peking but could even provoke war with one or the other of those powers. So planners of Duck Hook contemplated the mining for early May, allowing Nixon and Kissinger enough time to attempt to soften possible Soviet and Chinese reactions to such an attack.

One day in early April, Anatoly Dobrynin, the Soviet ambassador to the U.S., suggested that Kissinger fly to Moscow secretly in advance of the Nixon-Brezhnev summit in May to discuss the agenda. The president at first balked at sending Kissinger, suspecting a Soviet ploy to delay the growing U.S. military campaign against North Vietnam. Reconsidering, however, Nixon and Kissinger saw the potential for exploiting Soviet desire to have the summit.

So the president agreed to the Kissinger visit but insisted that Vietnam be the first order of business. As Nixon wrote in his memoirs, he ordered the national security adviser to refuse to discuss anything that the Soviets wanted "until they specifically committed themselves to help end the war." The "anything" Nixon meant included the planned summit meeting with its agenda of détente and new cooperation between the U.S. and U.S.S.R.

Kissinger journeyed to the secret meeting in Moscow on April 20 and there found Soviet leader Leonid Brezhnev agreeable to applying pressure on the North Vietnamese. Chary of Washington's thawing relationship with Peking, Brezhnev seemed determined that events in Vietnam should not derail the summit meeting. However, he insisted that the Soviet Union, in spite of its role as North Vietnam's arms supplier, had much less influence on

Hanoi than the Nixon administration assumed. He offered to act as a go-between to transmit America's latest peace proposal to Hanoi: an offer to halt the bombing of North Vietnam and to withdraw U.S. forces introduced since the beginning of the NVA invasion, in exchange for a withdrawal of NVA troops introduced to the South since March 29; immediate return of some American prisoners; and "serious negotiations to end the war." Kissinger considered some of his terms as "throwaways" and had accepted that the U.S. would eventually have to recognize the PRG and allow NVA troops to stay in the South. He did not, by his account, delude himself that the North would withdraw voluntarily from its hard-won gains. But he believed an initially tough stance provided more bargaining room. Kissinger asked Brezhnev to convey the U.S. proposal to Hanoi and to arrange a secret meeting for May 2 in Paris, adding that the U.S. would not bomb Hanoi and Haiphong pending that meeting.

The Russians quickly sent a delegation to Hanoi. Headed by Konstantin Katushev, leader of the Soviet Central Committee section dealing with foreign Communist parties, the group won approval for yet another meeting between Le Duc Tho and Kissinger on May 2, three weeks before the scheduled summit in Moscow.

Kissinger had accomplished two things: He knew that the Soviets would go to great lengths—and possibly show great restraint—in order to hold the summit; the national security adviser now had the Russians actively helping the United States seek a solution to the war. The next move by the U.S. would depend on how the North Vietnamese reacted on May 2.

## Retreat from Quang Tri

In late April, as Kissinger dickered with the Russians for three days, the military situation south of the DMZ in MR 1 steadied. The defensive line the South Vietnamese had patched together along the Cua Viet River and parallel to Route 1 was holding against continued NVA attacks. Still, the line of firebases and base camps along the DMZ and across north-central Quang Tri Province had all been lost, and counterattacks to regain them had failed. The 3d Division had been stabilized and reinforced by more marines and Rangers, and the southern soldiers had learned to "kill" the big Russian-made T54 tanks with their American-supplied LAWs. For three weeks in April, the ARVN 3d Division and all its attached units had battled the invading divisions to a standstill.

On April 27, however, the ARVN defenses began to un-

*Remnants of trucks, tractors, and warehouses dot a section of Haiphong's shipyard destroyed by a B-52 raid in April 1972.*

ravel. "Somebody started a rumor there had been a breakthrough from the west [that] was headed toward the Quang Tri [Ai Tu] Combat Base," recollected Major General Frederick J. Kroesen, who had become the commander of FRAC and senior U.S. adviser to I Corps just two weeks before the Easter attack. Now, in one of the few times General Lam roused himself from operational paralysis to take command, the former armor officer bypassed Giai and the 3d Division headquarters to order his pet unit—the 20th Tanks—out of the defensive line in the north near Dong Ha. Lam sent the tank regiment south to intercept, cut off, and contain the rumored NVA thrust.

This cavalier avoidance of the chain of command by Lam produced grim consequences. There was no enemy penetration, a fact that could have quickly been confirmed by checking with the 3d Division command. Instead, the first indication division staff officers had of the I Corps order was a line of tanks driving past the Ai Tu headquarters headed south. When the 20th Tanks pulled out of the line, they left a gaping hole. Worse, the infantry units on both sides of the hole left by the armored unit were unnerved by what they perceived as a retreat by the tanks. They, in turn, began streaming to the south. The line that had held against enemy attack for almost a month now fell to a rumor, abetted by the senior ARVN commander. Giai threw up his hands in frustration at the chaos created by his direct superior and, like a wronged character in a Greek tragedy, turned morose and withdrew to his quar-

ters. His effectiveness, undermined by Lam's endless politicking and erratic attempts at command, neared an end as Giai once again was forced to rally confused and disorganized troops.

The Vietnamese Marine units, still intact, halted the flight and began sorting the retreating soldiers into units. They slipped the ARVN soldiers into a new temporary line north of the Thach Han River with its center point the Ai Tu Combat Base. However, Giai realized that he needed to position his troops behind the river. Disposed as they were, with their backs to the Thach Han, there was no room for maneuver, a potentially disastrous position. The 3d Division commander announced April 30 to Lam and I Corps that he would withdraw behind the river the next day. Once more quiescent, Lam received the message without comment, thereby presumably giving his assent. The next morning the troops began withdrawing. Soon, however, an order from the JGS in Saigon to hold the present line passed without objection through Lam and I Corps to the hapless Giai. The 3d Division commander tried to stop the pullback, but the conflicting orders only created confusion. Huge gaps appeared once again in the defensive line. Within four hours the original positions had been abandoned, and the troops expected to stop and hold at the Thach Han River continued south toward Hue as a mob. Artillery pieces were spiked and abandoned. Tanks and APCs ran out of gas and sputtered to a halt.

As the ARVN fell back in disarray, local civilians also

began to flee. Clutching what possessions they could carry, thousands poured out of Quang Tri aboard buses, motor scooters, and bicycles and on foot. They mixed with the men, machines, and families of the 3d Division pushing and shoving down Route 1 toward the My Chanh River and the safety of Hue beyond. The narrow exits from the battle zone forced the South Vietnamese to queue up and stay on the main highway. Soon hundreds of military and civilian vehicles were cemented into a traffic jam that stretched for miles south of Quang Tri and presented too good a target for the NVA to ignore. The teeming mass was first hit by 130MM artillery fire, but most of the soldiers and civilians continued lemminglike down the main road. Later, looking over the carnage, military men agreed, it appeared that a "regimental-sized ambush" occurred: "The NVA went to the flank and began shooting." The South Vietnamese soldiers, with all cohesion and leadership gone, could muster no organized defense. Abandoned and destroyed vehicles were found various directions and distances from the main road, but few machines escaped. Survivors of the 3d Division arrived south of the My Chanh with only a tiny fraction of their equipment.

Not all Giai's units had collapsed. The two brigades of marines attached to the 3d had continued to defend the big base at Ai Tu and now withdrew in good order as the rear guard of the retreating division. Premature destruction of the bridges across the Thach Han forced the marines to cross at a neck-high ford in the river, but they

soon joined the remnants of the 20th Tanks and some other units at a helicopter pad near the fortresslike citadel in Quang Tri City. There they awaited Giai's next orders. Surrendering to the chaos around him, the 3d Division commander released his troops to make their way as best they could to yet another defensive line, this time along the My Chanh River, thirteen kilometers to the south. Giai also prepared for his own escape from the disaster at Quang Tri. His staff informed the marines that the general planned to leave with them.

The following day, May 2, hours passed as the NVA drew nearer and the column waited for the general to join them. In fact, Giai had already pushed his staff into three APCs and attempted to join his marines. But when he came under NVA fire near the citadel, the 3d Division commander returned to the fortress to join a hastily devised helicopter rescue that took out the last 132 men, including his staff. No word of the change in plans was passed to the waiting marines. "The first indication we had that Giai and his staff weren't coming was when we saw the Jolly Greens [CH–53 helicopters] going in to the Citadel," remembered Major Emmett Huff, U.S. Marine Corps adviser to the Vietnamese Marines, who were by then the tail end of the division.

The marines were in a difficult situation. The NVA was closing in quickly from the north and west. The main road south to the My Chanh River was under brutal direct fire from the enemy. They needed a plan that would enable

## Exodus on Highway 1

During the Easter offensive, as in most wars, the fighting also victimized civilians, many of whom had to flee their homes to avoid the crossfire. In the northernmost South Vietnamese provinces, Quang Tri and Thua Thien, the majority of the population lived on the coast and in towns along Highway 1, which became the invasion route for the Communist army. As the NVA pressed the attack, by the tens of thousands, the refugees fled south, sometimes joined by South Vietnamese troops escaping the battle.

Right. *With Quang Tri falling to the Communists during the first days of May, ARVN soldiers and civilians trudge along Route 1 to Hue and safety; within hours the road became a gauntlet of NVA artillery fire and ambushes.*

Below. *Homeless women and children fleeing the NVA offensive huddle near a small river just south of Quang Tri. There they await passage across the stream and toward Hue.*

148

them to travel safely the thirteen kilometers to the My Chanh, where the surviving ARVN and Marine troops were beginning to dig in once again. Huff and the other senior marine officers decided they might gain surprise for their patched-together unit and possibly escape the NVA by avoiding the predictable route south. Moving east toward the ocean first, the column later picked a secondary road leading south. For a day and a half the ruse worked. The NVA did not expect anyone to be that near the coast. But as the party neared the My Chanh, its luck ended, and the unit was struck by heavy fire as the NVA caught up to them. Groups of enemy soldiers were maneuvering to attack and break up the column.

The group of Americans, including one civilian, traveling at the very tail of the South Vietnamese unit, turned and climbed a small hill. From there they could see the NVA movements and direct air and naval gunfire on them, slowing the enemy enough to allow the column to escape. Meanwhile, the soldiers of the 20th Tanks had used up their remaining courage. They panicked and ran their tanks and APCs the length of the column, scattering the infantry and carrying off the headquarters staff and communications gear still aboard. As the remnants of the retreating column fought their way clear of the NVA attack and headed for the nearby My Chanh River, the now isolated Americans continued to call in fire support. But the dozen Americans were surrounded, and the North Vietnamese were moving in on their hilltop observation post.

Brigadier General Thomas W. Bowen, deputy senior adviser for I Corps, aloft in his helicopter trying to monitor the battle for the staff in Hue, heard the Americans describe their plight on the advisers' radio network. He knew they had to be extricated quickly or they were lost. Bowen had his pilot hedgehop their UH-1 north to reach the group before the NVA did. Bowen won the race but faced a new dilemma. There were, he recollected, seventeen men crammed aboard and standing on the skids when the small aircraft struggled into the air from the hilltop. Horsing the helicopter into flight was difficult. At one point a marine slipped from the landing gear. Grabbing desperately, Major Huff caught the radio strapped to the falling marine's back and held on until they sat back down and pulled him aboard. "Fortunately, [Bowen's helicopter] was so loaded and so shot up he couldn't get much altitude," Huff noted of the second attempt. As a result, the SA-7 missiles carried by the NVA could not lock onto the fleeing helicopter. The craft, riddled by small-arms fire, stayed airborne just long enough to cross the My Chanh River. They were the last Americans out. Those north of the My Chanh were either dead or prisoners.

During the 3d Division's debacle, Major General Kroesen, senior adviser to I Corps, and General Bowen talked several times with General Abrams in Saigon telling the MACV commander of their dismay with the corps command. Abrams then carried their message to President

Thieu. On May 2, as Giai evacuated Quang Tri, General Lam was summoned to Saigon to meet with the president. It was a private meeting and no record of it emerged, but Lam's military incompetence was now painfully evident and the general himself had little stomach for a continued combat role. Lam still had political prowess, however, and it saved him once again. "When he came back from Saigon, Lam was a changed man," Kroesen said. "The weight of the world had been removed from his shoulders. He was happy and cheerful at the briefing that evening." He told everyone that he was being replaced by Lieutenant General Ngo Quang Truong, the IV Corps commander. Thieu still felt he needed the loyalty of the politically important Lam. Instead of sacking him for poor leadership, Thieu had promoted him to the Ministry of Defense in Saigon as head of the anticorruption campaign.

General Giai was not so fortunate. Constantly countermanded by superiors and saddled with mostly raw troops, he nonetheless had conducted a reasonably good fight. But Lam had been promoted, and someone had to take the blame. Although Truong, with a good eye for fighting men, wanted to keep Giai in command of the 3d, Thieu needed a scapegoat. By order of the JGS, Giai was tried for "desertion in the face of the enemy." Unfairly, but as "standard practice in ARVN," said Truong, General Giai was held personally responsible for the defeat of his division. He received a five-year prison sentence. When Vietnam fell in 1975, his new captors transferred the general from a GVN jail to a Communist reeducation camp.

## Attack on An Loc

If the Easter offensive was over for Generals Lam and Giai and the 3d Division, it was still underway for the rest of the South Vietnamese army. North Vietnam's invasion entered its second phase when, before dawn on April 5, the 5th VC/NVA Division moved out of Cambodia and struck the ARVN outpost of Loc Ninh. Moving with tanks and armored personnel carriers, the Communist soldiers advanced through rows of rubber trees into the South Vietnamese positions. The 2,000 men of the 9th ARVN Regiment and a Ranger battalion, along with their handful of U.S. advisers, beat back the tanks on five occasions, but in the end they were overwhelmed. By the morning of April 7, all were dead, captured, or escaping into the jungle.

Loc Ninh was at the northern tip of Highway 13, which led straight south to the nation's capital. Some twenty-five kilometers south stood An Loc, capital of Binh Long Province, Vietnam's most fertile rubber-producing area and the next major town on the route to Saigon. Anticipating An Loc as the next target, President Thieu promptly ordered the province capital "held at all costs." He was concerned that the attack in MR 1 might have been a ruse and that the main goal of the entire offensive was Saigon.

With the loss of Loc Ninh, the South Vietnamese high

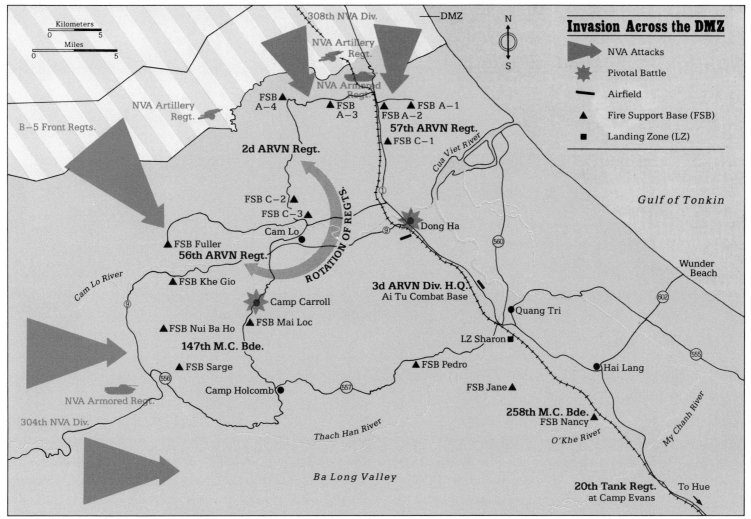

In 1972 the three regiments of the 3d ARVN Division deployed along the DMZ and two attached marine brigades manned the defenses of the western flank in Quang Tri Province. Little realizing the division faced attack by more than three NVA divisions, the 56th and 2d Regiments of the 3d Division were ordered to exchange positions (center) on March 30. At noon that day, the Communists attacked. Disorganized and surprised by the NVA invasion, the ARVN units fell back before the tank—led northern juggernaut.

command shifted the 5th ARVN Division from Lai Khe, some thirty–five kilometers away, to An Loc. Meanwhile, the 21st ARVN Division and a regiment of the 9th Division pulled out of the Mekong Delta and hustled north to the now–deserted base at Lai Khe to form a second line of defense between An Loc and Saigon. As the ARVN command made its adjustments, the Communists continued their attack. The VC/NVA 9th Division pinched off the remaining small outposts ringing An Loc and began shelling the city. Much of the fire came from U.S.–made 105MM and 155MM howitzers captured from the Cambodian army and from ARVN during Lam Son 719. Just as the ARVN 5th Division finished its move to An Loc, the VC/NVA 9th completed its encirclement of the town. At the same time, a third Communist division, the 7th, moved into place south of An Loc, blocking the route for reinforcements from Saigon. It now faced the ARVN 21st assembling at Lai Khe. The siege of An Loc had begun. As the 5th VC/NVA Division regrouped after taking Loc Ninh and started its own move toward An Loc, the word among the North Vietnamese was that An Loc would fall by April 20.

The senior adviser for III Corps and head of the Third Regional Assistance Command (TRAC), Major General James Hollingsworth, thought otherwise. A gruff, former subordinate of General George S. Patton, Jr., Hollingsworth immediately committed the fifty–odd American combat advisers in III Corps to staying with the ARVN units and sharing their fate. Next, from his headquarters near Saigon, he ordered his advisory teams to plan bombing strikes to blanket possible enemy locations or assembly areas around An Loc. With his plans in hand, the general then appealed to General Abrams, another Patton protégé, to provide extra air support. After considerable haggling, because of the other demands for the heavy bombers, Abrams agreed.

Next, Hollingsworth, who doubted the ARVN's capability to hold An Loc, called around the country, looking for more advisers who were sent for the embattled ARVN units. He believed that an American presence was necessary to the survival of An Loc. "Once the Communists decided to take An Loc, and I could get a handful of soldiers to hold and a lot of American advisers to keep them from

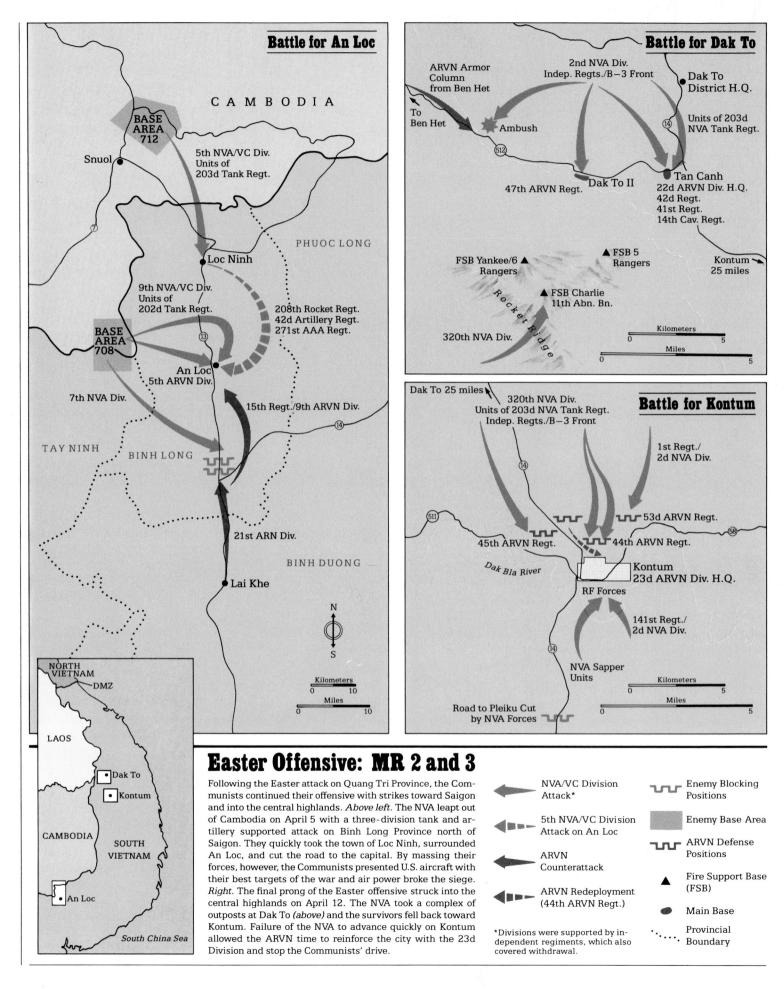

### Battle for An Loc

CAMBODIA

BASE AREA 712

Snuol

5th NVA/VC Div. Units of 203d Tank Regt.

PHUOC LONG

Loc Ninh

9th NVA/VC Div. Units of 202d Tank Regt.

208th Rocket Regt. 42d Artillery Regt. 271st AAA Regt.

BASE AREA 708

An Loc 5th ARVN Div.

7th NVA Div.

15th Regt./9th ARVN Div.

TAY NINH

BINH LONG

21st ARN Div.

BINH DUONG

Lai Khe

N

S

Kilometers
0          10

Miles
0          10

NORTH VIETNAM

DMZ

LAOS

Dak To

Kontum

CAMBODIA

SOUTH VIETNAM

An Loc

South China Sea

### Battle for Dak To

ARVN Armor Column from Ben Het

2nd NVA Div. Indep. Regts./B—3 Front

Dak To District H.Q.

To Ben Het

Ambush

Units of 203d NVA Tank Regt.

512

47th ARVN Regt.

Dak To II

Tan Canh
22d ARVN Div. H.Q.
42d Regt.
41st Regt.
14th Cav. Regt.

FSB Yankee/6 ▲ Rangers

▲ FSB 5 Rangers

Kontum 25 miles

▲ FSB Charlie 11th Abn. Bn.

Rocket Ridge

320th NVA Div.

Kilometers
0          5

Miles
0          5

### Battle for Kontum

Dak To 25 miles

320th NVA Div. Units of 203d NVA Tank Regt. Indep. Regts./B—3 Front

1st Regt./ 2d NVA Div.

14

511

53d ARVN Regt.

45th ARVN Regt.

44th ARVN Regt.

Dak Bla River

Kontum
23d ARVN Div. H.Q.

RF Forces

141st Regt./ 2d NVA Div.

14

NVA Sapper Units

Road to Pleiku Cut by NVA Forces

Kilometers
0          5

Miles
0          5

# Easter Offensive: MR 2 and 3

Following the Easter attack on Quang Tri Province, the Communists continued their offensive with strikes toward Saigon and into the central highlands. *Above left.* The NVA leapt out of Cambodia on April 5 with a three-division tank and artillery supported attack on Binh Long Province north of Saigon. They quickly took the town of Loc Ninh, surrounded An Loc, and cut the road to the capital. By massing their forces, however, the Communists presented U.S. aircraft with their best targets of the war and air power broke the siege. *Right.* The final prong of the Easter offensive struck into the central highlands on April 12. The NVA took a complex of outposts at Dak To (*above*) and the survivors fell back toward Kontum. Failure of the NVA to advance quickly on Kontum allowed the ARVN time to reinforce the city with the 23d Division and stop the Communists' drive.

NVA/VC Division Attack*

5th NVA/VC Division Attack on An Loc

ARVN Counterattack

ARVN Redeployment (44th ARVN Regt.)

Enemy Blocking Positions

Enemy Base Area

ARVN Defense Positions

▲ Fire Support Base (FSB)

Main Base

Provincial Boundary

*Divisions were supported by independent regiments, which also covered withdrawal.

running off, that's all I needed," Hollingsworth declared. "Hold them and I'll kill them with airpower. Give me something to bomb and I'll win."

When the main NVA assaults against An Loc began on April 13, Hollingsworth and his advisers forced the enemy troops to advance through a rain of cannon fire, rockets, and bombs delivered by U.S. aircraft. But the Communist soldiers, supported by massed artillery, tanks, and APCs, were relentless. Slowly they battered their way into the town and took the airfield, reducing the allied perimeter to about a square kilometer. But, as in I Corps, the ARVN soldiers learned they could knock out the fearsome tanks with their LAWs and gradually they stopped the advance, littering the streets of the city with destroyed enemy tanks. The NVA's April 20 deadline slipped by and the tenacious South Vietnamese held. A status report from the 5th Division's senior U.S. adviser reflected how desperate the situation had become, however:

The [5th ARVN] division is tired and worn out; supplies minimal, casualties continue to mount, medical supplies coverage low. Wounded a major problem, mass burials for military and civilian, morale at a low ebb. In spite of incurring heavy losses from U.S. air strikes, the enemy continues to persist.

Twenty-four hours a day, rotating shifts, three Americans huddled around a plywood map table in the central bunker functioning as the "conscience" of the 5th Division command. The Vietnamese had little of the training necessary for complicated big-unit functions. What the U.S. officers routinely learned at Command and General Staff College was not available to most ARVN staff officers. The Americans offered alternatives and worked as a staff: advising, ordering artillery support, juggling logistics, and linking all these elements to current intelligence of enemy activity. But most important, they directed the torrent of bombs that continually shook the earth during daylight hours. At night, even as they planned the next day's air bombardment, the advisers directed the specially equipped gunships that probed the darkness with electronic "eyes" looking for more targets. They also helped organize air supply drops, the only way the surrounded garrison could be supplied, and the distribution of supplies, which had initially gone, as one adviser noted, to "the strongest, swiftest, and the closest to the pallet drop."

Another of the Americans' tasks was to monitor the daily progress of the relief column of the 21st Division now fighting its way up Route 13 from Lai Khe. The 21st Division's attack had foundered because of the last-minute appointment of a new, inexperienced division commander who launched uncoordinated, piecemeal attacks in the morning and devoted the rest of the daylight hours to recovering and evacuating casualties. The senior U.S. adviser to the division, Colonel J. Ross Franklin, knew from radio intercepts that the enemy suffered from lack of supplies, bad morale, illness, and casualties. But the NVA remained a formidable foe. "It doesn't take a lot of guys in bunkers to stop an uncoordinated attack," he said.

One unit, however, did get behind the Communist positions on Route 13 and break through to An Loc, but it was a harrowing passage. The 15th Regiment of the 9th ARVN Division swept east around Franklin's stalled 21st and the enemy flank and back onto the highway, only to find itself trapped between the VC/NVA 7th and 9th Divisions. For three weeks the South Vietnamese were struck with tanks, infantry, and artillery. The troops sometimes moved only fifty meters a day, mostly on their stomachs through rubber plantations and open fields. "Because the contact was so [heavy], the bodies would just lie there," recalled Major Craig Mandeville, who served as assistant senior adviser to the regiment. "You couldn't get up and bury them." The wounded who could not advance were left behind. Ravaged by dysentery from the diet of rice and untreated water, the 120 survivors of the 15th, all of them wounded at least once, were the first troops to break through to An Loc, but the road had closed behind them.

## Bombing on the hour

The enemy was also having its problems, more than the allies imagined. A political officer from the Central Office for South Vietnam (COSVN) died in an ambush near An Loc. His body yielded a letter detailing the difficulties faced by the 9th VC/NVA Division. The division had failed to take the city because the B-52 and tactical air strikes had been unbelievably devastating. Sometimes the armor left the infantry and other times the infantry failed to advance with the tanks. The letter ended with severe criticism of the 9th Division commander. In early May the commander of the 9th suffered an official reprimand for failing to take An Loc, and the job of capturing An Loc was handed to the commander of the 5th VC/NVA—successful at Loc Ninh.

Hollingsworth, seeing the probing attacks and shellfire that heralded the new attack, once again went to Abrams for more B-52 strikes. Once more, supported by the new air chief in Vietnam, air force General John W. Vogt, Hollingsworth received his extra missions for An Loc. The air force proceeded to lay on a B-52 strike every fifty-five minutes for twenty-five hours beginning at 5:30 A.M. on May 11. By the end of the day the Communist troops began to stream from the field, abandoning some of their tanks. For the next three days, each time they assembled for an attack, enemy troops endured bombing raids, some of them within a few hundred meters of friendly lines.

A Communist soldier captured early on the first morning of the air strikes revealed that his regiment had been ordered into the craters of an earlier strike as a jumping-off point for an attack, his commanders betting that a second strike would not be called on the same site. The results of the interrogation quickly reached the III Corps senior adviser. Looking over his strike schedule, Hollingsworth brushed aside red tape and directed a second raid on the original target. "I'm so proud of that strategic air force," the general said. "That crew diverted the strike in 20 minutes, put it in . . . and destroyed that whole damn regiment, right in the same holes where they had gone to reorganize when I'd missed them in the morning."

Continuing pressure from air strikes and the efforts of the 5th Division's new senior adviser, Colonel Walt Ulmer, and his fellow advisers to do "everything we could to thump people on the back and tell . . . all of the Vietnamese friends of ours . . . to keep hanging in there," brought the attack to its climax on the fourteenth. The NVA had attacked directly the ARVN positions and failed. They were "simply trying to pile on and pile on and pile on. They frittered away an awful lot of manpower," Ulmer said.

Although it would be weeks before it became apparent because of the NVA's continued shelling and stubborn defense, the 5th VC/NVA Division had failed as had the 9th. The decimated units now started slipping west toward Cambodia and the rice granaries of the Mekong Delta as other units moved in to cover their withdrawal.

## Fight for the central highlands

While the battles raged in Quang Tri and An Loc in early April, the central highlands area of MR 2 had remained quiet. Yet John Vann, the former army officer who had become civilian senior adviser for South Vietnam's MR 2, and ARVN commander Lieutenant General Ngo Dzu worried about intelligence reports arriving in their Pleiku headquarters that suggested an NVA attack would come in the Dak To area near the Cambodian border.

To counter the threat, Dzu shifted two infantry regiments of the 22d Division and two armored squadrons into the three military compounds at Tan Canh, Dak To II, and Ben Het. The region had been a battleground more than once before. Here the Americans of the U.S. 173d Brigade and 4th Infantry Division had battled the North Vietnamese in November 1967—their biggest battle of the war to that time. Building defenses around Dak To presented logistical problems. The region was linked to the supply and command centers at Kontum and Pleiku by a single road, Highway 14. Since the rest of the 22d Division was on the coast and the 23d Division was scattered in the south of MR 2, there were few additional troops available to defend Kontum and Pleiku if the ARVN forces around Dak To were cut off.

On April 12 the NVA ended speculation by attacking "Rocket Ridge," the high ground overlooking Dak To. The third phase of the Easter offensive was underway. Advancing behind a curtain of artillery fire, the Communists broke into the outlying ARVN positions and overran them after four days of heavy fighting. After regrouping and then moving into encircling positions around the three for-

tified bases, the NVA loosed barrages of artillery on the valley camps the morning of April 23.

Early in the fighting, Colonel Phillip Kaplan, senior adviser to Colonel Le Duc Dat, the commander of the 22d Division at Tan Canh, received reports of ARVN M41 light tanks being knocked out on the perimeter of his camp. He and two other advisers scrambled out of the command bunker to survey the damage. As they moved toward the disabled armor, the Americans suddenly heard a new sound, something rushing through the air with a "whooping" sound. Next to a destroyed tank, they located strands of wire and some metal parts and took them back to their bunker to try to learn what was hitting them.

What they had were scraps from a Russian-made AT-3 "Sagger" antitank rocket. As the rocket flew through the air, two extremely fine control wires spun out behind it. These wires connected to a control box from which an NVA soldier could accurately guide the flight of the missile. The range of the Sagger was from 500 to 3,000 meters, and the missile traveled visibly enough and slowly enough (120 meters per second) so that an intended victim had between four and twenty-five seconds to move out of its path.

As Kaplan and the rest of the division staff, including Dat, studied the find, an enemy artillery shell, or perhaps another Sagger, scored a bull's eye when it came through a narrow slit window of the sandbagged position. The explosion wounded most of the staff, including Kaplan, and destroyed all the radios and antennas with which the division headquarters communicated.

The discovery of the new weapon, the brush with death, the destruction of his bunker, and the continuing assaults by the NVA caused Col. Dat to lose control of himself. "Dat was really demoralized," Kaplan recalled. "He told me, 'We're going to lose, we're going to be overrun, we will all be killed or captured,' yet we had roughly 1,200 men inside of that compound." In Kaplan's opinion, the regiment could still mount a credible defense. Through the night Kaplan argued with Dat, but the ARVN commander was paralyzed by fear. He did nothing to prepare a defense.

At breaking light, Kaplan made his decision. He gathered the advisers and told them they were getting out. As they moved toward the perimeter, the first NVA tank rolled over the camp's wire and into the compound. Kaplan's men tried to stop the T54s with LAWs, but the weapons had corroded while stored in the damp bunkers. Now they all failed to fire. Giving up the futile effort to fight the tanks, the nine escaping Americans began picking their way through the camp's wire and into a surrounding minefield to elude the attackers. At that moment two small OH-58 observation helicopters, one of them piloted by John Vann, swooped from the sky to rescue the Americans. Vann had been following events on the command radio and had flown to the battle from Pleiku at first light. By shuttling the helicopters into the minefield, Vann's flight completed the evacuation of the Americans.

*Wounded South Vietnamese troops close in on a helicopter taking off from An Loc while others cling to the skids to escape the encircled town on April 29, 1972. Disembarking reinforcements push through the rush.*

The leaderless South Vietnamese put up a brief disorganized fight and then scattered before the NVA attacks. The survivors trickled to the south under cover of a driving rain to arrive in Kontum days later. The nearby camp at Dak To II had also come under attack. In an attempt to break up the Communist assault, the armored units at Ben Het, a little farther to the west, headed for the sound of the guns. Then in the midst of these conventional battles, the NVA put their guerrilla tactics to use. While crossing a bridge halfway to Dak To II, the armored force fell into an ambush and disintegrated under the concentrated NVA fire. The armor unit was the last major reserve in the area, so the regiment at Dak To II had no hope of rescue. Under heavy attack, the ARVN soldiers split into small groups and began breaking out toward Kontum.

Events were transpiring as the American and Vietnamese II Corps planners had feared. With the ARVN 23d Division scattered throughout the south of the military region, half of the 22d on the coast, and the other half destroyed as a fighting force in the Dak To region, no ARVN units stood between the attacking Communists and the provincial capital of Kontum. Improbably, the NVA did not move to press its advantage. Instead, the Communists delayed and allowed the South Vietnamese to build a redoubt around Kontum. "It was the dumbest possible thing they could have done," said U.S. Army Colonel Joseph Pizzi, "and I'm very grateful they did because there was nobody to stop them except a few people like me with pistols."

Under the pressure, Gen. Dzu, ensconced at his headquarters at Pleiku, began to unravel. "Tense, exhausted, and unable to pull himself together," Lt. Gen. Ngo Quang Truong later wrote, "he spent his time calling President Thieu on the telephone . . . begging for instructions even on the most trivial things." Major General John Hill, newly appointed adviser to Dzu, arrived at Pleiku to find a commander with no control of the situation or his troops. "Dzu was a beaten man," he said. "He wished to be relieved and said so to Vann and others."

As the crisis at Kontum waxed and Vietnamese leadership there waned, the role of II Corps senior adviser John Paul Vann became paramount. The retired infantry lieutenant colonel worked day and night, using all his civilian and military connections to channel U.S. support to the region. He also flew dangerous reconnaissance flights himself after the withdrawal of U.S. air cavalry units and continually made trips deep behind enemy lines to resupply or rescue isolated American advisers.

In Vann's opinion, the ARVN had enough equipment and trained men to defend itself. What it lacked was a strong, charismatic leader. Vann used his influence and the trust he had built up to seize that role during the defense of Kontum. "The rest of us organized around Vann's personal efforts," explained Gen. Hill, "and concentrated on getting the resources marshalled to take advantage of the leadership he was exerting with the Vietnamese."

Quickly the 23d Division and Ranger groups poured into Kontum to dig trenches and dugouts for a line to halt the slowly gathering NVA force to their north. With the reinforcements also came a new Corps commander, Major General Nguyen Van Toan, replacing Dzu. Physically large, confident, and self-assertive, Toan allowed Colonel Ly Tong Ba, commander of the 23d ARVN Division, to juggle his troops by moving the Rangers into blocking positions outside of town while his own regiments constructed the defenses in Kontum City.

On May 16, the NVA attacked Kontum from the north, driving into the strongest section of the ARVN lines. The tank-supported assault was mounted straight ahead down Highway 14 and totally without finesse. These concentrated units attacking in the open once more presented ideal targets for the B–52. The strategic bombers began to pound the advancing North Vietnamese.

In one of the ARVN trenches, Lieutenant Colonel James McKenna, senior adviser with the 44th ARVN Regiment, felt the power of the air attacks. Col. McKenna remembers, "We couldn't hear the airplanes, but suddenly you heard the bombs whistling down. When they hit it was like they came from the center of the earth—just like the bowels of the earth exploding." When the South Vietnamese rushed forward in counterattack, the men of the NVA attacking force under the bombs had either been killed or had fled. This type of action characterized the next two weeks as the attacking NVA was whittled away by the firepower of the ARVN soldiers and U.S. air support.

The intensive bombing and resulting losses left the North Vietnamese in a critical position. They had either to win a quick victory or to withdraw to refit, resupply, and replace their heavy casualties. They retained enough strength for only one more big push.

In late May the 44th ARVN Regiment was pulled back into reserve while the other two regiments of the 23d Division took over the defense of Kontum's front lines. The 44th occupied a bunker and small perimeter on the edge of a bombed-out hospital complex, safely back from the front lines. Throughout the night of the twenty-sixth, the men's sleep was interrupted by the sounds of what they took to be more South Vietnamese troops and tanks moving around them, but about 5:00 A.M. one of the ARVN soldiers on perimeter guard shouted an alarm. An NVA tank was coming through the barbed wire. During the night the NVA had found a big hole in the division's forward defenses and pushed into the rear area. An ARVN soldier destroyed the tank with a LAW and killed the crewmen as they tried to escape, but the T54 was only one of many. The NVA struck the surprised 44th Regiment with more tanks and infantry simultaneously from the north and east flanks. Fighting from a perimeter of bunkers on the east and shallow trenches on the north, the 44th sought to maintain its punctured lines. A break for the ARVN came when Gen. Hill's personal helicopter, especially fitted with

# The Indispensable Man

On the night of June 9, 1972, South Vietnamese troops at a firebase sixteen kilometers north of Pleiku saw a flaming helicopter go down into the hills outside Kontum. Next morning, when government troops located the site of the wreck, they discovered that John Paul Vann, an American who had given ten years to helping the war-torn country, had also given his life. Senior U.S. adviser to II Corps and one of the most experienced and respected Americans in Vietnam, Vann was making a routine flight when the helicopter crashed, killing all aboard.

Vann, a familiar figure in Vietnam, had first served as commander of an airborne ranger company sent to fight in Korea, where the unit carried out operations behind enemy lines and against North Korean guerrillas. This heightened his interest in guerrilla warfare, and he had volunteered eagerly for duty in Vietnam. But soon after Vann's arrival in Vietnam in 1962 as an army lieutenant colonel advising the 7th ARVN Division, he began alienating many with his outspoken criticisms of U.S. policy.

Vann served as a candid source of information and analysis for reporters, and he always spoke on the record. "If I had been a young lad growing up in Vietnam between 1961 and 1965, I would have been a Vietcong," Vann once told a reporter, explaining that he thought the majority of the population during that period supported the NLF. After his twelve-month tour, Vann retired from the army as a gesture of protest of his country's support for the Diem regime.

Yet Vann remained committed to an independent South Vietnam, and in 1965 he was drawn back to the country to work as the civilian AID representative in the Vietcong-controlled Hau Nghia Province. For a year Vann drove the back roads in his jeep visiting hamlets to gather information about the needs of the rural population. He refused to surrender the roads or the night to the enemy. With an AR15 and several hand grenades by his side, he drove at high speed—up to seventy mph—to thwart ambushers and, in fact, survived three attacks during his year at Hau Nghia. Those familiar with Vann's work were even more impressed by his belief in pacification and by his demands for government reform and stronger leadership. Despite being inde-

*John Paul Vann, senior U.S. adviser for II Corps, aboard his OH–58 Kiowa the day before he was killed.*

pendent and outspoken, Vann was promoted in 1966 to director of civil operations in III Corps and then to deputy for CORDS in IV Corps.

After the bloody 1968 Tet offensive, Vann concluded that the war had changed from a civil war to an outright invasion by the North Vietnamese. Once firmly in favor of fighting a guerrilla force with guerrilla tactics, Vann became a strong advocate of preparing ARVN to fight a conventional war and of continuing U.S. support until the South Vietnamese were completely ready to take over. The United States' use of overwhelming firepower to defeat the enemy, which in the early stages of the war Vann found countereffective, was now the key to victory, Vann concluded, against an invading force that could not count on real support in the countryside. Those closest to Vann observed that while he had once expressed admiration for the Vietcong, he despised the North Vietnamese. He expressed satisfaction in accounts of enemy forces caught in the open and destroyed by air strikes.

In May 1971, Vann had gained such prominence for his work that as a civilian he was named senior adviser to II Corps, normally a two-star (or major general) billet. Full of energy, often impatient and domineering, barking orders to his staff, Vann seemed at times to hold II Corps together by the very strength of his will. More than any other American in Vietnam, Vann had won the respect and confidence of the Vietnamese. He was able to make demands that would have been resented coming from any other American.

When the North Vietnamese launched their offensive into II Corps in April 1972, Vann's career seemed to have come full circle. Once again he became the quintessential military commander, piloting his own helicopter behind enemy lines to aid isolated U.S. advisers and encouraging ARVN commanders who faltered during the enemy attacks.

Vann's hopes for the Vietnamese were embodied in Colonel Ly Tong Ba, with whom he worked closely during the battle for Kontum. As a captain during the pivotal battle at Ap Bac in 1963, Ba had performed dismally. When aggressive action would have trapped a large VC force, Vann, then an adviser, had pleaded with Ba to advance and finally ordered him to do so. But Ba failed to move, and later Vann singled out his performance as a major factor in the South Vietnamese defeat.

Vann, however, did not give up on Ba. Most U.S. advisers worked with an ARVN commander for a year, but Vann advised Ba on and off for ten years. During the Tet offensive that patience paid off when Ba proved himself a strong leader. After Vann became senior adviser to II Corps, he requested that Ba serve as commander of the 23d ARVN Division. Under Vann, Ba fought bravely at Kontum and was promoted to brigadier general.

But if advisers who stayed a year had less impact on the Vietnamese than Vann, at least they could be easily replaced. The same was not true for Vann. "John is too good," a friend of his said only days before Vann's death. "When he finally gets killed, and he will be one of these days, I shudder to think what will happen to those people he's been advising. He has come closer to being the indispensable man than any other in Vietnam, and that's a very dangerous thing."

*A Communist soldier wounded and captured in Kontum in May is carried by a member of the 23d ARVN Division to a rear area for treatment and questioning.*

heavy .50-caliber machine guns, drove the NVA infantry away from their attacking tanks. The fight once again mounted in fury, and North Vietnamese tanks threatened anew to break through.

Suddenly, wheeling into the fight through the thick smoke of burning storage dumps and around the water tower occupied by the enemy flew two ten-year-old UH-1B helicopters, underpowered and slowed to a top speed of about sixty knots by the strange equipment they carried. A team of veteran pilots was bringing to battle the new experimental airborne TOW (for tube-launched, optically tracked, wire-guided) missile. A test unit at Fort Lewis, Washington, the 1st Aerial Tow Team, was ordered to Vietnam soon after the Easter offensive started. John Vann had persuaded his superior to send the unit and its new weapon to the central highlands. They were there to prove they could knock out tanks with the new missiles and sophisticated thirteen-power, gyrostabilized sights that were linked together by computer.

When they got to Kontum that day, the TOW team quickly spotted ten tanks "running around in one building and out the other," pilot-gunner Chief Warrant Officer 2 Danny Rowe remembered. Boring through the thick smoke, Rowe locked his sights on a tank near the defensive wire. The missile roared from the craft and burned through the tank's armor in a shower of sparks. The U.S. now had provided a long-range tank killer to support the South Vietnamese. The two choppers stayed over the battlefield most of the day, occasionally returning to Pleiku to refuel and change crews. While the pilot maneuvered to dodge enemy machine-gun fire, the gunner kept his sights trained on the tanks skittering through the battlefield. Even aboard the jinking, explosion-buffeted helicopters, if the gunner could keep the sight on the tank, the computer made certain the missile hit the target. The two ships bagged ten tanks before dark; a total of twenty-four was destroyed during the three-day fight. The new weapon and the old, slow choppers provided part of what was needed to break the NVA armored spearhead.

For General Hill, the decisive point of the battle for Kontum came on May 27 with "the destruction of the enemy tanks by the TOW birds." But there were other important factors as well. One of the U.S. advisers with the 44th Regiment, Major Wade B. Lovings, found an abandoned tank near the hospital. The T54 was undamaged. Puzzling over this he checked the gas tanks and found them empty. The air power unleashed against the NVA had cut off its resupply, and lack of fuel was at least a partial reason the attack against the 44th had foundered.

As the NVA forces pulled back, they were again hit by the heavy bombers and tactical aircraft. "The B-52s came in parallel to our front line," remembered Major Lovings. The bombs fell so close "they were blowing us out of our foxholes with the concussion." Afterward, as ARVN soldiers counterattacked through the bomb craters, they wore gas masks to avoid the stench from the many decomposing NVA bodies. The corpses were so mangled by the bombing, said Lovings, "we couldn't count the bodies." Still a great deal of dirty, hard fighting lay ahead, but General Hill believed the "enemy's offensive potential had been exhausted."

John Paul Vann did not survive the end of his greatest battle. He died on the night of June 9 when his helicopter crashed.

## A "brutal" secret meeting

The battle marked a turning point in the North Vietnamese offensive, but that was not immediately clear to the defenders of the three battlefields of South Vietnam and it was even less obvious to the politicians and officials in Washington, Hanoi, and Paris.

The day—May 2—came for the meeting that Moscow had persuaded Le Duc Tho to hold with Henry Kissinger in Paris. The national security adviser went to the secret gathering with great expectations but was quickly disillusioned. The DRV representatives were never more obdurate than when they had a military advantage, and on May 2, 1972, it looked as if they held a large one—Quang Tri had just fallen, An Loc was surrounded, and the outer posts of Kontum had collapsed. As Kissinger put it afterward: "For all Le Duc Tho knew, a complete South Vietnamese collapse was imminent."

In a curious turn of logic, Le Duc Tho began the meeting by declaring there was no North Vietnamese offensive. Instead, northern forces were merely responding to provocation by the United States. He then read from a long series of newspaper clippings, droning on about North Vietnamese successes in South Vietnam. Kissinger complained that he had not traveled thousands of miles to listen to press reports. According to the national security adviser, Le Duc Tho then said that if the reports of the North Vietnamese Army's battlefield victories were true, "What difference does it make" what they did as negotiators in Paris? After that, the two men went through the motions of offer and counteroffer, but the meeting, which Kissinger later described as brutal and insulting, ended in impasse.

The U.S. held another card, however. U.S. officials had withheld a major blow against the North while trying to negotiate an end to the NVA invasion. With those hopes now dashed, Kissinger and Nixon decided that it was time for the United States to strike again at the North. Their hope, and their gamble, was that in their mutual desire for improved relations with the United States, neither the Soviet Union nor China would choose to retaliate on behalf of their North Vietnamese ally.

*An NVA soldier lies dead in a section of Kontum shattered by battle in May 1972.*

# An Loc Besieged

When three NVA divisions burst out of Cambodia in early April 1972 to surround An Loc and begin round two of the Easter offensive, it seemed their ultimate target was Saigon itself. If the Communists took the provincial capital, which they announced they would do by April 20, Saigon would be but a ninety-kilometer march away down Highway 13. To answer the threat, Major General James Hollingsworth, the senior adviser to ARVN in MR 3, which encompassed An Loc, called for heavy air support. He later said, "I took no excuse as to why I could not have the airpower necessary to win. I brought B-52 strikes to within 500 meters of the friendlies. . . . [I didn't] pay attention to rules written for amateurs." Despite the power of U.S. and South Vietnamese bombing, the defenders had to hold out under daytime shelling and nighttime tank and infantry attacks from April 8 through July 11—ninety-five days.

*An O-2 spotter plane with a forward air controller on board dives toward An Loc to mark targets with white phosphorous rockets so that U.S. fighter-bombers can attack tank-supported NVA troops surrounding the city. The FACs were the defenders' link to the outside world.*

## The fight on Route 13

While the intensive air support encouraged An Loc's defenders to hold the fort, the knowledge that a division-sized rescue force was fighting its way north along Highway 13 proved a mixed blessing for morale. On days the column advanced, spirits in the city soared; when the NVA counterattacked or stopped the ARVN relief column, however, they plunged. "Once in a while we would break through and push a mile," said Colonel J. Ross Franklin, senior U.S. adviser to the relief force, the 21st ARVN Division. "But the attack was being fought piecemeal ... the good leaders had been killed." The highway was never cleared, and before the battle's end only one regiment managed to push into the city.

Right. *Infantry of the 21st ARVN Division advance near Route 13, the road to An Loc.*

Above. *Sergeant First Class Ronald Macauley, an adviser to the relief force, calls in an air strike about ten kilometers north of Lai Khe.*

## Relief from the air

The unrelieved ARVN force at An Loc held through April only to face renewed enemy attacks in early May. The response: stepped up air attacks by U.S. aircraft, which kept the enemy at bay.

Life inside the city was grim. Colonel Walt Ulmer, senior adviser to the 5th ARVN Division when it defended An Loc, remembers: "It was indescribable: People of all ages inadequately nourished, wounded, crying. They were all over the city way down in the cellars and the bottom of houses."

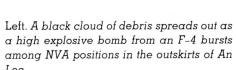

Left. *A black cloud of debris spreads out as a high explosive bomb from an F-4 bursts among NVA positions in the outskirts of An Loc.*

Above. *Soldiers of the 21st ARVN Division watch a "ripple" of bombs dropped by a B-52 strike along Route 13 in support of the troops' advance.*

## The battle's flotsam

An Loc's determined defenders, propped up by their U.S. advisers, persevered, despite facing for the first time the NVA's sophisticated Soviet weaponry. An Loc's narrow streets had become a death trap for the North Vietnamese, inexperienced in using the new tanks and self-propelled artillery. A regimental adviser to the 5th ARVN, Lieutenant Colonel Edward Benedit, recalls: "The tanks came in like they owned the world. The commanders were hanging out of the command cupolas. . . . But the NVA sending in the armor without infantry support gave the [South] Vietnamese the opportunity to kill the tanks with their LAWs."

Above. *Children investigate the wreckage of a Russian-made T-54 tank, one of a string that was destroyed along this narrow street.*

Right. *The NVA offensive out of Cambodia was stopped at An Loc, but the city was left in rubble.*

# Counterattack

In the warm darkness of a spring evening along the Potomac, three men sat around the wardroom table of the presidential yacht *Sequoia*, tied up in the Washington Navy Yard only a dozen blocks from the Capitol dome. Henry Kissinger, just returned from Paris, told his aide Alexander Haig and President Nixon of his meeting with Le Duc Tho earlier in the day. After learning of the North Vietnamese representative's hauteur and intransigence stemming from the Communist military victories, they agreed that a major military move was called for if they were to force the DRV to negotiate. Kissinger advocated delivering a "shock" that would shatter North Vietnamese confidence and rally the South Vietnamese. Nixon agreed. He had earlier declared: "The bastards have never been bombed like they're going to be bombed this time."

It was not believed wise at that time to step up B-52 bombing raids on Hanoi and Haiphong.

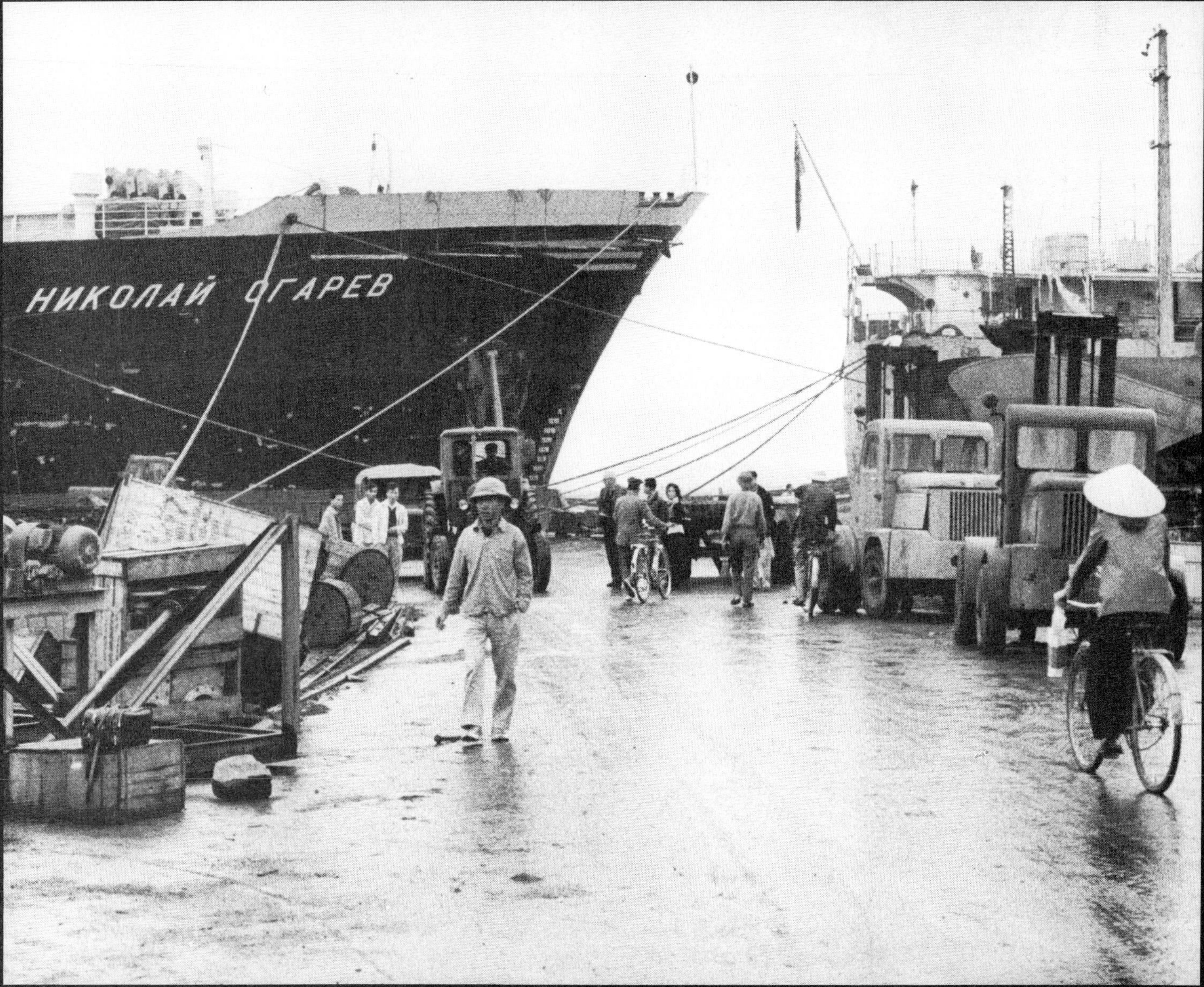
НИКОЛАЙ ОГАРЕВ

General Abrams insisted that he needed all available B-52s to hammer the NVA forces then attacking in the South. Kissinger and Haig reached instead for the updated version of "Duck Hook," the plan for mining North Vietnam's major harbors to cut off shipments of supplies. Kissinger's analysts estimated that Hanoi had received 2.1 million tons of supplies and all its oil through Haiphong Harbor in preparation for the Easter offensive. The two railroads and eight highways linking North Vietnam with China and the Soviet Union carried only one-seventh of the total tonnage entering the DRV.

At shortly after 2:00 P.M. on Monday, May 8, President Nixon asked Kissinger to go over the pros and cons of the mining raid, then signed the order to proceed. That evening, Nixon briefed Congressional leaders before making a 9:00 P.M. radio and television speech announcing the mining. He told the nation that the only way to stop the killing was "to keep the weapons of war out of the hands of the international outlaws of North Vietnam."

As he spoke, jets were already launched from the deck of the U.S.S. *Coral Sea*, which was steaming with a large task force of U.S. cruisers and destroyers in the Gulf of Tonkin close to the coast of North Vietnam. Nine A-6 Intruders and A-7 Corsair IIs, loaded with four 2,000-pound mines each, catapulted from the deck of the aircraft carrier for a twenty-minute trip to the 200-foot-wide, twelve-mile-long channel connecting the port facilities of Haiphong to the deep water of the Gulf of Tonkin.

Commander Roger Sheets led the nine crews, all picked from among the best fliers in the *Coral Sea*'s three attack squadrons. Flying in radio silence and with radar off, the aircraft slipped over the waves at a height of no more than fifty feet to avoid detection by coastal radar. As they neared land, the pilots tensed in expectation of fierce enemy opposition; they knew the Joint Chiefs of Staff had predicted that three of the planes would probably be lost to enemy fire. The planes' 8,000-pound payloads took away some of their maneuverability, making them vulnerable to North Vietnamese fighters and antiaircraft guns.

As the low-flying U.S. aircraft swept toward the target, the cruiser U.S.S. *Chicago*'s radar spotted a flight of four Migs at high altitudes coming toward the fleet from airfields near Hanoi. The ship fired a salvo of long-range Talos antiaircraft missiles. One missile destroyed the lead Mig and drove the other three back toward Hanoi. Any pretense of surprise was now past. Arriving over the coast, the American aircraft split into two groups and climbed to 350 feet for their mining runs. Enemy antiaircraft batteries along the shore now began to seek out the intruders. The first wave of three marine A-6s flew straight down the channel and dropped mines. A few seconds later six navy A-7s, having moved away, banked back toward the wa-

terway and arrived on a cross-channel course to deliver their mines. The crossing pattern, flown through heavy enemy fire, guaranteed that the mines were broadly distributed across the channel leaving no gaps through which a ship might maneuver. The first mine splashed into the water at 8:59 A.M., May 9—one minute before President Nixon took to the airwaves half a world away—and the last followed two minutes later. Thirty-six were planted in 120 seconds. No U.S. aircraft was hit.

The thirty-six mines that blocked entry to Haiphong Harbor were a mix of one-ton Mark-52s and Mark-55s, which resemble giant milk cans: nine feet in length and one-and-a-half feet in diameter. The mines dropped in Haiphong's ship channel were slowed in their descent by small parachutes that kept the weapon from burying itself too deeply in the floor of the channel. These sophisticated weapons contained sensors that monitored a variety of underwater signals such as a ship's magnetic field, the noise of its engines and propellers, and decreased water pressure from a ship's passage. The proper mix of signals would trigger an explosion powerful enough to rip open the hull of any cargo ship.

Vice Admiral William Mack, commander of the U.S. 7th Fleet, thought that even one of these mines might have served the purpose since the North Vietnamese had no mine sweepers to clear the channel. "The threat," he later said, "was what stopped the ships from going out through the field, not the number of mines." At Haiphong, twenty-seven ships were bottled up. For the next three days U.S. Navy aircraft mined the ports of Thanh Hoa, Phuc Loi, Quang Khe, and Dong Hoi, in addition to several inland waterways, with a total nearing 11,000 smaller 500-pound Mark-82 destructors (a cross between a bomb and a mine). The bombs' and mines' internal controls were set to deactivate their explosives in 100 days. Until then craft in those waters ran the risk of being blown up.

## Silence from Moscow

As Nixon and Kissinger planned the mining, one thought had gnawed at them. Would the mining blockade push the Soviets into canceling the May summit with the U.S.? If so, the work of the last few years, the effort to build rapprochement, might be wasted. The president's first impulse was to cancel the summit himself and avoid the embarrassment of having the Russians do so. "The summit isn't worth a damn if the price for it is losing Vietnam," Nixon said to his advisers. "My instinct tells me that the country can take losing the summit, but it can't take losing the war."

A few hours before the president's speech announcing the raid on Haiphong, Henry Kissinger had met with the Soviet ambassador to the U.S., Anatoly Dobrynin, and had given him a letter for Soviet leader Leonid Brezhnev. It outlined the measures the president planned to take but

Preceding page. *The Soviet freighter* Nikolai Ogarev *looms over a dock at Haiphong, North Vietnam's busiest port.*

In a U.S. reconnaissance picture, three supply-laden ships crowd the piers along Haiphong's waterfront in August 1968. U.S. mining halted sea traffic to the port in May 1972.

made clear his willingness to proceed with a summit meeting. Dobrynin, gloomy about the news, predicted that Moscow's reaction to the mining would be drastic. He envisioned, Kissinger recalled, that U.S.–Soviet relations "were likely to be in for a long chilly period."

But Kissinger had carefully prepared the ground for this eventuality when he recruited the Russians to act as go-between for the U.S. and North Vietnam and made the Soviets party to his offers of peace for Indochina. At the same time he had whetted their appetite for the political and commercial benefits of détente. On reflection, Nixon and Kissinger were convinced that the Russians would go to great lengths to make sure the summit went off as scheduled. They decided to wait for the Russians to act.

In the end, the Soviets did nothing. As Hanoi ranted in its press about the "insolent challenge" presented by the mining blockade and demanded increased support from its Communist arms suppliers, the reaction from Moscow

and Peking was cool. The only Soviet comment on May 9 was a summary of President Nixon's speech by Tass, followed the next day by the text of a brief Soviet note of protest about damage to Soviet ships caused by bombing. The Soviet mine sweeper fleet, more than 350 ships capable of sweeping away the American mines, did not venture toward North Vietnamese waters. The Chinese also did nothing to reverse their new relationship with the U.S., although the government issued a statement conveying "utmost indignation" over the blockade and "strongly" condemned the American escalation of the war. As Kissinger later wrote: "Peking's priority was not the war on its southern border, but its relationship with us."

Bitterly, North Vietnam's Lao Dong party newspaper *Nhan Dan* characterized the summits as "throwing life preservers to a drowning pirate." In any event, Washington interpreted the mild response of China and the Soviet Union to the mining as proof that its gambit had worked;

## In Search of Détente

Above. President Nixon cajoles a smile from a small girl holding the hand of Chinese Prime Minister Chou En-lai during his visit to China in February 1972.

Left. Nixon and Leonid Brezhnev, the Soviet Communist party leader, toast each other at the end of their summit meeting in Moscow in May 1972.

The ice breaks. For the first time, an American president visits the Forbidden City in Peking.

the lack of reaction was tantamount to approval from the two big Communist powers. The U.S. could react as it pleased to Hanoi.

Early in May, while the South Vietnamese of I Corps dug into their tenuous defensive line along the My Chanh River, Lieutenant General Ngo Quang Truong, a short, slim, ramrod-straight man with knifelike creases in his olive drab fatigues, listened to the voice coming from the telephone in his Mekong Delta headquarters at Can Tho. The speaker, South Vietnamese President Thieu, was ordering him to take command of I Corps after General Lam's debacle with the 3d Division. It came as no surprise to Truong, who had served under Lam as commander of the 1st Division. He had no confidence in the ability of Lam or his staff to maneuver or inspire large forces in combat. Truong, with very little enemy activity in MR 4 to occupy him, had followed the events in MR 1 from the start of the Easter offensive. As the situation soured he anticipated Thieu's call. In fact, he wrote, "I had already selected the staff I would take with me when the President told me of his decision." That afternoon, May 3, he flew to Hue and immediately began to reorganize the shambles left by the departing Lam and to plan a counterattack by South Vietnamese ground forces.

As the first step, Truong had to throw the NVA off balance and break its pattern of dictating the direction and pace of the fighting. Truong intended to hold the line of firebases west of Hue with the 1st Division while the bulk of the available air support, materiel, and troops moved north to retake the lost province of Quang Tri. To bolster his forces, Truong was given two brigades of the reserve Airborne Division. They were refitting in Saigon after fights along Rocket Ridge near Dak To and at An Loc, where they had attempted to lift the siege. While waiting for the Airborne to complete the transfer, Truong threw two of his three marine brigades into a series of attacks that caught the victory-flushed NVA flat-footed.

## Counterattack

Using American-piloted helicopters and landing craft belonging to the U.S. fleet stationed in the South China Sea, the South Vietnamese Marines raided behind enemy lines twice in May. The first attack on May 13 employed helicopters to land two battalions of marines six kilometers north of the My Chanh River (see map, page 181). The second, on May 24, was even more ambitious, with one battalion assaulting from naval landing craft on "Wunder Beach," fourteen kilometers due east of Quang Tri, as another battalion landed by helicopter behind the beach. At-

At FSB Birmingham. Howitzers of the 54th ARVN Regiment blast away at NVA units in early May 1972. Inset. Later that month, soldiers of the 1st ARVN Division prepare for the June counterattack.

tacking through the NVA's rear areas, they fought their way back to the allied lines. On the way the marines disrupted delivery of supplies, terrorized rear echelon units, and attacked the NVA front lines from the rear.

For once the South's efforts were also blessed with perfect weather that permitted air support. U.S. tactical aircraft started a "gun hunt" program to find and destroy enemy artillery and simultaneously begin striking at NVA troops and vehicle movement on the roads to the north. In one convoy the allied air force destroyed more than 100 trucks stranded between two destroyed bridges. When the Communists switched to moving their tanks along the beach, the air force followed them. Daytime movement carried a death warrant for the NVA vehicles.

In mid–June, Truong's troops and supplies were assembled, and he presented MACV and the JGS with a plan for a two–division counterattack along Route 1 and past Quang Tri City to the Cua Viet River. After a day or two of rumination, the plan was rejected by both commands as overly ambitious and premature. Discouraged, Truong folded his maps and flew back to Hue. Through the night he pondered his problem and the next morning sent a message to Saigon indicating that he would prepare no more plans. If the president or the JGS wanted any military activity in I Corps, they, or MACV, must do the plan-

ning and send a copy in Vietnamese to Truong. The general's fit of pique worked. Thieu, conciliatory to his best fighting general, called Truong back to Saigon, and after a brief discussion he recanted and endorsed the counterattack plan. Truong left Saigon with approval for a plan called Lam Son 72, directed at the recapture of eastern Quang Tri Province.

The operation began with an attack by the 1st Division to the west of Hue—an attempt to draw NVA attention away from Quang Tri Province—and two seaborne feints along the coast north of the Cua Viet River. There followed a nighttime attack on June 27 and 28 by the Airborne Division, which, after a stealthy approach across the My Chanh River, pounced on unsuspecting NVA soldiers snug in their bunkers on the north side of the river. The NVA defensive line quickly cracked. Simultaneously, helicopter assaults put four ARVN and marine battalions in the NVA rear to occupy river crossings and prevent reinforcements from reaching the front. With opposing troops running through their rear areas and artillery positions, sitting astride their supply lines, and shoving past prepared defenses, the North Vietnamese soldiers broke and ran for a new line of defense. Audacity and surprise had for once become a weapon of the ARVN, and for the first time the NVA suffered from the weaknesses that can beset a conventional army. The primitive supply system, light arms, and fast movement that made the NVA and VC almost impossible to trap in the past had been replaced by the vulnerable logistics of a mechanized army. Instead of slipping away into the jungles or mountains, the NVA had to retreat to a new line of defense that would protect the life lines of supplies and troops that stretched all the way back to North Vietnam. They fell back, and before the week passed a new defensive line formed around Quang Tri City and the Thach Han River, territory the South Vietnamese had lost two months before.

## Rats were fat from the carrion

A number of the Americans who had survived the ordeal of An Loc with the paratroopers joined them in the overland assault to recapture Quang Tri Province. Colonel Art Taylor recalled that the attack moved so fast that it overran some of the NVA artillery positions. Major John How-

ard noted that the paratroopers covered most of the twenty kilometers between the My Chanh and Thach Han rivers and arrived on the outskirts of Quang Tri "within three or four days." The satisfaction of recapturing their own territory with only light battle casualties was tempered by the scenes of destruction they passed on Route 1. As the soldiers marched north along the highway, they had to pick their way through the horrific remnants left from the headlong ARVN retreat in May. The NVA had cleared a path through the detritus to move its own columns but did not remove or bury the thousands of civilian and military victims. Now, at the end of June, the southern soldiers passed rows of burned and mangled vehicles. At first the passing soldiers barely noticed small bundles of rags lying in the carnage that seemed to flap and move. Animals were picking over the tatters of clothing, feeding on the remains of the refugees from Quang Tri. "The rats were fat from eating the carrion in the fields," remarked Captain Jim Butler, a member of the Airborne advisory

*Above and right. Death and destruction litter Highway 1 south of Quang Tri City in late June. The carnage was discovered by South Vietnamese soldiers counterattacking to seize Quang Tri from the Communists.*

team. The men passed knocked out tanks serving as tombs for their crews, ambulances with the long-dead occupants still inside on litters, and seemingly endless numbers of desiccated, disfigured bodies. "As far as you could see there was the litter of war," Major Howard said. "The ARVN and civilians had got on the road and bunched up." The scene of the disaster stretched on for some ten kilometers. Retreating NVA piled more onto the carnage of May as they abandoned large quantities of ammunition, small arms, crew-served weapons, and even tanks and APCs so new that the leather on the seats was not yet stained from the sweat of their occupants.

Through the first week of July, the South's counter-offensive had been well executed, but upon reaching the outskirts of Quang Tri the Airborne troops in the vanguard of the attack stopped. It is a maxim of war that once an enemy is routed the aggressor pursues him, allowing no opportunity for reorganization; the enemy must be destroyed in small groups before he can rally. Ignoring this

imperative, Truong allowed the senior officers in the Airborne Division to give their troops a few days to rest, resupply, and celebrate their victory. Given such a respite, the NVA was able to reform its units and man the formidable defenses of Quang Tri City.

Quang Tri, a small city of 15,000, was arrayed around its central citadel—a miniature of the great fortress at Hue from within which besieged NVA troops had carried on a month-long fight against the U.S. Marines during the Tet offensive (see chapter three of *Nineteen Sixty-Eight*, another volume in THE VIETNAM EXPERIENCE). With its thick stone walls, ramparts, and wide moat it might have looked familiar to a crusader of the Middle Ages, even though it was built in the nineteenth century. The NVA had used the two months since it captured the city to weave a system of bunkers and strong points around this defensive centerpiece. Interlocking fields of fire for machine guns, mortars, and artillery covered the Airborne and Marine troops' avenues of attack. As the lead ARVN troops ap-

proached the Thach Han River, which wound around Quang Tri, the North Vietnamese, regrouped and dug into the defenses of the city, opened fire.

Initially the city of Quang Tri itself had not been a primary target of the counterattack. Truong had envisioned sweeping past the city to the banks of the Cua Viet. After the NVA forces in the open ground around the city of Quang Tri had been destroyed or pushed to the North and the Communist reinforcements and supply lines to the citadel cut, whatever NVA defenders remained in the city could be starved out or captured at a cautious pace by the surrounding South Vietnamese force.

## A symbol and a challenge

At this crucial moment politics intruded on the battlefield. As he had with the village of Tchepone during Operation Lam Son 719, President Thieu made Quang Tri into a symbol. "Thieu demanded the city be seized," said I Corps's new senior adviser, Major General Howard H. Cooksey. "The city, which was to be by-passed, suddenly became an emotionally inspired, national objective." Truong obviously preferred a different method of continuing the attack. "Although it had not been a primary objective, Quang Tri City had become a symbol and a major challenge," General Truong noted. "Pushed by public opinion on one side and faced with the enemy's determination to hold the city on the other, I was hard-pressed to seek a satisfactory way out."

Truong bent to Thieu's pressures and thereby compounded his error in allowing the troops a rest period before continuing the counteroffensive. If Truong's men had continued the assault to the open country in the north, the loss of momentum would probably have had small effect on his corps's progress. But with the city as the primary target, each day's delay gave the NVA more time to improve its defenses in the city. The South Vietnamese held only two sides of the city; through the other two sides, the NVA continued to move in supplies and reinforcements from the north. Regimental commanders of the 320B NVA Division even made plans to rotate their units in defense of the city. The citadel was not the only obstacle. The suburbs, honeycombed with bunkers, trenches, and observation posts, threatened a bloody prelude to any final assault on the fortress. NVA artillery observers called down mortar and 130MM howitzer fire on the advancing paratroopers. Counting their progress house by house, the South Vietnamese battled toward the center of the town through an uninterrupted barrage.

In Hue's ancient citadel, the South Vietnamese and American officers set up their headquarters to organize the fight for MR 1. Within the walls of the fortress, Truong had established his forward command post and the inner city teemed with the camouflaged fatigues and the brightly colored shoulder patches and neckerchiefs that identified Marine, Ranger, Airborne, and 1st Division troops. Hammocks hung between ancient brass cannons that once guarded the royalty of Annam, and officers hurried through the halls of the sacred temple that was once the inviolate home of the Sacred Virgins.

## Isolating Quang Tri

U.S. Marine Corps Major Emmett Huff, who had survived the retreat and counteroffensive with the Vietnamese Marines, was in Hue to plan yet another behind-the-enemy-lines attack, this time north and east of Quang Tri City. If successful, the raid would cut the remaining road into the city and force the NVA to cross the Thach Han River to enter Quang Tri, a difficult task even without having to reckon with the bombing of the South Vietnamese air force. Huff had been called on to brief a group of U.S. Marine Corps pilots stationed aboard ships offshore who were to fly the troop-carrying CH-53 and CH-46 helicopters in the raid. But as he talked to the young fliers he became uneasy. Instead of the seasoned veterans he expected, Huff found that 90 percent of the airmen had never flown in combat before. In the short time available, the major tried to pass on what he had learned in three Vietnam tours about staying alive in the situation they faced. Behind enemy lines they must stay below fifty feet and fly between the sand dunes and trees to shield their aircraft from small-arms fire and antiaircraft missiles; they must never lose sight of the U.S. Army Air Cavalry Cobra gunships assigned to lead them to landing zones. Although the pilots listened intently, Major Huff worried about the evident overconfidence of some of the pilots as he left the briefing room.

At dawn on July 11, the sun at their backs, the U.S. helicopters flew with their loads of Vietnamese Marines into the territory behind enemy lines after two B-52 strikes had prepared the way. Riding back in the long column of helicopters that snaked between the low hills, Huff's fears for the inexperienced fliers were realized when he saw one of the CH-53 Jolly Green Giants drift back from the army helicopter that was leading it. To Huff's horror the young pilot rose above the trees, evidently to look around for the lead ship. At once a small black missile, one of the Russian-built, shoulder-fired SA-7 Strelas, homed in on the helicopter's exhaust, exploding as it made contact with the helicopter. Shrapnel from the surface-to-air missile riddled the engine and the chopper lost power. "At first he kept it level and I thought he was going to make it," Huff said, "but as he neared the trees he let the tail drop." The craft crashed into the ground, tail first. The impact crushed the cargo door shut, trapping forty Vietnamese and two U.S. Marines inside. The fuel lines ruptured and ignited, turning the helicopter into a torch. Only the pilot and co-pilot escaped. The CH-53 was the first U.S. Marine aircraft shot down by North Vietnam's new weapon.

*House-to-house in Quang Tri. During the ARVN drive to retake Quang Tri City in July, a paratrooper dashes toward a building as his buddies cover him.*

Flying around the black plume of smoke from the wreckage, the remaining helicopters of the attack force landed their cargo of marines. From the landing zone, two kilometers north of Quang Tri, the battalion of infantrymen attacked a complex of trenches occupied by the 48th Regiment of the NVA 320B Division. For three days the fight went on, the Communists counterattacking with tanks. But on the fourteenth day of July, with their main line broken and marines moving behind them, the NVA forces began to break up and withdraw. The South Vietnamese now occupied three sides of Quang Tri and had cut the last road to the north.

After the marines' success, the Airborne Division planned its own assault. Having fought through the suburbs, the paratroopers were within 100 meters of the walls of Quang Tri's citadel. U.S. aircraft opened the way for the infantry by punching a breech in the northeast face of the thick wall with laser-guided bombs. Attacking at dusk on July 23, three companies of the 5th Airborne Battalion, per-

haps 500 men, crossed the moat and pressed through the hole. Fighting aggressively, the men of the 51st, 52d, and 53d Companies quickly gained the enemy positions. Then poor coordination between the Vietnamese army and air force produced a disaster. An after-dark air strike meant for the NVA rolled in over the paratroopers. The planes dropped three 500-pound bombs on the friendly troops now in the NVA positions, killing forty-five soldiers and wounding a score of others. The attack came to a halt. Stunned survivors of the chopped-up Airborne force fell back before NVA fire, and by morning the Communists had regained control of the citadel. The 5th Battalion's foray had been costly. That night's casualties to the Airborne Division, coupled with previous losses suffered in the fight for the city, finished the ability of the division to continue the attack.

Worried about the state of the Airborne Division and his long, exposed western flank—behind which lurked the portions of North Vietnam's 304th, 308th, 325th, 320B, and

*The NVA occupation of Quang Tri almost at an end, South Vietnamese Marines rush toward a pocket of Communist resistance. Their cover is a military truck wrecked during the NVA's assault of the city four months earlier. The map at right gives an overview of the South Vietnamese counterattack.*

312th Divisions not engaged around Quang Tri—Truong decided to change the assignments of the units in his command. Rangers were moved into the marine positions, the marines took on the assault of the city, and the paratroopers retired to form a line on the west. The general also decided to use the full support of U.S. air power. American air had been used sparingly because Thieu had wanted the recapture of the city to be chiefly a Vietnamese affair. Now that both sides had concentrated their forces at Quang Tri City, Thieu lifted his ban and gave Truong an "opportunity to accomplish my mission employing the superior firepower of our American ally."

On September 9 the ARVN command concentrated its forces for an assault on the citadel. Five battalions of marines from the 147th and 258th Brigades attacked from three sides behind tactical air and B–52 bombings. During the night and early morning of the eleventh, a platoon of the 6th Battalion scrambled over the southern corner of the citadel's wall. After the platoon gained the interior, more

of the battalion followed to establish a foothold inside the fortress. As the air strikes and artillery continued to pound the 500-meter-square citadel, at dawn on the fifteenth the 3d Battalion carried its attack over the eastern corner of the wall. Throughout the early part of the day, the two battalions fought toward each other down the length of the southeast wall. After linking up, the forces turned and attacked across the fortress, killing or capturing its last defenders by 5:00 P.M. The South Vietnamese flag was raised over the citadel at noon on the sixteenth, and the capture of the rest of the city was completed the next day. In the final weeks of the fight, one of every five of the 8,000 South Vietnamese Marines had been killed or wounded in their relentless attack.

With the recapture of the citadel, the South Vietnamese counterattack came to a halt. The South Vietnamese continued minor attacks to protect their flanks and destroy small units of NVA, but the battle lines became the effective boundaries of occupation for the two armies. Both the

## Counterattack on Quang Tri

The recapture of Quang Tri Province began on May 13 when South Vietnamese Marines carried out a series of behind-the-lines raids around Wunder Beach. South Vietnamese forces then began a series of attacks *(below right)* intended first to recapture territory up to Phase Line Gold, then Brown, and finally Blue. The attacks moved quickly until they reached Quang Tri City, which President Thieu had made the new objective of the counterattack, rather than all of Quang Tri Province. Four months after the attack began, Quang Tri City was again in ARVN hands, but the offensive had fallen short of its original objectives.

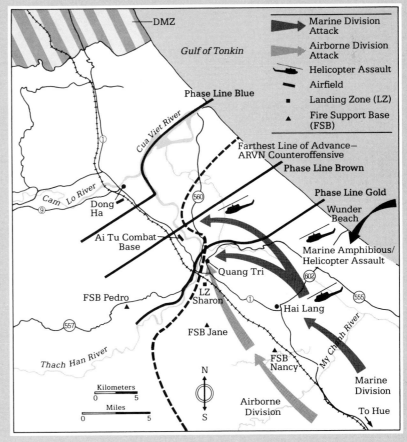

*Originally an all-Vietnamese operation, the counterattack on Quang Tri produced such heavy casualties that U.S. strikes were called in. Here a bomb from an F-4 Phantom bursts on an NVA position 1,000 yards ahead of advancing ARVN troops.*

North and South Vietnamese armies, Major Howard said, were like "two fighters in the 14th or 15th round; they could hardly do anything but hold on to each other." North Vietnam's bold Easter offensive into the South was over. The rumble of war gave way to a rumor of peace.

# A grim conclusion

At An Loc, Kontum, and Quang Tri the attacks and counterattacks had sputtered to an end. With the exception of the capture of the citadel at Quang Tri there were no epic final battles. Each side had fought with diminishing vigor and resources until neither was capable of budging the other.

After the firing stopped, two high-ranking North Vietnamese, To Huu, a member of the Central Committee, and army Chief of Staff General Van Tien Dung, inspected the areas of South Vietnam held by the North, about 10 percent of the country. At the end of the tour the pair met with officers of COSVN, whose headquarters were now in northern Tay Ninh Province not far from the battlefield at An Loc where the Communist 5th, 7th, and 9th Divisions had bled so heavily. Their conclusions were grim. The outlook for a quick end to the war was gone, Huu told the COSVN assembly, and because of heavy losses and the budding détente between the U.S., the Soviet Union, and China, there could be no new large-scale offensive for another three to five years.

Hanoi had severely miscalculated both the fighting ability of the South Vietnamese army and the strength of the American response. The North Vietnamese had committed more than 200,000 men to the attack, but their attempt to use this mass to destroy South Vietnam's forces had proven disastrous because of the terrible toll exacted by U.S. air power. Deaths among the invaders and their southern supporters were estimated by one military historian to be more than 100,000. NVA commanders had thrown away their numerical superiority by making repeated frontal assaults into heavy defensive fire that caused massive casualties and tilted the manpower balance in favor of the RVNAF.

The North had gained enough territory—half of the four northermost provinces of Quang Tri, Thua Thien, Quang Nam, and Quang Tin, as well as the western border fringes of MR 2 and 3—to provide ample supply corridors from Laos and Cambodia into the A Shau Valley, the highlands, and the fringes of the Mekong Delta. But by their own account the holdings amounted to little more than "rubber trees and bricks"—jungle and a few small, heavily damaged towns.

Moreover, their allies had disappointed them. Contrary to Hanoi's hopes, the American bombing and mining did nothing to slow the thaw in U.S.-Chinese relations nor did it keep the Moscow summit from proceeding on schedule. Privately, during that meeting the Russians told Nixon they

felt the North Vietnamese had bungled the offensive and that they were furious at the tactical misuse to which Hanoi had put the Russian-supplied tanks. They affected to be fed up with the North's strategy and questioned Giap's reputation as a military genius.

But Hanoi's discouraged mood did not mean the leadership had ceased to anticipate victory and work toward it. They put their minor gains to good use. Logisticians set thousands of workers to improving the roads in Laos and Cambodia. The improvements were so effective that reinforcements were soon able to move from bases in North Vietnam to the Saigon area in less than twenty-five days. The NVA rapidly expanded port facilities in the small, newly captured river town of Dong Ha just below the DMZ, and within a year over 20 percent of the war materiel destined for the front lines flowed across its docks. As the year ended, Vietnamese Marines would still be trying to capture the banks of the Cua Viet River in order to stop this ship-borne traffic.

In the meantime, the negotiating conditions that followed the Easter offensive were, if not perfect, at least some of what the North wanted. Even as the leadership in Hanoi had planned the Easter offensive, it anticipated there would be negotiations when the fighting was over. Early in the fighting Hanoi had prepared a list of acceptable conditions for an end to fighting with the U.S.: a continuation of the war without American troops, the replacement of President Thieu with a coalition government, or, less attractive, an agreement that allowed Thieu to remain in power but that recognized the PRG as a legitimate and equal political force in the South. But by battle's end, Hanoi's assault had not forced the U.S. into accepting a coalition government or eliminating Thieu. The North Vietnamese, battered by the bombing and crippled by the mining, were also aware that Nixon might prove much more difficult to bargain with after his nearly certain election victory over George McGovern in November. They therefore decided to work toward a negotiated settlement in 1972 even if they had to settle for an agreement that merely recognized the PRG as a political reality in the South. A North Vietnamese spokesman later explained that Hanoi expected to end the war "even if there was a compromise, but a compromise which permits us to take a step forward."

In fact, the concessions they wanted, with the exception of a replacement for Thieu, had been unofficially offered through America's Russian emissaries. Implicit in what Kissinger was offering were a cease-fire in place, recognition of the PRG by Saigon, acceptance of the North Vietnamese presence in the South, and American withdrawal. They would be enough to meet the minimum criteria for "victory" that North Vietnam's leaders had established before the offensive.

Why then did Hanoi not seize on Kissinger's offerings and proceed toward a settlement? Two obstacles still remained. One, of course, was that Nixon and Kissinger could not at that time be sure of delivering President Thieu's and his government's assent to such a settlement. Another was the fact that Hanoi still believed that time was on its side. If their offensive, at the cost of tens of thousands of North Vietnamese soldiers, had failed to produce spectacular results, Hanoi at least had learned much about conducting mechanized warfare. If they were patient, perhaps in their next big battle they would be facing only one foe instead of two.

## A tough decision

For the South Vietnamese, the results were also equivocal. The offensive gave the government opportunities to replace many poor military leaders with young, battle-tested soldiers. One of them, General Truong, had led his outnumbered units on to recapture Quang Tri, thereby reversing a rout and gaining a measure of respect for the South Vietnamese armed forces and also for the prospects of Vietnamization. Few would have believed in May that the South Vietnamese, with only three divisions against six, could have recaptured Quang Tri. As ARVN Captain Do Cuong observed, "After this battle, we became masters of the situation again. The morale of all the soldiers seemed to be high. We seemed to be confident in the fighting ability of the South Vietnamese armed forces—and in our own unit. We thought that . . . we could defend a free South Vietnam by ourselves."

Although morale may have been high, other problems abounded for the South Vietnamese military. Air force helicopter units did not respond to army needs, refusing to fly certain missions and on occasion leaving ground units in jeopardy. The air transport fleet was sufficient only for emergency resupply missions. Artillery tended to substitute massive, undirected barrages for carefully placed, well-timed fire. Communications, security, and intelligence were poor. It was also apparent that the South Vietnamese supply system was not going to function once the U.S. stopped supporting it. The U.S. had either to repair much of the Vietnamese military equipment at American bases in the western Pacific, such as Okinawa, or arrange to have it done by civilian companies in Taiwan or Singapore. There was simply no way the South Vietnamese could afford to duplicate this expensive process, and there were no facilities for sophisticated repairs available to ARVN within Vietnam.

Also, South Vietnam was running out of men. The general reserves, men of the Airborne and Marine divisions, were too few. The offensive proved there were not enough forces to meet emergencies on three widely separated battlefields. Despite the general mobilization of South Vietnamese males, the pool of draft-age men was drying up. Even though South Vietnamese losses—perhaps 30,000 dead—were only one-third that of the NVA, the nation was unable to replace all of the men it lost in 1972. Just as important, the constant losses of the better officers and NCOs produced a new leadership crisis. This problem was compounded by the tendency of ARVN officers, particularly in the senior ranks, to keep authority to themselves. Often they would not delegate command to their assistants. If the commander was then wounded or killed, it was difficult for a subordinate to step in and fill the role of leader.

The final inescapable truth to emerge from the offensive was that ARVN soldiers and their U.S. advisers could neither stop the enemy without significant American air support nor could the counteroffensive have succeeded without it. "Anyone who disputes this," said I Corps senior adviser Maj. Gen. Howard Cooksey, "just does not have the facts." British adviser Sir Robert Thompson agreed: "It is untrue to say that the battles were won solely by American air power, it would be true to say they could not have been won without it."

That put the whole disengagement process at an awkward tilt. As General Cooksey pointed out in surveying the results of the offensive, if the North Vietnamese renewed hostilities on a scale of the 1972 invasion, "the U.S. will be confronted with a tough decision." Would Washington be willing or able to commit the nation's strength on such a scale once again? It was obvious to Cooksey such intervention would be necessary for the survival of South Vietnam. He stated in a MACV after action report, "I am convinced that in northern Military Region 1, U.S. air support would be required to withstand an assault by the forces available to the enemy in that area." This meant defeat of the 1972 NVA offensive was not a definitive test of Vietnamization. The South Vietnamese had to stand alone before the results would be conclusive.

That time was coming, made inevitable by the United States' Vietnamization policy. The man responsible for presiding over that complex program—building up Vietnam's military and political capabilities and successfully holding back the North's forces, while at the same time steadily withdrawing American resources from Vietnam—held few illusions about what would happen with South Vietnam on its own. Lieutenant Colonel Donald Marshall, who had worked under General Abrams for a long time, recalled the frustration mounting in Abrams as he watched events proceed. It was wrenching, he said, to have Abrams "look at you and say, 'By God, I hate to lose!' and you would deduce from that he knew the direction things were going."

*A victory and an uncertain future. A young South Vietnamese Marine brandishes a captured AK47 from atop the ruins of the Quang Tri Citadel, which was finally retaken in mid–September to mark the end of the Communists' Easter invasion.*

# Bibliography

## I. Books and Articles

"Air Support Not Reduced in Speeded 'Nam' Pullout." *Air Force Times*, December 1, 1971.

Bamford, James. *The Puzzle Palace.* Penguin, 1983.

Battreall, Col. Raymond R., Jr. "Ky Binh Viet Nam–Muon Nam." *Armor* (July–August 1974).

Berger, Carl, ed. *The United States Air Force in Southeast Asia, 1961–1973.* Office of Air Force History, 1977.

Bonds, Ray, ed. *The Vietnam War.* Crown, 1979.

———. *Weapons of the Modern Soviet Ground Forces.* ARCO, 1981.

Boyle, Richard. *The Flower of the Dragon.* Ramparts Pr., 1972.

Bradford, Lt. Col. Zeb B. "U.S. Tactics in Vietnam." *Military Review* (February 1972).

Buckley, Tom. "The ARVN Is Bigger And Better, But–." *New York Times Magazine,* October 12, 1969.

Candlin, A.H.S. "The Spring Offensive in Vietnam." *The Army Quarterly and Defense Journal* (July 1972).

Chen, King C. "Hanoi vs. Peking: Policies and Relations—A Survey." *Asian Survey* 12(1972).

Critchfield, Richard. "Impact in Hanoi." *The Nation,* August 16, 1971.

Dawkins, Peter M. "The United States Army and the 'Other' War in Vietnam." Diss., Princeton University, 1979.

Dommen, Arthur J. "The Future of North Vietnam." *Current History* (April 1970).

Donnell, John C., and Charles Joiner, eds. *Electoral Politics in South Vietnam.* Lexington Bks., 1974.

Dornan, Dr. James E., Jr., and Nigel de Lee. *The Chinese War Machine.* Crown, 1979.

———. *The U.S. War Machine.* Crown, 1978.

Edmonds, Robin. *Soviet Foreign Policy, 1962–1973: The Paradox of Superpower.* Oxford Univ. Pr., 1975.

Ellsberg, Daniel. *Papers on the War.* Simon & Schuster, 1972.

Emerson, Gloria. *Winners and Losers.* Harcourt Brace Jovanovich, 1978.

Frisbee, John L. "The Air War in Vietnam." *Air Force* 55 (September 1972).

*From Khe Sanh to Chepone.* Foreign Languages Publishing House, 1971.

Gabriel, Richard A. "Professionalism Versus Managerialism in Vietnam." *Air Univ. Review* (January–February 1981).

———, and Paul Savage. *Crisis in Command.* Hill & Wang, 1978.

"Gap Cac Si Quan Phan Chien Trung Doan 56." (Meeting with Antiwar Officers of the 56th Regiment.) *Doan Ket,* May 10, 1972.

Goldstein, Joseph, Burke Marshall, and Jack Schwartz, eds. *The My Lai Massacre and Its Cover-up: Beyond the Reach of the Law?* Free Pr., 1976.

Goodman, Allan E. *The Lost Peace: America's Search for a Negotiated Settlement of the Vietnam War.* Hoover Inst. Pr., 1978.

———. "South Vietnam and the New Security." *Asian Survey* 12(1972).

Halberstam, David. *The Best and the Brightest.* Random, 1972.

———. *The Making of a Quagmire.* Random, 1964.

———. "Ugliest American in Vietnam." *Esquire,* November 1964.

Halloran, Bernard F. "Soviet Armor Comes to Vietnam." *Army* (August 1973).

Hauser, Lt. Col. William L. *America's Army in Crisis.* Johns Hopkins Univ. Pr., 1973.

Hays, Col. Samuel H. "The Growing Leadership Crisis." *Army* (February 1970).

Heinl, Robert D., Jr. "The Collapse of the Armed Forces." *Armed Forces Journal* 19 (June 7, 1971).

———. "On Basis of Pacification, Vietnam War Has Been Won." *Armed Forces Journal* (February 1972).

Herring, George C. *America's Longest War.* Wiley, 1979.

Hersh, Seymour. *The Price of Power.* Summit Bks., 1983.

Hodgson, Godfrey. *America in Our Time.* Vintage Bks., 1976.

Holmes, Lt. Col. David R. "Some Tentative Thoughts about Indochina." *Military Review* (August 1977).

Howard, Maj. John. "A Study of U.S. Power." *Army* (September 1975).

———. "They Were Good Ol' Boys." *Air University Review* (January–February 1975).

Hsiao, Gene T., ed. *The Role of External Powers in the Indochina Crisis.* Andronicus Publishing Co., 1973.

Isby, David. *Weapons and Tactics of the Soviet Army.* Janes Publishing Co., 1981.

Just, Ward. *Military Men.* Knopf, 1970.

Kalb, Bernard, and Marvin Kalb. *Kissinger.* Little, Brown, 1974.

Kinnard, Brig. Gen. Douglas. *The Secretary of Defense.* Univ. Pr. of Kentucky, 1980.

———. *The War Managers.* Univ. of New England Pr., 1977.

Kirk, Donald. "How Major Buu of South Vietnam Fights His War." *New York Times Magazine,* August 20, 1972.

Kissinger, Henry. *The White House Years.* Little, Brown, 1979.

Knappman, Edward W. *South Vietnam. U.S.–Communist Confrontation in Southeast Asia.* Vol. 7, *1972–1973.* Facts on File, 1973.

Langguth, A.J. "The Vietnamization of General Di." *New York Times Magazine,* September 6, 1970.

Lewy, Guenter. *America in Vietnam.* Oxford Univ. Pr., 1978.

Linden, Eugene. "Fragging and other Withdrawal Symptoms." *Saturday Review,* January 8, 1972.

Littauer, Raphael, and Norman Uphoff, eds. *The Air War in Indo China.* Beacon Pr., 1972.

Loory, Stuart. *Defeated.* Random, 1973.

Luckow, Ulrik. "Victory Over Ignorance and Fear: The U.S. Minelaying Attack on North Vietnam." *Naval War College Review* (January–February 1982).

Luttwak, Edward. *The Decline of American Military Leadership.* Parameters, 1980.

McCaffrey, Lt. Gen. William J. "Wrapping It Up in South Vietnam." *Army* (October 1972).

McClellan, Maj. Gen. Stan L. "Vietnamization—A Point of View." Paper, no date.

Mack, William P. "As I Recall . . ." *U.S. Naval Institute Proceedings,* August 1980.

Maclear, Michael. *The Ten Thousand Day War.* St. Martin's, 1981.

Marshall, S.L.A. *Bringing Up the Rear.* Presidio Pr., 1979.

Moskin, J. Robert. "The Hard-Line Demand = Victory." *Look,* December 29, 1970.

Moskos, Charles C., Jr. "The American Combat Soldier in Vietnam." *Journal of Social Issues* (1975).

Nihart, Brooke. "Army Reports Helicopter Success in Laos, Air Force Skeptical." *Armed Forces Journal,* April 5, 1971.

Nixon, Richard M. *RN: The Memoirs of Richard Nixon.* Warner Bks., 1978.

Osborne, Arthur M. "Air Defense for the Mining of Haiphong." *U.S. Naval Institute Proceedings* 100 (September 1974).

Palmer, Col. David R. *Summons of the Trumpet.* Presidio Pr., 1978.

Parks, Maj. W. Hayes. "Crimes in Hostilities." *Marine Corps Gazette* 60 (August–September 1976).

Peachey, Lt. Col. William N. Diary, no date.

Peck, Winslow. "U.S. Electronic Espionage: A Memoir." *Ramparts* (August 1972).

Peers, Lt. Gen. W.R. *The My Lai Inquiry.* Norton, 1979.

Phan Thien Chau. "Leadership in the Vietnam Workers Party: The Process of Transition." *Asian Survey* 12 (September 1972).

Pike, Douglas. "North Vietnam in 1971." *Asian Survey* 12 (January 1972).

———. "North Vietnam in the Year 1972." *Asian Survey* 13 (January 1973).

Pimlott, John, ed. *Vietnam: The History and the Tactics.* Crescent Bks., 1982.

Porter, Gareth. *A Peace Denied.* Indiana Univ. Pr., 1975.

———, ed. *Vietnam, A History in Documents.* NAL, 1981.

Powers, Thomas. *The Man Who Kept the Secrets.* Pocket Bks., 1981.

Prosterman, Roy L. "Land Reform as Foreign Aid." *Foreign Policy* (Spring 1972).

Reed, David. "Mission: Mine Haiphong." *Reader's Digest,* February 1973.

———. "Vietnamization, Can It Succeed?" *Reader's Digest,* April 1970.

Safire, William. *Before the Fall: An Inside View of the Pre-Watergate White House.* Doubleday, 1975.

Schell, Jonathan. *The Time of Illusion.* Vintage Bks., 1975.

Serong, Brigadier F.P. "The 1972 Easter Offensive." *Southeast Asia Perspectives* (Summer 1974).

Shaplen, Robert. "Letter from Saigon." *New Yorker,* September 2, 1971.

———. "Letter from Vietnam." *New Yorker,* November 1, 1971.

———. *The Road From War.* Harper & Row, 1970.

Shawcross, William. *Sideshow: Kissinger, Nixon and the Destruction of Cambodia.* Simon & Schuster, 1979.

Shultz, Richard H., Jr., and Richard A. Hunt. *Lessons from an Unconventional War.* Perkamon Pr., 1982.

Simon, Sheldon W. *War and Politics in Cambodia: A Communications Analysis.* Duke Univ. Pr., 1974.

Snepp, Frank. *Decent Interval.* Random, 1977.

Sobel, L.A., ed. *South Vietnam: U.S.–Communist Confrontation in Southeast Asia.* Vol. 5, *1970.* Facts on File, 1970.

Stanton, Shelby L. *Vietnam Order of Battle.* U.S. News Books, 1981.

Stilwell, Lt. Gen. Richard G. "Evolution in Tactics: The Vietnam Experience." *Army* (February 1970).

Sulzberger, C.L. *Postscript with a Chinese Accent.* Macmillan, 1974.

Summers, Harry G., Jr. *On Strategy.* Presidio Pr., 1982.

Sutter, Robert G. *Chinese Foreign Policy after the Cultural Revolution: 1966–1977.* Westview Pr., 1978.

Szulc, Ted. *The Illusion of Peace.* Viking Pr., 1978.

terHorst, J.F. *The Flying White House.* Coward, McCann & Geoghegan, 1979.

Thompson, Sir Robert. *Peace is Not at Hand.* Chatto & Windus, 1974.

Thompson, W. Scott, and Donaldson D. Frizzell, eds. *The Lessons of Vietnam.* Crane, Russak & Co., 1977.

Turley, Lt. Col. Gerald, and Capt. M.R. Wells. "Easter Invasion: 1972." *Marine Corps Gazette* (March 1973).

Turner, Robert F. *Vietnamese Communism: Its Origins and Developments.* Hoover Inst. Pr., 1975.

Ulmer, Col. Walt, Sr. "Notes on Enemy Armor at An Loc." *Armor* (January–February 1973).

Ulsamer, Edgar. "Adding Another Dimension to Airpower." *Air Force* 55(August 1972).

———. "Airpower Halts an Invasion." *Air Force* (September 1972).

Van Dyke, Jon M. *North Vietnam's Strategy for Survival.* Pacific Bks., 1972.

Van Vlest, Clarke. "Year of Action, 1972." *Naval Aviation News* (February 1973).

Walters, Maj. Gen. Vernon A. *Silent Missions.* Doubleday, 1978.

Ward, Ian. "North Vietnam's Blitzkreig." *Conflict Studies* (October 1972).

Weiss, George. "Co 2/17 Air Cav: 'Gunships Took Tanks, Survived Flak' in Laos." *Armed Forces Journal* (April 19, 1971).

Weller, Jac. "RVNAF Training: The Vital Element in Vietnamization." *Military Review* (October 1972).

Westmoreland, Gen. William C. *A Soldier Reports.* Doubleday, 1976.

Zasloff, Joseph J., and Allan E. Goodman, eds. *Indochina in Conflict: A Political Assessment.* Lexington Bks., 1972.

Zorza, Victor. "Is Hanoi Ready To End the Vietnam War?" *Current History* (August 1970).

## II. Government and Government-Sponsored Published Reports

BDM Corporation. *A Study of Strategic Lessons Learned in Vietnam.* Vols. 1–8. National Technical Information Service, 1980.

Gen. Cao Van Vien. *Leadership*. Indochina Monographs, U.S. Army Center of Military History, 1981.

———, and Lt. Gen. Dong Van Khuyen. *Reflections on the Vietnam War*. Indochina Monographs, U.S. Army Center of Military History, 1980.

Cosmas, Graham A. *U.S. Marines in Vietnam 1970–1971*. Draft manuscript. U.S. Marine Corps, Headquarters, History and Museums Division, 1983.

Goodman, Allan E. *An Institutional Profile of the South Vietnamese Officer Corps*. Rand Corporation RM–6189–ARPA, 1970.

Col. Hoang Ngoc Lung. *Intelligence*. Indochina Monographs, U.S. Army Center of Military History, 1983.

Holt, Pat, Richard M. Moose, and James G. Lowenstein. "Laos: April 1971." Report prepared for the Committee on Foreign Relations. U.S. Senate, 92d Congress, 1st sess., 1971.

Hosmer, Stephen T., Konrad Kellen, and Brian M. Jenkins. *The Fall of South Vietnam: Statements by Vietnamese Military and Civilian Leaders*. Rand Corporation R–2208–OSD, December 1978.

Komer, Robert. *Bureaucracy Does Its Thing: Institutional Constraints on U.S.–GVN Performance in Vietnam*. Rand Corporation R–967–ARPA, 1972.

———. *Impact of Pacification on Insurgency in South Vietnam*. Rand Corporation P–4443, 1970.

Kroesen, Maj. Gen. Frederick J. *Selected Readings in Tactics: Quang Tri*. U.S. Army Command and General Staff College, April 1974.

Lavalle, Maj. A.J.C., ed. *Airpower and the 1972 Spring Invasion*. Vol. 2, Monograph 3, USAF Southeast Asia Monograph Series, 1976.

LeGro, Col. William E. *Vietnam from Cease-Fire to Capitulation*. U.S. Army Center of Military History, 1980.

Lowenstein, James G., and Richard M. Moose. "Cambodia: May 1970." Report prepared for the Committee on Foreign Relations. U.S. Senate, 91st Congress, 2d sess., 1970.

Momyer, Gen. William W. *Air Power in Three Wars*. United States Air Force, 1978.

Lt. Gen. Ngo Quang Truong. *The Easter Offensive of 1972*. Indochina Monographs, U.S. Army Center of Military History, 1980.

Maj. Gen. Nguyen Duy Hinh. *Lam Son 719*. Indochina Monographs, U.S. Army Center of Military History, 1979.

———. *Vietnamization and the Cease-Fire*. Indochina Monographs, U.S. Army Center of Military History, 1983.

Simmons, Brig. Gen. Edwin H. "Marine Corps Operations in Vietnam 1969–1972." *Marines in Vietnam, 1954–1973: An Anthology and Annotated Bibliography*. U.S. Marine Corps, History and Museums Division, 1974.

Special National Intelligence Estimate. "The Outlook from Hanoi: Factors Affecting North Vietnam's Policy on the War in Vietnam." No. 14.3–70, Carrollton Pr. Declassified Documents Reference System, February 5, 1970.

Starry, Gen. Donn A. *Mounted Combat in Vietnam*. Department of the Army, Vietnam Studies Series, 1978.

Sutsakhan, Lt. Gen. Sak. *The Khmer Republic at War and the Final Collapse*. Indochina Monographs, U.S. Army Center of Military History, 1980.

Sweetland, Anders. *Rallying Potential Among the North Vietnamese Armed Forces*. Rand Corporation RM–6375–1–ARPA, December 1970.

Thayer, Thomas C. "How To Analyze a War Without Fronts: Vietnam 1965–1972." Journal of Defense Research 7B (Fall 1975).

Tolson, Lt. Gen. John J. *Airmobility, 1961–1971*. Department of the Army, Vietnam Studies Series, 1973.

Brig. Gen. Tran Dinh Tho. *Pacification*. Indochina Monographs, U.S. Army Center of Military History, 1977.

U.S. Congress. House. Committee on Armed Services. *Hearings on Military Posture*. 92d Congress, 1st sess., 1971.

U.S. Congress. House. Subcommittee of Committee on Appropriations. *Foreign Assistance and Related Agencies Appropriations for 1972*. Part 1. 92d Congress, 1st sess., 1970.

U.S. Congress. Senate. Committee on Foreign Relations. *Vietnam: Policy and Prospects*. 91st Congress, 2d sess., 1970.

U.S. Department of State. *Vietnam Documents and Research Notes*, Nos. 53–117. GPO, 1969–1972.

*Vietnam: The Anti-U.S. Resistance War for National Salvation 1954–1975: Military Events*. FBIS, GPO, 1982.

Vongsavanh, Brig. Gen. Southchay. *RLG Operations and Activities in the Laotian Panhandle*. Indochina Monographs, U.S. Army Center of Military History, 1979.

### III. Unpublished Government and Military Documents

Department of Defense

*Communist Military and Economic Aid to North Vietnam, 1970–1974*. Memorandum prepared by Defense Intelligence Agency and Central Intelligence Agency. SC 01600, 1975.

*Southeast Asia Analysis Reports*. Office of the Assistant Secretary of Defense (Systems Analysis), 1969–1972.

U.S. Military Assistance Command, Vietnam

Battreall, Col. Raymond R. *ARVN 1st Armor Brigade Operations*. March 26, 1971.

———. Interview. Military History Branch, January 14, 1973.

Baughman, Maj. Kendal L. *Comments and Observations on the 20th Tank Squadron*. October 12, 1972.

Duffy, Maj. John. After Action Report, H.Q. 11th Airborne Battalion, Combat Assistance Team, March 30–April 15, 1972. May 1, 1972.

Evergam, Capt. Michael H. Memorandum for Senior Adviser, III Corps Ranger Command. May 29, 1972.

Finn, Maj. John M., II. After Action Report, 20th Tank Regiment, May 20, 1972. Follow-up to After Action Report MACT-ARMC of May 23, 1972.

Hatcher, Maj. Michael, Sr. *Activities of 20th Tank Regiment, April 8–May 2, 1972*.

*MACCORDS Provincial Reports*. February and March 1972.

*MACDI Command History: The 1972 Spring Offensive*. No date.

*MACDI: The Nguyen Hue Offensive*. No date.

*1970 Summary*. Office of Information, no date.

*One War*. MACV Command Overview, 1968–1972.

*Report of Investigation To Assess the Effectiveness of the Functioning of Command Within the 23rd Infantry Division as it Pertains to the Attack Against FSB Mary Ann*. Office of the Inspector General, July 1971. Portions still classified.

Wagner, Lt. Col. Lewis. *Comments of 1st Armored Brigade's Senior Advisor*.

XXIV Corps

Lam Son 719 After Action Report, January 30–April 6, 1971. No date.

23d Infantry Division

Intelligence Summaries. March 1971.

Operational Report. Lessons Learned, February–April 1971.

1st Battalion, 46th Infantry. Daily Journal Files. March 1971.

196th Brigade. Situation Reports. March 1971.

101st Airborne Division

Combat Operations After Action Reports:

Airmobile Operations in Support of Operation Lam Son 719, February 1971–April 6, 1971. 2 vols. May 1971.

Operation Jefferson Glen, September 5, 1970–October 8, 1971.

Harrison, Col. Ben, and Lt. Col. O.H. Wells. *Lam Son 719: Airmobile Concept Questioned*. No date.

Operational Report. Lessons Learned, for three-month periods ending January 1970, April 1970, July 1970, October 1970, April 1971, and October 1971.

U.S. Air Force—Project CHECO Interviews and Reports

Broadway, Col. Roy D. Chief Air Force Advisory Team 5.

Ingalsbe, Col. Orville D. Plans Adviser, Air Force Advisory Team 5.

Landman, Maj. Ronald T. Chief of Staff, Training, Air Force Advisory Team 5.

Mann, Capt. David K. *The NVA 1972 Invasion of Military Region 1: Fall of Quang Tri and Defense of Hue*.

Osborne, Lt. Col. Jimmie R. Material Adviser, Air Force Advisory Team 5.

U.S. Army—Center of Military History, Washington, D.C.

Howard, Maj. John. *The War We Came to Fight: A Study of the Battle of An Loc*. Command and General Staff College.

Oral History Interviews:

Hathaway, Col. William S. Commanding Officer, 196th Infantry Brigade.

Ogilvy, Maj. David L. New Zealand Army.

Pence, Col. A.W., Jr. Senior Airborne Advisory Detachment Commander.

Vaught, Col. James B. Senior Airborne Advisory Detachment Commander.

Vann, John Paul, Sr. Letter dated April 12, 1972.

U.S. Army War College, Carlisle, PA

Howard, Maj. John. *The Easter Offensive, 1972: A Strategic Appraisal*.

Kroesen, Maj. Gen. Frederick J. *Quang Tri, The Lost Province*.

*Study on Military Professionalism*. June 30, 1970.

U.S. Marine Corps—History and Museums Division, Washington, D.C.

Oral History Collection, Marine Corps Historical Center:

Dabney, Col. William (USMC).

Darron, Lt. Col. Robert R. (USMC).

Lt. Gen. Le Nguyen Khanh (VNMC).

Ripley, Capt. John (USMC).

Robertson, Lt. Gen. Donn J. (USMC).

Turley, Lt. Col. Gerald (USMC). Combat Situations/Actions for period of March 30–April 2, 1971.

U.S. Navy

Commander 7th Fleet. Command History, 1972.

*Documentation and Analysis of U.S. Marine Corps Activity in Southeast Asia, April 1–July 31, 1972*. Center for Naval Analysis; affiliate of the University of Rochester.

Operations of U.S. Marine Forces in Southeast Asia, July 1, 1971–March 31, 1973.

OPNAV Report 5750–1. May 9, 1972, p. 25.

Salzer, Vice Adm. Robert S. Oral History Interview. U.S. Naval Institute.

Smock, Maj. James, Sr. Memorandum for Record: May 16, 1972; Memorandum for Record: March 19, 1976; Letter to the Navy Historical Division, Washington Naval Yard, March 23, 1976.

### IV. Newspapers and Periodicals

The authors consulted the following newspapers and periodicals:

*Air Force Times, Army Times, The Christian Science Monitor, Life, Newsweek, The New York Times, Time, U.S. News and World Report, The Washington Post*. (1969–1972 issues used for all of these periodicals.)

### V. Interviews

Military interviewees are identified by current rank or highest rank attained (if retired). Noncareer veterans and civilians are listed without rank or title. Vietnam experience listed pertains to the period of this volume.

Samuel A. Adams, CIA Analyst.

Steve Adolph, U.S. Army Company Commander.

George Allen, CIA Area Chief.
James Bamford, author of *The Puzzle Palace.*
Col. Raymond R. Battreall, Jr., Chief of Staff, U.S. Army Advisory Group, Vietnam.
Lt. Col. Frank Benedict, MACV Plans Officer.
Col. Edward B. Benedit, Adviser, 7th Regiment, 5th ARVN Division.
Tom Bernard, USAF 6908 Security Squadron.
Brig. Gen. Thomas W. Bowen, Deputy Senior Adviser, First Regional Assistance Command (MR 1).
James E. Butler, MACV SOG.
James D. Cain, 525 Military Intelligence Group (MR 2).
Col. William C. Camper, Sr., Adviser, 2d & 56th Regiments, 3d ARVN Division.
Col. William Cathey, U.S. Air Force Fighter Pilot.
Lt. Gen. Howard H. Cooksey, Senior Adviser, First Regional Assistance Command from May 1972.
Vice Adm. Damon W. Cooper, Commander, Task Force 77.
Lt. Gen. Donald H. Cowles, MACV Chief of Staff, Operations.
Col. William H. Dabney, Vietnamese Marine Corps.
Lt. Gen. Wellborn G. Dolvin, Senior Adviser, First Regional Assistance Command to March 1972.
Maj. Gen. George S. Eckhardt, CG Delta MACV, 1968–1969.
Lt. Ellis Edwards, Adviser, Third Regional Assistance Command.
Edward Eskelson, USAF 6908 Security Squadron.
Lt. Gen. Julian J. Ewell, Division and Corps Commander.
Maj. Jack Finch, Adviser, 23d ARVN Division.
Maj. Hugh F. Foster, III, B Company Commander, 1st Battalion, 5th Cavalry.
Col. J. Ross Franklin, Ph.D., Adviser, 21st ARVN Division.
Maj. Gen. Niels Fulwyler, Third Regional Assistance Command, Operations (MR 3).
Richard A. Gabriel, coauthor of *Crisis in Command.*
Brig. Gen. James Herbert, Assistant Chief of Staff, CORDS.
Maj. Gen. John G. Hill, Jr., Deputy Senior Adviser, Second Regional Assistance Command (MR 2).
Lt. Gen. James F. Hollingsworth, Senior Adviser, Third Regional Assistance Command (MR 3).
Col. John Howard, Adviser, 1st ARVN Airborne Brigade.
Watson M. Howell, CORDS Phoenix Program.
Col. Emmett S. Huff, USMC, Adviser, Vietnamese Marine Corps Division.
William Joy, U.S. Army Platoon Leader.
Maj. Gen. Phillip Kaplan, Adviser, 22d ARVN Division.
Col Richard J. Kattar, Commander, 1st Battalion, 5th Cavalry.
Brig. Gen. Douglas Kinnard, Chief of Staff, II Field Force.
Maj. Gen. Frederick J. Kroesen, Acting Senior Adviser, First Regional Assistance Command, March–May 1972.
Lt. Col. Wade Lovings, Adviser, 44th Regiment, 23d ARVN Division.
Maj. Gen. Stan L. McClellan, Chief, U.S. Army Advisory Group.
Vice Adm. William P. Mack, Commander, 7th Fleet.
Lt. Col. Thomas McKenna, Adviser, 55th Regiment, 23d ARVN Division.
Col. Donald S. Marshall, Ph.D., member of Defense Department's Vietnam Task Force.
Col. John Miller, Adviser, Vietnamese Marine Corps.
Richard Moose, Senate Committee on Foreign Relations.
Vincent Morgan, USN, MACV naval intelligence.
Gen. Bruce Palmer, Vice Chief of Staff, U.S. Army.
Lt. Col. William N. Peachey, Commanding Officer, 158th Aviation Battalion.
Lt. Gen William R. Peers, Division and Corps Commander, head of My Lai inquiry panel.
Col. Joseph Pizzi, Chief of Staff, Second Regional Assistance Command (MR 2).
Maj. Gen. George W. Putnam, Jr., Commander, 1st Cavalry Division (Airmobile).
CW02 Danny Rowe, 1st Aerial TOW Team.
Paul W. Savage, coauthor of *Crisis in Command.*
Capt. Roger Sheets, USN, Commanding Officer, Air Wing, U.S.S. *Coral Sea.*
Frank Snepp, CIA Analyst.
Maj. Paul Spilberg, Assistant Operations Officer, 196th Brigade.
Maj. John D. Stube, Operations Officer, 1st Battalion, 5th Cavalry.
Col. Arthur E. Taylor, Jr., Adviser, 1st ARVN Airborne Brigade.
Col. John Truby, Senior Military Adviser, CORDS, MR 2.
Lt. Col. Gerald Turley, USMC, Adviser, 3d ARVN Division.
Lt. Gen. Walt Ulmer, Adviser, 5th ARVN Division.
Gen. John W. Vogt, USAF, Commander, 7th Air Force.
Col. Thomas A. Ware, Commander, 2d Brigade, 101st Airborne Division.
Brig. Gen. George Wear, Senior Military Adviser, Second Regional Assistance Command (MR 2).
Maj. Eugene J. White, Jr., A Company Commander, 1st Battalion, 5th Cavalry.

# Acknowledgements

Boston Publishing Company would like to acknowledge the kind assistance of the following people: James A. Alexander, Carlisle, Pennsylvania; Dr. Jeffrey Clarke of the Army Center of Military History, who read parts of the manuscript; Col. Dale Dorman, Development Center, Quantico, Virginia; Charles W. Dunn, professor and chairman, Department of Celtic Languages, Harvard University; Gladys Maeser and Joyce Wiesner, Retired U.S. Army Reserve Components Personnel and Administration Center, St. Louis, Missouri; Benis M. Frank, Col. John Miller, and Jack Shulimson, Marine Corps Historical Center, Washington, D.C.; Jeff Powell, Center of Military History, Washington, D.C.; Paul Taborn, Office of the Army Adjutant General; Steven J. Zaloga; and numerous veterans of the Vietnam War who wish to remain anonymous.

The index was prepared by Elizabeth Campbell Peters.

# Photography Credits

**Cover Photo**
Sovfoto

**Chapter 1**
p. 7, ©1984 David Burnett/CONTACT. p. 10, U.S. Army. p. 11, Burt Glinn—Magnum. pp. 12–3, Roger Pic. pp. 14–7, U.S. Army. p. 18, ©1984 David Burnett/CONTACT. p. 19, top, U.S. Army; bottom, UPI/Bettmann Archive. pp. 20–1, AP/Wide World. p. 25, Major Hugh F. Foster III Collection.

**An Army Departs**
pp. 26–7, U.S. Army. p. 28, top, Raymond Depardon—Magnum; bottom, Philip Jones Griffiths—Magnum. pp. 28–9, U.S. Army. p. 30, top, Ian Berry—Magnum; bottom, Harold Ellithorpe—Black Star. pp. 30–1, ©1984 David Burnett/CONTACT. pp. 32–3, Ralph Crane—LIFE Magazine, ©1971, Time Inc.

**Chapter 2**
p. 35, UPI/Bettmann Archive. p. 38, Robert MacCrate Collection. p. 40, U.S. Military Academy Archives. pp. 40–1, James H. Karales. p. 41, Roger Malloch—Magnum. p. 42, left, UPI/Bettmann Archive; right, AP/Wide World. p. 43, Lynn Pelham—LIFE Magazine, ©1971 Time Inc. p. 44, U.S. Army Recruiting—TIME Magazine. p. 46, Richard L. Swanson—LIFE Magazine, ©1970, Time Inc. pp. 48–9, © David Hume Kennerly.

**Chapter 3**
p. 51, Marc Riboud—Magnum. p. 53, UPI/Bettmann Archive. pp. 54–5, Larry Burrows—LIFE Magazine, ©1969, Time Inc. p. 58, Thomas Koeniges—The LOOK Collection, Library of Congress. p. 59, James Hansen—The LOOK Collection, Library of Congress. p. 60, Le Minh—TIME Magazine. pp. 62–3, Mark Godfrey—Archive Pictures Inc. p. 67, Sovfoto.

**Chapter 4**
p. 69, Jacques Tonnaire—Gamma/Liaison. p. 71, AP/Wide World. p. 73, Larry Burrows—LIFE Magazine, ©1971, Time Inc. pp. 74–5, ©1984 David Burnett/CONTACT. pp. 77–9, Akihiko Okamura—Pan-Asia. pp. 82–3, ©1984 David Burnett/CONTACT. p. 84, UPI/Bettmann Archive. pp. 86–7, Akihiko Okamura—Pan-Asia. p. 89, Library of Congress.

**End of a Mission**
pp. 92–3, UPI/Bettmann Archive. p. 93, inset, Akihiko Okamura—Pan-Asia. pp. 94–5, Mark Godfrey—Archive Pictures Inc. pp. 96–7, ©1984 David Burnett/CONTACT. p. 96, inset, Mark Godfrey—Archive Pictures Inc.

**Chapter 5**
p. 99, Dieter Ludwig—Gamma/Liaison. p. 100, left, © Steve Murez 1984; right, Agence France-Presse. p. 101, left, Henri Bureau—Sygma; middle, Ngo Vinh Long Collection; right, Henri Bureau—Sygma. p. 105, © David Hume Kennerly. p. 106, Wallace Driver—Camera Press Ltd. p. 107, Nancy Moran—NYT PICTURES. pp. 108–9, Ngo Vinh Long Collection. p. 110, top, David Burnett—LIFE Magazine, ©1971 Time Inc.; inset, Ngo Vinh Long Collection. p. 112, Ngo Vinh Long Collection. p. 113, U.S. Army.

**Chapter 6**
pp. 115–7, Marc Riboud. p. 118, top, Camera Press Ltd.; bottom, Ngo Vinh Long Collection. p. 119, Camera Press Ltd. p. 121, Sovfoto. p. 124, inset, Nihon Denpa News. pp. 124–5, Agence France-Presse. p. 129, AP/Wide World.

**The North's New Weapons**
pp. 130–5, Illustrations © Profile Publications Ltd.

**Chapter 7**
p. 137, Eastfoto. pp. 138–9, AP/Wide World. p. 141, Eastfoto. p. 143, U.S. Navy. pp. 144–5, Ngo Vinh Long Collection. pp. 146–7, p. 148, inset, © David Burnett/CONTACT. pp. 148–9, Henri Huet—Sygma. p. 155, 157, UPI/Bettmann Archive. pp. 158–9, MACV Advisory Team 33, courtesy Major John Finch.

**An Loc Besieged**
pp. 160–1, ©1984 David Burnett/CONTACT. p. 162, inset, Dirck Halstead—Gamma/Liaison. pp. 162–3, Henri Bureau—Sygma. pp. 164–5, ©1984 David Burnett/CONTACT. p. 165, inset, Dirck Halstead—Gamma/Liaison. pp. 166–7, Bruno Barbey—Magnum.

**Chapter 8**
p. 169, Roger Pic. p. 171, U.S. Air Force. p. 172, top, Camera Press Ltd.; bottom, AP/Wide World. p. 173, Roger Pic—Gamma/Liaison. pp. 174–5, AP/Wide World. p. 176, inset, Yves Guy Berges—Gamma/Liaison. pp. 176–7, Ken Wagner—Black Star. pp. 179–81, AP/Wide World. p. 182, Lee Rudakewych—Camera Press Ltd. p. 185, Claude LaFontan—Gamma/Liaison.

# Map Credits

Map Credits
All maps prepared by Diane McCaffery. Sources are as follows:
p. 65—Department of the Army.
p. 81—Department of the Army.
p. 151—*Marine Corps Gazette.*
p. 152—Department of the Army.
p. 181—*Marine Corps Gazette.*

# Index

Note: Military units are listed according to the general organizational structure of the U.S. Armed Forces. The following chart summarizes that structure for the U.S. Army. The principal difference between the army and the Marine Corps structures in Vietnam lay at the regimental level. The army eliminated the regimental command structure after World War II (although battalions retained a regimental designation for purposes of historical continuity, *e.g.,* 1st Battalion, 7th Cavalry [Regiment]). Marine Corps battalions were organized into regiments instead of brigades except under a few unusual circumstances. The marines, however, do not use the word "regiment" to designate their units; *e.g.,* 1st Marines refers to the 1st Marine Regiment.

**U.S. Army structure**
(to company level)

| Unit | Size | Commanding officer |
| --- | --- | --- |
| Division | 12,000–18,000 troops or 3 brigades | Major General |
| Brigade | 3,000 troops or 2–4 battalions | Colonel |
| Battalion* | 600–1,000 troops or 3–5 companies | Lieutenant Colonel |
| Company | 150 troops** or 3–4 platoons | Captain |

* Squadron equivalent to battalion.
** Size varies based on type of unit.

# Names, Acronyms, Terms

**APC**—armored personnel carrier.

**ARVN**—Army of the Republic of Vietnam (South Vietnam).

**base area**—Communist base camp. Usually containing fortifications, supply depots, hospitals, and training facilities.

**B-5 Front**—Communist military command operating in the two northernmost provinces of South Vietnam.

*binh tram*—North Vietnamese logistical unit responsible for defense and maintenance for a section of the Ho Chi Minh Trail.

**Cambodian Liberation Army**—also called Khmer Liberation Army. Communist armed forces of National United Front of Kampuchea (FUNK).

**Chieu Hoi**—The GVN "open arms" program promising clemency and financial aid to VC guerrillas and NVA regulars who gave themselves up.

**CIA**—Central Intelligence Agency.

**Cobra**—Bell AH-1G Huey Cobra. Fast attack helicopter armed with machine guns, grenade launchers, and rockets.

**concertina barbed wire**—coiled barbed wire used as infantry obstacles.

**CORDS**—The Civil Operations and Revolutionary Development Support was established under MACV in 1967. CORDS organized U.S. civilian agencies in Vietnam within the military chain of command.

**corps**—two or more divisions, responsible for the defense of a Military Region.

**COSVN**—Central Office for South Vietnam. Communist military and political headquarters for southern South Vietnam.

**DEROS**—date eligible for return from overseas. The date a soldier's tour of duty was to end.

**DMZ**—demilitarized zone. Established by the 1954 Geneva accords, provisionally dividing North Vietnam from South Vietnam along the seventeenth parallel.

**DRV**—Democratic Republic of Vietnam. North Vietnam.

**FAC**—forward air controller. Pilot or observer who directs strike aircraft and artillery.

**IV Corps**—RVNAF military command controlling forces in Military Region 4, the Mekong Delta region.

**FRAC**—First Regional Assistance Command. U.S. Advisory command that replaced XXIV Corps in Military Region 1 during withdrawal period.

**fragging**—killing or attempting to kill a fellow soldier or officer, usually with a fragmentation grenade.

**FSB**—fire support base. Semifixed artillery base established to increase indirect fire coverage of an area and to provide security for the firing unit.

**FUNK**—National United Front of Kampuchea. Popular front established in 1970 and nominally headed by Prince Norodom Sihanouk, dedicated to the overthrow of the Lon Nol government in Phnom Penh.

**GVN**—U.S. abbreviation for the government of South Vietnam.

**high points**—CIA and MACV term for brief periods (usually about three days) of intense enemy activity, such as attacks against population centers or military posts.

**indirect fire**—bombardment by mortars or artillery in which shells travel on a trajectory to an unseen target.

**JCS**—Joint Chiefs of Staff. Consisting of chairman, U.S. Army chief of staff, U.S. Navy chief of naval operations, U.S. Air Force chief of staff, and the U.S. Marine Corps commandant. Advises the president, the National Security Council, and the secretary of defense.

**JGS**—Joint General Staff. South Vietnamese counterpart to U.S. Joint Chiefs of Staff.

**Lao Dong party**—Vietnam Worker's party, Marxist-Leninist party of North Vietnam. Founded by Ho Chi Minh in May 1951. Absorbed the Vietminh and was the ruling party of the DRV. Extended into South Vietnam as the People's Revolutionary party in January 1962.

**LAW**—M72 light antitank weapon. A shoulder-fired 66MM rocket with a one-time, disposable fiber glass launcher.

**LOCs**—lines of communication. Land, water, and air routes along which supplies and reinforcements move from rear bases to troops in the field.

**MACV**—Military Assistance Command, Vietnam. U.S. command for all U.S. military activities in Vietnam.

**MR**—Military Region. Term that replaced Corps Tactical Zone. One of four geographic zones into which South Vietnam was divided for purposes of military and civil administration.

**NCO**—noncommissioned officer (noncom). Enlisted ranks including corporal and sergeant up to command sergeant major.

**NLF**—National Liberation Front, officially the National Front for the Liberation of the South. Formed on December 20, 1960, it aimed to overthrow South Vietnam's government and reunite the North and the South. NLF included Communists and non-Communists.

**NSA**—National Security Agency. Intelligence-gathering agency established in 1952, responsible to the executive branch and specializing in code breaking and electronic surveillance.

**NVA**—North Vietnamese Army.

**OER**—officer efficiency reports, a primary basis for officer evaluations and promotions.

**I Corps**—"Eye" Corps. RVNAF military command controlling forces in Military Region 1, South Vietnam's five northernmost provinces.

**PF**—Popular Forces. South Vietnamese village defense units.

**Phoenix program**—*(Phung Hoang)*. A South Vietnamese intelligence-gathering program advised by CORDS, designed to neutralize the Vietcong infrastructure through identification and arrest of key party cadres.

**Politburo**—policy-making and executive committee of the Communist party.

**PRG**—Provisional Revolutionary Government. Established in 1969 as the government of the NLF as a means to challenge the legitimacy of the Saigon government and to act as a political entity to share in any coalition government.

**RF**—Regional Forces. South Vietnamese provincial defense units.

**RVNAF**—Republic of Vietnam Armed Forces, including ARVN, PFs, RFs, VNAF, VNMC, and VNN.

**SAM**—surface-to-air missile.

**sapper**—originally, in European wars, a soldier who built and repaired fortifications. NVA/VC sappers were commando raiders adept at penetrating allied defenses.

**70th Corps**—North Vietnamese military command activated in 1970 to control defense of base areas in Laotian panhandle.

**SRAC**—Second Regional Assistance Command. U.S. advisory command that replaced I Field Force in Military Region 2 during withdrawal period.

**III Corps**—RVNAF military command controlling forces in Military Region 3, the area from the northern Mekong Delta to the southern central highlands.

**III MAF**—III Marine Amphibious Force. U.S. Command responsible for defense of I Corps Tactical Zone until redeployed in 1971.

**TRAC**—Third Regional Assistance Command. U.S. advisory command that replaced II Field Force in Military Region 3 during withdrawal period.

**XXIV Corps**—U.S. Army command activated in 1968 to operate in I Corps Tactical Zone.

**II Corps**—RVNAF military command controlling forces in Military Region 2, the central highlands, and adjoining coastal lowlands.

**Vietcong**—a contraction of Vietnam Cong San (Vietnamese Communist).

**VNAF**—South Vietnamese Air Force.

**VNMC**—South Vietnamese Marine Corps.

**VNN**—South Vietnamese Navy.